Freedom of Protest, Public Order and the Law

Freedom of Protest, Public Order and the Law

Avrom Sherr

Basil Blackwell

First published 1989

Basil Blackwell Ltd
108 Cowley Road, Oxford, OX4 1JF, UK

Basil Blackwell Inc
432 Park Avenue South, Suite 1503
New York, NY 10016, USA

British Library Cataloguing in Publication Data

Sherr, Avrom
Freedom, of protest public order and the law.
1. Great Britain. Public order. Law
I. Title
344.104′53

ISBN 0–631–15809–X
ISBN 0–631–15811–1 Pbk

Library of Congress Cataloging in Publication Data

Sherr, Avrom.
Freedom, of protest public order and the law.

Bibliography: p.
Includes index.
1. Public policy (Law)—Great Britain. 2. Police
regulations—Great Britain. I. Title.
KD703.P9S53 1988   344.41′052   88–16744
ISBN 0–631–15809–X   344.10452
ISBN 0–631–15811–1 (pbk.)

Typeset in 10½ on 12 pt Plantin
by Photo-Graphics, Honiton, Devon
Printed in Great Britain by Billing and Sons Ltd, Worcester

To
Lorraine

'For in reason, all government without the consent of the governed is the very definition of slavery. But in fact, eleven men well armed will certainly subdue one single man in his shirt. But I have done. For those who have used power to cramp liberty have gone so far as to resent even the liberty of complaining, although a man upon the rack was never known to be refused the liberty of roaring as loud as he thought fit.'

'A Letter to the Whole People of Ireland'
(the fourth of the 'Drapier's Letters')
Jonathan Swift, 22nd October 1724

Contents

Acknowledgements

My thanks are due to a number of generations of students who have suffered, and (I hope) enjoyed, the course out of which this book has come. They have mainly been students at the University of Warwick, but there have also been a number of students from law schools at UCLA, the University of San Francisco and the University of Syracuse, whose involvement in the course has informed my understanding of the subject area. In particular I wish to thank Nicky Pittam, Charlie Donaldson and John Meacock for reading the chapters and making helpful suggestions; and Nicky Pittam for her characteristically painstaking work on the index. Debi Gould also suggested a particularly good idea relating to 'victimless crimes' under the new Public Order Act.

Professor David Kretzmer helped to spark off some of the original ideas and also assisted by reading and commenting on early drafts of the first few chapters. His work in the Israeli Civil Liberties Union provided an interesting perspective from which to view both the English and American constitutional positions. Special thanks are also due to Professor John Miller at Warwick who provided detailed criticism on drafts of all chapters with speed and helpfulness. Laurence Lustgarten also read and commented on an early draft.

Chapter 9, in an earlier draft, was first delivered to the Law Faculty at UCLA as a seminar, and I am grateful to the Dean and Faculty for a productive visiting year there. Otherwise, Paul Bergman has nothing to do with this book, which probably accounts for its lack of humour.

Thanks are due to Dr Daniel Eilon of the English Department at Warwick for numerous pleasant evenings of moderately alcoholic discussion, the Swiftian quote, and the aborted titular attempt. David Lewi's incredulity only continued. David Lowry brought Zinn to my attention, David Kader the Skokie cases.

Tom Hervey's remarks about ambition were a spur. Even Ari, Ilan and Yoni Sherr allowed me pretty much to work in peace – whilst proving continuously that protest is either genetic or nurtured from an early age.

Most important of all, Carol Chapman, with a little help from Helen Beresford and Philippa Ross-White, did all the careful word processing involved in the book and dealt with fiddly tables, and a much more fiddly author, with pleasantness, accuracy and speed. Any faults in the text, either major or minor, may be blamed on computer virus.

Table of Statutes

Table of Cases

Introduction

This book was written to fit into a particular niche in the literature of freedom of expression in England and Wales. It attempts to bridge the gap between works dealing only with legal exposition of what is usually described as the 'law of public order', and works from other disciplines, including history, politics, sociology and psychology, showing the context of demonstrations in which the law of public order operates.

The book is based on a course taught for some twelve years at Warwick University. The factor precipitating its production now has been the difficulties facing teachers with an eclectic approach in their attempts to include material from more than one discipline in courses prepared for their students, without requiring those students to buy considerable numbers of books. A tightening up of publishers' reactions to photocopying for academic purposes and the clarification of the laws of copyright by some recent cases have meant that it is now much more difficult to put together sets of materials for students from widely differing disciplines. Accordingly, the birth of this book was forced rather than incidental.

As a study (and as a course) it is intended to be rather more than a book specifically about parts of the law of public order, or simply the law relating to demonstrations. This particularly difficult area of state control is also seen as a metaphor for a number of aspects of our legal, political and social system, of which it is an excellent example. As such, it is intended to introduce the reader to the English system of dealing with 'rights' and 'freedoms', not supported by a written constitution but relying on the discretion operated by police officers, prosecutors, magistrates and judges generally. It is also an introduction to our system of policing, controlled neither by law, nor by political masters at central or local government level, nor by a police complaints body. The system of judicial precedent also comes under review, showing how it is possible for our courts to enunciate rights and freedoms at the same time as they deny them to the people involved in the cases they are deciding.

The central focus of the book is the subject matter of demonstrations and protest. It deals specifically with demonstrations outside the context of industrial disputes which have, to a great extent, become a subject of their own within the disciplines of law, politics and sociology in recent years. Although much of what is to be found here will also be applicable to industrial disputes, and some of the law arising out of those disputes will be applicable here, a separation has been drawn where this has been possible. The rights of the workplace appear to be different from the rights of general protest.

A number of books have appeared since the Public Order Act 1986, mostly dealing primarily with the workings of that Act. This book takes a wider view, looking at the law of demonstrations more generally as well as the context in which that law operates. It therefore begins with a chapter outlining some of the political and legal theory regarding demonstrations and protest, followed by a chapter of case studies in terms of both historiography and individual demonstrations in order to exhibit the subject matter more clearly. Later chapters, beyond a statement of the law, discuss the problems of violence and police control; and the book ends with a chapter discussing whether the enactment of fundamental constitutional rights in this area would be likely to solve the major problems which the book exposes.

The subject is important because protest and demonstration are seen to constitute a safety valve for western democratic society. Protest or demonstration seems to take place where the normal political machinery fails because minority opinion does not receive sufficient publicity and cannot find other forms of expression in order to persuade a target audience. If such protest is subject to the discretion of the police, prosecutors and judicial officials, then the fundamental theory of the safety valve begins to break down. This is the major question posed by the book.

It has proved a somewhat difficult subject to study. Brownlie's excellent text and Supperstone's second edition of it have provided the reader with a strong encyclopaedic approach to the law. Williams's *Breach of the Peace* provided a useful background in historical terms and a much easier approach to understanding and evaluating modern problems. But both the law and the issues themselves seem to slip through one's fingers like grains of sand as soon as they are clutched. This seems to arise out of the peculiar dichotomy which is the distinguishing feature of the subject area. As a society we maintain on the one hand the sense, ideal or chimera of freedom of expression whilst at the same time desiring to maintain the reality of no right to protest. There is no fine line to walk between the two since no clear dividing 'Chinese wall' exists. Political viewpoint also causes some major difficulties in this area. It is more difficult here than elsewhere to provide an attempt at objectivity, and it will be seen from chapter 2 that most writers do not even make the attempt. For this reason the case studies have been confined to demonstrations and protests which are removed a little in time from the heat of the present, with the year 1978 taken as the cut-off point for this purpose. Material written about later events has been taken into account, and where those events have precipitated action, this too is acknowledged. However, in terms of detail of case study a little distance in time has proved a useful lens through which to view those happenings.

The final chapter considers in some detail how constitutional rights, such as those existing in the United States of America, work, and how they might work in England and Wales. A major comparison is undertaken of some detailed parts of the law as well as a detailed case study of materials arising out of the 'Skokie–Nazi cases' in Chicago in 1977. A number of attempts have been made to import and legislate the European Convention on Human Rights into the law of England and Wales, and the last chapter questions whether this will provide the solutions articulated by its advocates.

As far as the law is concerned, two major reviews of public order law through a Home Affairs green paper and a Law Commission Working Paper have been followed up by what was intended to be a major revision of the law in the form of the Public Order Act 1986. It is questionable whether this revision has changed the nature of the law in this area, or whether the new framework will operate effectively. This is an issue to which the book gives attention in chapters 3–7, the section dealing with legal regulation.

The book, in draft form, has already been used as a course for one year of students. In a still earlier form it has also proved a useful eye-opener to law students on many of the problems of our constitutional, legal and enforcement systems which might otherwise have needed recourse to much more comprehensive studies. It has also proved to be an exceptionally useful introduction to the way in which the law operates for many non-law students who have opted to take the course after some introduction to law and legal system. I hope that the book will be equally useful to both of these groups. I also hope that the way of looking at the right of freedom of protest and the law of public order demonstrated in this book will also provide something of novelty and perhaps originality to researchers and teachers in this area.

The law is intended to be stated as at 1 January 1988.

Avrom Sherr
Coventry

1

Thinkers and Doers

The English legal culture and the British constitutional system encourage the imagery of civil rights and liberties, but contain very little legal basis, if any, for such notions. Though many an English person believes in the ethos of 'a free country', it is uncertain what this may mean. The beliefs and the imagery are, however, powerful in themselves whether or not they are strengthened by legal underpinnings. The 'mother of parliaments' and the 'cradle of democracy' are based on a fair degree of unarticulated convention, habit and presumption about human nature. These allow, and perhaps even encourage, the spirit of freedom if not the letter of it.

However, it is not clear what we mean when we talk of 'freedoms' or 'rights'. Often the expression that 'we have' freedoms and rights is simply an expression of a belief about our particular political form of government compared with another. Such statements seem therefore to be made in terms more comparative than absolute.[1] In the first part of this opening chapter the thoughts of some legal, and other, philosophers are discussed in order to see whether one can find, in theory, including legal theory, some foundations and arguments for the vague notions or beliefs of freedom in relation to protest in the jurisdiction of England and Wales. In order to do this it may be useful to look at the legal philosophy which has engendered, or been engendered by, periods of great struggle and change in society. It is helpful in this context to compare the situation in England with the position in a country with some more obvious constitutional base such as the United States of America.

---

[1] For a review of the major 'free speech theories', the general literature and a comparative law approach see E. Barendt, *Freedom of Speech* (Oxford University Press, 1985). See also J. S. Mill's essay 'On Liberty' in *John Stuart Mill: Utilitarianism, Liberty and Representative Government*, ed. H. B. Acton (London, Dent, 1982), pp. 65–170; Sir Isaiah Berlin, *Four Essays on Liberty* (Oxford University Press, 1969) and R. Dworkin, *Taking Rights Seriously* (London, Duckworth, 1977). Rousseau's classic *Social Contract* (London, Dent, 1973) provides a basis for much of the later writings.

After entertaining this theory the chapter begins to look at the nature of protest and protestors in order to understand how the practice and theory march, or do not march, together.

Civil Disobedience, Protest and Revolution

Each era produces or rediscovers the political and legal theorists it needs in order to justify events. The revolutions of the eighteenth century fostered the literature of Rousseau's 'Social Contract' and helped to produce J. S. Mill's 'On Liberty'. These found their place next to ideas of 'natural law' and 'natural rights' which had been proposed by religious philosophers and adapted to the legal field.

Many of the natural law and natural rights theorists base themselves on the hypothesis that all law is based on morality. Since the law often becomes fossilized once it is created or peculiarly affected by the accidents of litigation, it is necessary to return to the moral basis of the law rather than the way in which the law itself had progressed. 'Morality' is therefore more important than 'law'; but who is to decide what is moral?

These are among the issues to be found in the literature regarding the American War of Independence, the American Civil War, American involvement in the war in Vietnam, and internal conflict over poverty and racism in America. These were also the issues sparked off by the incidence of the evil Nazi regime in Europe, and the changes fostered by the youth and student 'revolutions' of the 1960s and 1970s. One such major issue was whether it was not a moral (and therefore a legal?) obligation to overthrow an evil, but formally legal, government and system. Another such issue involved the question of disobedience to individual laws in an otherwise (generally) moral regime, often referred to as 'civil disobedience'.

Civil Disobedience

One of the more memorable and articulate legal debates arising out of the changes occurring in American society in the late sixties and early seventies was the debate between Supreme Court Justice Abe Fortas in his booklet, *Concerning Dissent and Civil Disobedience*[2] and Howard

---

[2] Abe Fortas, *Concerning Dissent and Civil Disobedience* (New York, New American Library, 1968).

Zinn, *Disobedience and Democracy: Nine Fallacies on Law and Order*.[3]
This debate is interesting because it sets out the major issues well, and
although it emanates from a 'constitutional' system, it still exposes the
problems of applying legal regulation to this area of human activity.
Both of the protagonists seem to occupy fairly traditional and not
extreme standpoints. This exhibits the political diversity operating within
one legal culture and perhaps goes some way to explain how such
divergent judicial opinions are arrived at, as appears in some of the
cases.

Rule of Law   Zinn first takes exception to Fortas's assertion that 'the
rule of law has an intrinsic value'[4] whether or not it is in itself moral.
In other words, even if one should believe that a particular law or laws
is or are immoral, obedience to the rule of law is in itself a value which
is equally, if not more, important.

While Fortas admits that he would have disobeyed Hitler's laws and
the Southern segregation laws, he feels that even in disobedience there
should be an acquiescence in 'the ultimate judgments of the courts'.[5]
He sees the rule of law as 'the essential condition of individual liberty'.[6]
If every person were to obey the dictates of their own conscience then
individual liberty would suffer more from the inevitable chaos than if
each individual attempted to obtain their moral right through the force
of law alone.

In Zinn's view there can be no moral duty to obey an immoral law.
Some sort of balance must be achieved between the violation of human
rights or the protection of an evil condition, and breaking the law. He
counters the argument that disobedience of bad laws can lead to a
general disrespect of law by arguing that children are not made to eat
rotten fruit along with the good, lest they learn to throw all fruit away.
It is just as likely that somebody forced to obey a bad law would develop
a distaste for all law.

The level of general obedience is far higher than the likelihood of
rebellion. There are a greater number of 'instances of forbearance to
exploitation, and submission to authority, than we have examples of
revolt'.[7] Outbreaks of civil disobedience and disorder are not the 'cause'

---

[3] H. Zinn, *Disobedience and Democracy: Nine Fallacies on Law and Order* (New York, Vintage Bowes, 1968).
[4] Ibid., p. 12. This is a rather different formulation of the idea of the Rule of Law from that found in A. V. Dicey, *Introduction to the Study of the Law of the Constitution*, 10th edn (London, Macmillan, 1959), pp. 195ff or H. L. A. Hart, *Law, Liberty and Morality* (London, Oxford University Press, 1963).
[5] Fortas, *Concerning Dissent*, p. 34.
[6] Ibid.
[7] Zinn, *Disobedience*, p. 17.

of troubles, but the result of them. Reactions to poverty, racism, urban blight and the Vietnam War in America pointed the way to necessary change which was taken. Protests and demonstrations did not cause the problems; they merely reacted to them.

Zinn goes on to argue that the selective, deliberate violation of those involved in civil disobedience is based on careful thought and not reckless disregard. Domestic tranquillity (or the Queen's Peace as it would be known in the UK) is not an end in itself. It is only the result of state monopoly of power and information. 'The violence to body and spirit that may come from ill health, unemployment, humiliation, loneliness, a sense of impotence – those afflictions, which poor, or black, or sick or imprisoned persons may have, or healthy young people forced to fit into a money worshipping success idolizing culture'[8] are themselves another kind of disorder.

But, asks Fortas, if the government is supposed to be subject to the rule of law and therefore available to attack under the law by its citizens, how can individuals be in some sense above the law? However, the government and the citizen, according to Zinn, do not stand on equal ground. That the government is bound by law is 'an expectation', while the citizen's being bound by the law is 'a fact'. The law is, in effect, merely an arm or tool of the government and if the law should criticize the government, the government may change the law. Governments do pick and choose among those laws that they will enforce and they do not treat all laws equally. All of the science of government and the theory of democracy is based on competing values. If governments have difficulty in governing a society affected by disobedience then this is how it *should* be.

The 'rule of law' problem as argued between Fortas and Zinn is not faced in the same way under the English system. Since there is no 'higher rule' of constitutional effect within the system the only important question is whether a criminal or a civil law has been broken by the protesters. There is, therefore, not even a place for arguments regarding freedom to protest within our system. In chapter 9 the importance of the European Convention for the Protection of Human Rights will be discussed, together with other forms of written constitutional guarantees which are beginning to affect English law. For the purpose of this chapter it should be noted that the result has not been insignificant to date, in this particular area of the law.

The question of whether the government is circumscribed by the law, and therefore the rule of law, to the same extent as the individual is a rather different aspect. This has arisen most noticeably in some of the cases

[8] Ibid., p. 19.

arising out of the troubles in Northern Ireland. Overall, therefore, Zinn's form of philosophical or political argument in relation to the question of disobedience and the 'rule of law' can only be dealt with here in the academic court of moral justice, not as arguments in a legal case.[9] These are philosophical arguments which could not hold sway before an American court deciding constitutional issues unless he could find himself within the gateways of constitutional rights as expressed in the constitution, the amendments thereto and judicial decisions explaining their function.

Acceptance of Punishment   The next problem Zinn and Fortas discuss is whether protesters or others involved in civil disobedience should meekly accept punishment by law without complaint, as a form of martyrdom. Fortas sees the acceptance of normal punishment under law as part of the balance of democracy, whereas Zinn sees this punishment as an occasion for further civil disobedience in order to publicize the grievance.

Limitation on Forms of Civil Disobedience   Fortas takes the view that the only laws that may be broken by civil disobedients are those which in themselves are wrong. This would mean that those protesting against nuclear armament would not be allowed to trespass onto Ministry of Defence property or to sit down in a street since the laws of highway obstruction and trespass were not the issues aimed at by the action. Zinn asks whether Jews in Nazi Germany would have been justified in violating the yellow arm-band rule, but not in fighting back against those attempting to impose it. Zinn also suggests that some features of society are not there as a result of immediately identifiable laws, but are conditions arising out of the entire social framework or a number of disparate instances of legal regulation.

Non-Violence   Lastly, Fortas points out that many of the great theoreticians of protest, including Gandhi, Martin Luther King and Thoreau were against violence. However, it is difficult to see, according to Zinn, how the violence of the state can be tolerated without some tolerance of the violence of the oppressed against the oppressor. Breaking windows in the Pentagon seems to Zinn, 'a mild form of violence' compared with the Vietnam War in which 'thousands of American men [were] returning to their families in coffins'.[10] It is sometimes necessary to see violence in order to understand the depth of people's feelings

[9] Except, perhaps, in a plea in mitigation, with regard to sentence, although even that has not always been successful. See, e.g. *R* v. *Caird* (1970) 54 Crim. App. Rep. 499.
[10] Zinn, *Disobedience*, pp. 46–7.

and the need for change. According to Zinn, whilst the least violent plan possible should be chosen, in the event that violence occurs either as a result of the protestors or as a result of the forces of law and order, the morality of the issue protested should be taken into account in assessing the violence of the protest.

This issue is taken up by other North American legal theorists and an alternative view is presented in the work of Mark MacGuigan.[11] He draws a distinction between 'coercive and 'persuasive' conduct. Acts which he says tend to coerce people, even if non-violent, are wrong if they cause inconvenience to innocent members of society who have 'a purely arbitrary relationship to the injustice whose correction is sought'. Acts which tend to persuade rather than to coerce would, to him, be acceptable.

The Zinn–Fortas debate provides the first part of the backdrop to protest and the manner in which the law deals with protest. Their debate moves between the realms of moral and legal philosophy, and provides an approach to our subject matter which will not be found in the details of case studies of protest or the intricacies of the legal regulation.

It is especially interesting to note that their thoughts on legality come from within a constitutional system where it is possible to turn to an overall moral right such as the freedom of speech or the power of protest. Even with such a constitutional system the force of obedience to specific law is very strong. *A fortiori*, this must be so in a system such as ours without any higher rule governing, but a decision simply whether a crime has been committed or a law broken.

The Role and Function of Protest

With the above discussion on morality and law in mind we can begin to understand the role and function of protest in our society whilst reviewing how the issues of obedience, punishment and violence are dealt with here.

The Theory of Democracy and the Problem of Protest

Democratic theory suggests that in a Western democracy the view of the populace is observed and put into action through the ballot box. Although we all intuitively know that this is not so (and that, for

---

[11] M. R. MacGuigan, 'Obligation and Obedience' in *Political and Legal Obligation*, ed. J. R. Pennock and J. W. Chapman (New York University Press, 1970).

example, only a very small overall majority or even a minority often votes the government into power), the theory suggests that the ballot box and the normal political channels are the avenues for ensuring that the will of the people is observed.

A safety net is then proposed by traditional theory in the form of the possibility of protest and demonstration where the usual political channels are not sufficient because of the nature of the issue or its supporters. Where the mass media are often controlled by or subservient to those who have power in society it becomes even more difficult for those with different views to obtain publicity for them. Therefore, a right or freedom of protest is granted so that minority views may be taken into account and respected.

But what happens if the much vaunted freedoms of protest and speech do not exist as strongly as is supposed? It would be legally correct to say that there is no such right or freedom of speech, or protest or demonstration in England. We are therefore faced, as stated above, with the competition of the imagery of freedom versus the reality of law. This competition is mediated through the discretion of judgement of officials within the legal justice system from a policeman on the beat all the way up to a Lord of Appeal in Ordinary. Such discretion is available as a result of the apparent illegality of almost all forms of protest. Almost any demonstration will be a potential obstruction of the highway and any decision by a policeman to move demonstrators can precipitate a potential 'obstruction of a policeman in the exercise of his duty'. In the face of this presumed illegality it is up to the official to decide whether to enforce the law or to turn a blind eye.

This system, on paper, can be compared unfavourably with a constitutional system[12] in which such rights are in theory guaranteed. However, we have already seen some of the problems that exist in manipulating such theory into practice in the Fortas–Zinn debate above.

In our system, where no rights exist and large expanses of areas of 'no-right' exist, we have to be especially vigilant in limiting the force of the criminal law and understanding its boundaries. The function of the lawyer becomes not one of challenging evil morality and taking the part of 'the good', but of technically limiting the intricacies of the law as they affect the individual defendant.

The function of the theoreticians has been to understand in more practical terms how change occurs in society as a result of protest and to rationalize the need for change against the methods used to bring it about.

---

[12] This would include a system such as the Israeli sytem where the Supreme Court has imported and granted fundamental rights although no formal constitution in those terms exists. See Ch. 9 and D. Kretzmer, 'Demonstrations and the Law' [1984] 19 Israel LR p. 47.

The Heritage of Disorder – Protest in History

Many of those who write about the history of protest in England underplay the use of violence here in bringing about social change.[13] Comparisons between violent protest and revolution on the continent of Europe and protest in England, with seemingly a far smaller number of casualties here in terms of the death roll, are simplistic. Attention must also be given to the character of the issues which were the subject of the protest, the authorities protested against, and any oppression which attempted to prevent protests. Clutterbuck quotes Dr Johnson who, in 1780 after the Gordon riots, wrote 'the danger of unbounded liberty and the danger of bounding it have produced a problem in the science of government which human understanding seems hitherto unable to solve'.

One does not need to scratch far below the surface of our history of protest to see numerous occasions of violence and death. The English Civil War may have been fought in the seventeenth century rather than in the nineteenth but it was still bloody. The Peasants' Revolt with Jack Straw at its head needed more than kind words to turn them away from London at the top of Hampstead Hill. The 'Peterloo' massacre which left a number of women and children dead, the Gordon riots and Emily Pankhurst's efforts for female enfranchisement were not unnatural precursors of the Brixton disorders, Red Lion Square and the Broadwater Farm Estate. Divisions in modern society caused by differentiations in wealth and power may feel as crucial to those prejudiced thereby as the divisions which caused disorder in years gone by. In particular, divisions in society caused by unemployment and racialism nowadays[14] may be akin to those previously experienced by serfs, peasants, workers, suffragettes and early unionists. The strength of feeling involved and the force of the issues concerned, as well perhaps as the intransigence of respective governments in dealing with the protestors, would all have had an effect on the level of violence and general disorder which ensued both in the past and today. This may tend to call into question a particular view espoused by more conservative writers regarding the prime causes of violence on demonstrations and protests.

[13] See, for example, Richard Clutterbuck, *Protest and the Urban Guerrilla* (London, Cassell, 1973). They also underplay the effect of media attention, or lack of attention – see, e.g., R. Kilroy-Silk, 'Riots that Go Unremarked', *The Times*, 22 Aug. 1987.
[14] For a similar perspective see J. White, 'The Summer Riots of 1919', *New Society*, 13 Aug. 1985; P. Smith and G. Gaskill, 'The Crowd in History', *New Society*, 20 Aug. 1981; G. Pearson, *Hooligan* (London, Macmillan, 1983).

The Conspiracy Theory of Protest

The view which they voice is that twentieth century revolutionaries act as 'entryists' into other legitimate organizations, and somehow subvert the aims and objectives of those organizations to their own ends. If they do not act as 'entryists', and are more open about their views, they may still be *agents provocateurs* who take over demonstrations for wider political purposes which are often unrealized by the others who are taking part.[15] According to this theory, protestors, demonstrators and strikers are easy prey to such revolutionaries who wish to use all such opportunities in order to further their own 'ulterior' purposes. Agitators, according to Clutterbuck,[16] mingle with a crowd which has gathered 'for some non-political purpose' and 'induce them into disruption or violence for political ends'. An allied complaint is that protests are very often staffed and fuelled by a group of people who will always be prepared to go out and protest at anything. This 'rent-a-crowd' is sometimes portrayed as a set of mindless individuals who will protest simply for the sake of fighting authority. On other occasions the 'rent-a-crowd' is portrayed as a highly developed and cynical group who will join any protest for their own purposes.

This 'conspiracy theory' of demonstrations and protests needs careful scrutiny. Its adoption is a useful strategy for law enforcement agencies and officers in that it provides a simplistic excuse for not treating demonstrators and protestors with the merit deserved by the issues of their protest. It enables the police to arrest and mistreat demonstrators and protestors with impunity in the knowledge that the ones who they, the police, are dealing with are only the *agents provocateurs* or agitators.

This theory also shows little understanding of the complexity of individuals and groups of people who find the necessity to protest issues in public. Where public protest is embarked upon, usually as a last resort, the protestors will often be representatives of only a minority within the country. If they were not representative of a minority view the more normal political channels might have provided a better solution. The fact that the protestors are a minority does not necessarily mean that they are wrong, or that they are right, either morally or politically, in their endeavour. However, it is likely to mean that they care a great deal about the cause or would have given up fighting for that cause, before resorting to demonstration in the streets. In order to campaign, it will have been necessary to bring together as many people as possible

---

[15] For an interesting example of police acting as *agents provocateurs* see 'PC Joined Gang who Attacked Rival Fans', *The Times*, 8 Jan. 1987.

[16] Clutterbuck, *Protest and the Urban Guerrilla*, p. 8.

so that a good public showing can be made, and the media who will be asked to publicize the protest will feel that this minority is a significant one and not just a few people.

The business of organizing a campaign must therefore involve liaisons of numerous individuals and groups, not all of whom will share identical views, the same strength of interest in the issue or agree on the best method of airing their protest. It is, therefore, not surprising that there will usually be within larger protest groups some smaller groups whose views will be at opposing ends of the spectrum of views aired in the protest. If complete solidarity of action is not achieved then it is possible that certain groups within a protest movement may attempt to achieve further or different aims than the consolidated group had intended. Since the sorts of people who become involved in protest are likely to feel strongly about the issues they are fighting, it is surprising that there are not more internecine conflicts or more occasions of active violence on demonstrations.

Where violence has occurred it has often been all too easy to blame a particular group on one extreme of the demonstration as the 'agitators' who have tried to lead the rest of the demonstration astray in a cynical fashion, using the goodwill of the otherwise good people. This was the accusation in relation to events at Red Lion Square on 15 June 1974 when the International Marxist Group advanced in a different direction from the remainder of the march (although in the direction originally agreed). This also seems to have been the accusation at the Vietnam demonstration of 17 March 1968 when the breakaway group of Mr Manchanda of the British Vietnam Solidarity Front broke away from the main Vietnam march and began pressing the police at the south-west corner of Grosvenor Square in London which houses the American Embassy. On each occasion the splinter or breakaway group was accused of causing the main problems, received the blame for all violence that occurred and was separated off by the 'conspiracy theory' of demonstrations as being quite different from the other, peaceful protestors.

Without wishing necessarily to comment on whether in these two cases, and in other similar cases, the particular groups were acting as agitators and *agents provocateurs*, it is important to assess the effects of operating this theory. The importance of any violence which occurred is minimized. This seems to be because society will not tolerate violence in this form. However, the importance of the issue demonstrated against or protested about is also minimized, and the evil of that issue and any institutional violence associated with it, are forgotten when the protest and protestors are dealt with in this manner.

It is not suggested that the bulk of the protestors would prefer to have had violence occurring. However, if violence did occur its relationship to the issues needs to be taken into account in any moral calculus. The use of the conspiracy theory of protest prevents this happening. The conspiracy theory leads us to believe that society itself is not so evil that it could have caused an event or situation so bad that reasonable people would protest violently against it. The theory, therefore, ascribes blame for any violence or disruption which occurs to social renegades and outcasts, and not to the issues themselves.[17]

The conspiracy theorists, such as Clutterbuck and others, agree that protest itself is 'necessary' and see clearly that it is a way of maintaining 'a fair rate of change in the face of entrenched interests in any society'. However, whether or not one applauds the fact, effective protest is often protest which involves some disruption to others, or disorder or even violence. It appears that where protest becomes effective the conspiracy theorists withdraw their support. This clearly has to be seen as a moral issue, or a political one, as opposed to a legal one. However, we should not be beleaguered by an attitude towards violence or other disruption which does not take into account the nature of the issue protested against, and the manner in which the protest is handled by law enforcement officers and agencies.

We will return to the question of violence later.

The Nature of Demonstration

What then are demonstrations really about? Are they to be seen as a significant element in western democratic society which will always need to be there, whatever the organizational or political form society takes? Do we see the possibility of demonstration as merely an effective safety valve to let off the pressure of strongly felt dissent now and again? Or is it a means for the youthful testing out of a previous generation's ideals before reluctantly being socialized into accepting them? A brief encounter with some descriptions of the views of demonstrators and the atmosphere of demonstrations may begin to answer these questions.

Few have written directly on this subject.[18] John Berger in his somewhat idiosyncratic article 'The Nature of Mass Demonstrations'[19]

---

[17] As Professor David Kretzmer has pointed out to me, demonstration organizers may feed into this process themselves by blaming any violence on to a few 'outsiders'.
[18] One classic which first uses the term 'demonstration' in the manner used here is Amitai Etzioni, *Demonstration Democracy* (New York, Gordon and Breach, 1969), prepared for the US 'Task Force on Demonstrations, Protests and Group Violence' arising out of the 'long hot summers' of the late 1960s.
[19] J. Berger, 'The Nature of Mass Demonstrations', *New Society*, 23 May 1968.

suggests that mass demonstrations such as those that were seen in the late 1960s on the streets of London and Paris, were in some sense a special sort of gathering. He suggests that they are 'a metaphor of strengths' and a possible 'rehearsal for revolution'. Berger alludes to the atmosphere experienced on such demonstrations by the participants, suggesting that the 'rehearsal for revolution' element is neither strategic nor tactical, but more a question of 'revolutionary awareness'. Those involved 'become more positively aware of how they belong to a class' which does not necessarily have to suffer a common fate, but may in fact have 'a common opportunity'.

According to Berger, the symbolic use, with freedom and independence, of a city space is a creativity which may change the outlook of a group or groups who had previously considered themselves to lack such power, freedom or independence. The desperation which may have originated the activity is forgotten in their jointly declared strength. By this symbolic behaviour they force a classic dilemma upon 'the state authority'. If the authority allows the crowd to do as it wishes the 'symbolic' power 'suddenly becomes real' and effective. On the other hand, if authority attempts to prevent the mass demonstration then the authority shows itself as 'undemocratic' and proves the nature of the issues subject to protest. Berger differentiates this form of 'spontaneous mass demonstration' from those which are 'officially approved and controlled' which have a sensored symbolism.

Since often authority decides to use force in order to constrain or disperse the crowd, such mass demonstrations will often end in violence. Berger alleges that the 'tactical truth and an historical one' is that the demonstrators are more likely to suffer more violence than they inflict since demonstrations are primarily protests of innocence. Moving away from this political mysticism, he suggests that the demonstrations 'express political ambitions before the political means necessary to realise them have been created. Demonstrations predict the realisation of their own ambitions and thus may contribute to that realisation, but they cannot themselves achieve them'.

Another view of the 'atmospheric' effect of being on a demonstration can be found in the classic protest film 'Getting Straight' in which Elliott Gould portrays a somewhat ageing postgraduate student who had taken part in the freedom marches of the early 1960s in the south of USA and in the 1970s faces a group of students protesting against the governance of their university. The Gould character describes participation in demonstrations as being an earthy feeling of emotional closeness. The feeling of togetherness and the display of power against authority, he suggests, makes people taking part feel 'sexy'.

A more intellectually ordered approach appears in Paul Barker's

'Portrait of a Protest'.[20] Barker reports on the work of Humphrey Taylor, Emanuel de Kadt and Earl Hopper who looked at a representative sample of demonstrators on the anti-Vietnam march of 27 October 1968 from the London School of Economics to the United States Embassy in Grosvenor Square in London. An earlier demonstration in March of that year had produced scenes of violence which had been given great prominence in newspapers and the general media. The researchers were interested to find out how much this had affected the protestors who came on the march. They also wanted to find out about the character and background of the demonstrators involved. As this is one of the very few studies looking in detail at the demographic characteristics of a group of protestors, it seems worth reporting its findings in some detail.

Approximately 1 per cent of the demonstrators were questioned by fifteen interviewers during the march, resulting in 270 completed interviews. A number of 'myths' which had been circulating in the media were disproved. Eighty-five per cent of those marching were British, and there were no overwhelming 'mass of overseas activists' as had been suggested. Only one in forty of the people on the march were 'art school students' although it had been suggested that following massive demonstrations at Hornsey and Guildford, a larger proportion would be present. Students generally were only just over half the sample; and 10 per cent of that half were still at school.

People did not seem to have been much influenced by the media to attend the demonstration, with most people naming friends and political groups as being their sources of information about the march. Two-thirds of the sample had been on a demonstration before. Neither were the number of students studying social sciences as great as had been suggested. There were almost equal proportions who were studying science or technology, the humanities and the social sciences in the sample studied.

Ninety-six per cent of protesters said that they were there to protest at US policy in Vietnam. Sixty-nine per cent said they were against US policies in general. Eighty-five per cent were against British policy on Vietnam. Sixty-five per cent were there to protest at 'the general structure of British society' and 68 per cent against 'capitalism in general'. Only 23 per cent were there to protest at 'all forms of authority'.

The main distinctions found by the researchers were between students of working class backgrounds and the rest. The working class students were much more opposed to capitalism than any other group including their fellow students and even other 'workers' who were on the march.

[20] P. Barker, 'Portrait of a Protest', *New Society*, Oct. 1968.

However, they were not so hostile to authority as other marchers. It was the working class students who were most in favour of a Vietcong victory, rather than a compromise in Vietnam. They were the ones who had the strongest suspicion that there would be violence on the march and they were not as definite as others that they would be remaining out of it. Being at university seemed to act 'as a magnifying glass . . . enlarging their class consciousness'. Class generally seemed to be a stronger factor than age, quite opposite to the view that the youth movement of the 1960s had rendered society more split by age than class. The protestors were, in general, not interested in being involved in violence. Although 70 per cent expected violence 'perhaps because of the preceding news coverage', over 80 per cent did not expect to be involved in it themselves.

In terms of political party affiliation, the Labour party came out most strongly at 28 per cent with Communists at 24 per cent, Anarchists at 11 per cent, the Liberal party at 5 per cent and the Conservative party at 4 per cent. Forty-four per cent of people had belonged to the CND and 24 per cent to the Committee of One Hundred with 20 per cent belonging to the Revolutionary Socialists Students Federation and 17 per cent to other socialist groups. Labour party support was very much stronger for those over 24 who would have had a chance already to vote.

Sixty-four per cent of the demonstrators were aged between 18 and 24, 11 per cent under 18, 14 per cent between 25 and 34, and 11 per cent above 35. Forty-one per cent had been, or were still, grammar school attenders, 16 per cent public or independent schools and 27 per cent secondary modern or comprehensive schools. Forty-six per cent of the sample had been to university and another 29 per cent had been in some other higher or further education. Of the students on the march almost 60 per cent were at university rather than polytechnics or colleges of education.

Some indication of lifestyles and aspirations may be imagined from a question about hero figures (*sic*) which 'produced a joyful scatter'. Just over half of the respondents gave 'straight answers'. Che Guevara was mentioned by seventeen people, Marx and Lenin by sixteen each, Gandhi by eight and Mao by six. In the four to six range were Trotsky, Luther King, Bertrand Russell, President Kennedy, Shakespeare, Churchill and Christ. John Lennon was the only pop figure mentioned and D. H. Lawrence, Ataturk and Herbert Marcuse each obtained one or two votes.

Unfortunately, no other such empirical survey of a large demonstration in this country has been published. This particular piece of research must therefore serve as an historical snapshot of that era of demonstrators. It is, however, more useful than a simple black and white photograph devoid of context. By comparing the findings of this research with the then current mythology regarding such demonstrators and demonstrations it is possible to learn lessons which are also applicable to the present time. Media hype and general portrayals of such events and actors are not necessarily consonant with accuracy.

Christopher Driver's book *The Disarmers: A Study in Protest*[21] is not such an attempt at empirical observation of one demonstration, but it provides an earlier overview of a somewhat different group of post-war British protestors.

Driver's description of the early Campaign for Nuclear Disarmament marchers shows them as 'mainly middle class and professional'. The first march from Trafalgar Square to Aldermaston over the Easter weekend in 1958 had between 5000 and 10,000 people marching over the last mile. Alan Brien in the *Daily Mail* said,

> They were the sort of people who would normally spend Easter listening to a Beethoven concert on the Home Service, pouring dry sherry from a decanter for the neighbours, painting Picasso designs on hard boiled eggs, attempting the literary competitions in the weekly papers, or going to church with the children . . . the quiet suburbanites were on the march.

The many 'notabilities' included five Labour MPs, Fenner Brockway, Frank Allaun, Michael Foot, Ian Mikardo and Steven Swingler, as well as people from the arts such as Doris Lessing, Christopher Logue, Kenneth Tynan and Christopher Booker. The McWhirter brothers (one of whom was later to be killed by an IRA bomb) 'came to jeer, and had their car dented by impatient spectators'.

Another viewpoint on those involved in demonstrations appears from the proceedings of the Inquiry conducted by then Lord Justice Scarman into the events of 15 June 1974 in Red Lion Square, London. The details of the events which occurred will be dealt with in chapter 2. For the purposes of this chapter, the evidence of Martin Webster (who was the National Activities Organizer of the National Front, a neo-Fascist group), provides an interesting example of a rather different group of protestors and their form of organization.

Under cross-examination from Stephen Sedley who was representing the National Union of Students,[22] Martin Webster described the composition of the National Front march.[23] It apparently began with a 'flag party' carrying flag poles with pointed aluminium tops. Behind

[21] C. Driver, *The Disarmers: A Study in Protest* (London, Hodder & Stoughton, 1964).
[22] A student from Warwick University had died as a result of the events of that day.
[23] Tony Gilbert, *Only One Died: An Account of the Scarman Inquiry into the Events of 15th June 1974, in Red Lion Square* (London, Kay Beauchamp, 1975), pp. 33–8.

them came the main 'banner party' carrying a banner with the words 'Britons Unite with the N.F.'. After them were the drum corps, the platform and petition party, and then 'the first defence party' made up of 'men who were robust . . . in the event of an attack on our column'. Webster described what the 'first defence party' would do in the event of an 'attack'.

> I had scouts at the front of the column to watch out for people building up in side streets for this sort of activity, and in the event of such a force being built up by the opposition, I would be told about it and I would instruct the defence party to go forward from the column and block the entrance of that street by linking arms, so that no rush could be made on our column to break it up.

Beyond this 'defence party' was a loud speaker vehicle and then the main section of National Front members and supporters, followed by a second defence party bringing up the rear. Stephen Sedley asked whether it was within Webster's knowledge that the leader of the second defence party, a Mr Ken Merrit, was a man with a record of conviction for robbery with violence for which he had served 6 months imprisonment. Webster denied any knowledge of this.

One cannot limit the understanding of the aims and objectives of protestors to one political viewpoint or one side of the political spectrum. It is quite clear from their evidence that the fact of marching, and the manner of marching, together held a very different meaning for Webster's National Front from the views expressed (although they were with regard to mass demonstrations) by John Berger.

The supporters of the anti-racist collection of groups under the heading of 'Liberation' were also marching on 15 June 1974, and it was the clash or possible clash between the racialist National Front and the anti-racist 'Liberation' which caused the disorder.

The 'Liberation' supporters were a very different group from the National Front supporters. Liberation marched in a different manner and with very different objectives to those of the National Front. It is clear that any theory regarding rights of protest and demonstration, and any policing or law enforcement systems and attitudes, need to take into account a whole spectrum of demonstrations and demonstrators from the quiet suburbanites of the early CND, through the politically aware students of the anti-Vietnam marches, all the way over to the quasi-militaristic approach of the National Front.

A final view of the nature of protest can be obtained from the Tribunals of Inquiry associated with events in Northern Ireland, including the Widgery tribunal regarding the events of Sunday 30 January

1972 ('Bloody Sunday'),[24] and the Scarman inquiry into violence and civil disturbances in Northern Ireland in 1969.[25]

Here we see a picture of 'no go' areas and attempts by the armed forces to return such areas under their control. In these cases the army and the police worked together or separately in controlling disturbances. One interesting paragraph from the report by the then Mr Justice Scarman sums up some of the distinctions between demonstrations and outright 'riots', and the thin line that may be drawn between them.

> But the riots are a different matter. Neither the IRA nor any Protestant organisation or anybody else planned a campaign of riots. They were communal disturbances arising from a complex political, social and economic situation. More often than not they arose from slight beginnings: but the communal tensions were such that, once begun they could not be controlled. Young men threw a few stones at some policemen or at an Orange procession: there followed a confrontation between police and stone-throwers now backed by a sympathetic crowd . . . Their own interpretations of the events of 1968 and early 1969 had encouraged the belief amongst the minority that demonstrations did secure concessions, and that the police were their enemy and the main obstacle to a continuing programme of demonstrations, while the same events had convinced a large number of Protestants that a determined attempt already gaining a measure of success, was being made to undermine the constitutional position of Northern Ireland with the United Kingdom. In so tense a situation it needed very little to get going a major disturbance.[26]

Problems of Practice

Endemic to the nature of protest are a number of other issues which deserve recognition in this introductory chapter. They include the competing rights of protesters between themselves and with bystanders, the existence and nature of discretion in the legal system, and the problem of violence.

---

[24] 'Report of the Tribunal Appointed to Inquire into the Events on Sunday 30 January 1972, which Led to Loss of Life in Connection with the Procession in Londonderry on that day' [1972], HL101, HC220.
[25] 'Report of the Tribunal of Inquiry into Violence and Civil Disturbances in Northern Ireland in 1969', Cmnd. 566.
[26] 'Report of the Tribunal of Inquiry into Violence and Civil Disturbances in Northern Ireland in 1969', Cmnd. 566, 2.4.

Competing Rights

In relation to the material above it will be noted that there can be no singular prime 'right' in this area of human behaviour which does not in itself conflict with the rights of others. All rights, therefore, are comparative and interactive. This must clearly be true for demonstrations and protests by opposing groups at the same time and place, groups who are entirely ideologically opposed to each other or even, in part, ideologically opposed.

Similarly, comparative and interactive 'rights' must also exist between protestors and others who may be affected by the demonstration or protest in some way. This will include those people who are directly affected by a march or meeting who, for example, have fewer customers buying from their shops or cannot as a result drive their vehicle or walk along a highway. It will also include those affected in less immediate fashion, for example, by extra amounts of tax or local rates being imposed on them because of the necessity of extra police being available or present at demonstrations. Indeed, the cost of demonstrations, especially in the metropolis, has been a matter of some concern for a number of years and the Metropolitan Police Commissioner's reports specifically mention this as an increasing difficulty.[27]

This particular competition of rights between protesters and others should, in theory, be solved on the basis of policy through the normal political channels. A general initial decision could be made with regard to the importance of protests and demonstrations which would underwrite certain levels of police expenditure out of the public purse. However, the situation could arise that expenditure on these matters could become out of hand in the view of tax and rates or poll tax payers, or in the view of the police themselves. If this occurred, the expense of policing protest would then become an important element in deciding the validity of the democratic process.

Discretion

An element which is also implicit in the above discussion, and which will become more important in relation to legal doctrine, is the amount of discretion available to the police, the prosecutors, the courts and the government in dealing with protest. Where rights and freedoms actively compete with each other, and exist side by side with massive discretion

[27] See ch. 8.

in the hands of the authorities, a recipe for uncertainty exists. This, as we shall see, is the case in England and Wales. The law in itself is so all-encompassing that almost every form of protest and demonstration is, by its nature, a breach of some legal regulation. With this background, it is clear that any demonstration which is allowed to occur does so as a result of active or passive discretion on the part of the law enforcement agencies.

Although no right of protest exists at law, we have already noted that such a right is claimed to exist. Where protest is allowed the police report this act of discretion as their active involvement in promoting 'freedom of speech'. Where protests or demonstrations are banned or otherwise affected by police action, no lip service to such discretion or freedom of speech is paid, but a reference is made to the laws which have been, or may be, broken.

Recognition and understanding should be given to the nature of discretion and the power which arises from it. A positive use of discretion is equivalent to a negative use of discretion in that they are both an exercise of the same power. Where such power exists, it is not important that on occasion it is used wisely, if on other occasions it is not. As will be seen, it is the nature of this power and the manner of its use which makes this area of the law and human activity so fascinating.

The use of discretion is another issue through which our system may be compared with other countries with a written constitution[28] seeming to legislate for such freedoms to exist. Whereas under such systems reliance appears to be placed on rules,[29] in our system reliance appears to be placed on people in the form of the discretion of the police and others involved in law enforcement.

Violence

The question of violence on demonstrations and protests has been touched upon and will be returned to, but needs to be mentioned directly here. This is not the simple issue which it appears to be. As we have seen above, one cannot blandly state that a violent demonstration is immoral or a non-violent demonstration moral. Neither can one be certain of the causes or exact perpetrators of violence on demonstrations. There is some information which seems to suggest that the manner of

[28] See ch. 9 for a longer discussion of the 'constitutional' culture issue.
[29] Clearly, discretion also exists in a constitutionally based system, but may be subject to more control. See, e.g., L. Lustgarten, *The Governance of Police* (London, Sweet & Maxwell, 1986), pp. 7–8 and ch. 1 generally on the different discretion available to the 'British' police officer.

policing of demonstrations can directly cause or prevent violence by demonstrators and by police.

It also seems that preparation for violence in itself by either side (which appears to be only rational when the media have played up its likelihood) is a further cause of violence. As far as one can tell, as much violence seems to occur as a result of an immediate precipitating incident at the scene whilst feelings are running high, as occurs as a result of intentional conduct on the part of police or protesters. Violence, therefore, needs careful and considered study, and a beginning will be made in subsequent chapters.

Conclusion

This chapter has introduced some of the competing theories relating to the morality and legality of civil disobedience. It has considered the function of protest, and what sorts of people take to the streets in order to carry out protest and the nature of the protests involved. It has considered why people protest and some of the major issues which demonstrations present, including competing rights, expense of policing, discretion and violence.

With this background in mind we now turn to see, through a number of case studies, what is involved in the planning, carrying out and policing of demonstrations in more detail.

2

Case Studies

This chapter includes two types of case study of protest or demonstration. The first part considers some general histories of protest, noting how the specific views of the historians or commentators are played out in the history they portray. In the second part some specific case studies of demonstrations will be looked at in detail.

The objectives of setting out the information in this manner are many. Primarily, it is important for a better understanding of what is involved in a demonstration and in the policing of a demonstration. This should appear from the individual case studies. Secondly, it is important to note that history is really only historiography, i.e. that we as readers have very little idea of what actually occurred in history; all we know is what the historians say occurred. This is a truism not only for historical case studies, but it applies also within the legal context to the adversarial trial. In attempting, therefore, to make sense out of the empirical information of such case studies, one must necessarily view each item in the context of its writer and its writer's intention.

Thirdly, by setting out in detail some examples of the situations and behaviour to which the doctrinal law will then be applied a clearer understanding may be obtained of where the practical problems lie in applying the law of public order to the facts of public protest and demonstration.

Some General Histories of Protest

Any selection of histories or of particular authors cannot be entirely representative. This selection is based on a sample of different political opinions and does not attempt to represent all possible views, but merely a spectrum of them. The authors chosen for this purpose are Barry Cox, a writer on civil liberties; A. F. Wilcox, a policeman writing on the politics of prosecution before the Crown Prosecution Service was set up; Richard Clutterbuck, an ex-army officer who also taught Politics at Exeter University; Stuart Bowes, a political researcher into police roles and Ronald Kidd, a Member of Parliament who belonged to the National Council for Civil Liberties.

The British Genius – Clutterbuck

In chapter 1 reference was made to the work of Richard Clutterbuck. In this section his thesis will be developed further in order to provide an understanding of one view of protest, and especially its relationship to violence and role of the police.[1]

Clutterbuck describes the particular 'British genius' as being the ability to protest without violence. He suggests that the recipe for this lies in the special relationship which exists in Britain 'between the police and the people – both radical and conservative'. He suggests that this relationship goes far back to a collective responsibility existing in each community in Saxon times. He points out that each citizen after the Norman Conquest had liability for a compulsory 'police' duty of enforcing the law. When a professional police force finally emerged, it was never an agent of central or local government, but had a higher duty to the law itself and to 'the Queen's peace'. Each individual policeman has the question of judgment about the legality of protest available to him 'on the spot'.

Starting with John Wilkes in 1763, Clutterbuck charts the continuing effects of protest. He sees Wilkes as a 'provocateur', an ambitious and charismatic leader who exploited the real grievances of the people for his own ends. He encouraged riotous mobs to roam the streets of London and delighted them with his own exploits. Subsequently, 'he cashed in on his popularity by becoming an alderman and later Lord Mayor of London'. Apparently, during the Gordon Riots in 1780 it was Wilkes, in an about-face, who assumed command of the troops who fired on crowds outside the Bank of England.

The Gordon Riots, aimed at preventing the granting of certain rights to the Catholic minority, led to burning and looting of buildings, smashing down the gates of Newgate Jail to release the prisoners and the killing or wounding by George III's troops of several hundred people. The results of the violence, according to Clutterbuck, were simply a 'backlash'. A number of 'voluntary associations for defence of

[1] The major excerpts produced as Clutterbuck's thesis here are from *Protest and the Urban Guerrilla* (London, Cassell, 1973), pp. 13–32. His views have also been expounded in *Living with Terrorism* (London, Faber, 1975), *Britain in Agony* (London, Faber, 1978), *The Media and Political Violence* (London, Macmillan, 1981), *Industrial Conflict and Democracy* (London, Macmillan, 1984) and *The Future of Political Violence* (London, Macmillan, 1986).

property' appeared and restrictions under the Riot Act on troops opening fire were removed. From this he learns that the demonstration 'by turning violent, had certainly not advanced the liberty of the subject, but had set it back'.

Clutterbuck proceeds along the same tack describing the actions of the Luddite movement in 1811 to 1813. This was the beginning of the Industrial Revolution and textile workers were unhappy about the new technology of weaving frames appearing in the factories. Some 12,000 troops were eventually deployed, even though much of the violence was used against property. Three people died as a result of the Luddite riots, but thirty of their leaders were hanged. This seems to show again, according to Clutterbuck, that violence only begets a backlash.

However, his next example would appear to disprove his point. In Manchester in 1819, when 80,000 people gathered together peacefully to demand, among other things, freedom of assembly and universal suffrage, the crowd was charged by the Yeomanry and eleven of those assembled were killed. This massacre of 'Peterloo' in St Peters Fields in Manchester was not provoked by the violence of the demonstrators, and therefore the backlash appears to have been not so much to violence, but to protest itself.

Clutterbuck admits that the assemblies of the Reform League in the 1860s led to the reforms in voting rights of subsequent years. He also notes that the violence of the suffragettes, including assault on politicians, smashing windows, burning buildings and chaining themselves to railings, as well as Emily Davison's act of martyrdom under a horse on Derby Day in 1913 were finally to bring about female suffrage. However, Clutterbuck suggests that it was probably the energies they threw into recruiting and war work during the First World War which earned them the right of suffrage afterwards. He concludes, as does Roger Fulford,[2] that it was 'the public revulsion against their violence' which prevented women receiving the vote before the war. This is a question not readily susceptible to proof.

Clutterbuck then refers to the General Strike of 1926 showing, in his view, how little bitterness and violence occurred despite the polarization of views. He mentions the 'football matches between strikers and police' as 'an established highlight of English folklore'.

The 1930s brought the clashes between Oswald Mosley's British Union of Fascists, and protests by left wingers and Jewish groups. Clutterbuck points out that these led to the passing of the Public Order Act 1936 and he minimizes the amount of violence which was supposed to have occurred, or even the numbers of people involved by pointing

---

[2] R. Fulford, *Votes for Women* (London, White Lion, 1976).

out that 'the combined strength of both sides in the biggest demonstration [of that period] was less than the number of Londoners who turned out [in the same week] to cheer the beautiful Princess Marina when she arrived to marry the Duke of Kent'. He then passes off the entire Campaign for Nuclear Disarmament protest in this manner, 'the demonstrators were predominantly intellectuals, and as they offered no convincing suggestions as to how Russia might be motivated to ban her bomb, they were not taken very seriously'.

From then onwards he charts the growth of the 'New Left' with 'a wider aim than the particular political issue' for which they were fighting. He mentions the anti-apartheid demonstrations involved in the 'Stop the 70 Tour' protests organized by Hain and others. The previous year attempts had been made to stop the South African Rugby Football team playing at a number of venues in England. There were numerous arrests at these matches which are well charted by A. F. Wilcox (see below). In the event, the Labour government asked the Cricket Council to withdraw their invitation to the South African team. Once again Clutterbuck's grudging acquiescence that protest achieves its aim is accompanied by a number of other possible reasons why this occurred, quite apart from the protests themselves. Clutterbuck, therefore, explicitly states that he is in favour of public assembly and free speech as an 'outlet' which 'has always prevented the pressure of discontent from building up to a dangerous level'. He states himself explicitly to be against violence. However, his implicit message all along is that protest is not really successful for its own reasons, but that where success is achieved extraneous factors must have existed.

It is our unarmed police force which Clutterbuck sees as 'the biggest single contribution for keeping protest peaceful'. He compares this situation with the violence that has erupted in the United States and elsewhere as a result of protest. In 1968, when five people were killed and 1500 were injured in a single night and America had its 'long hot summer', including the assassinations of Robert Kennedy and Martin Luther King, and riots at the Democratic Convention in Chicago and Cleveland, England had its two Vietnam demonstrations of March and October, the latter being almost devoid of violence. This is, indeed, a striking comparison, as is the comparison with the position 'across the Irish Sea'. Clutterbuck puts this down to a rule of law which takes action against the forces of authority for going too far, as well as against protestors. As examples he cites the trial of Captain Porteous in 1737 who ordered his troops to fire on a rioting mob, thereby killing and wounding seventeen people. He also refers to the trial of Gillam, a magistrate, and Maclean, a soldier, involved in the Wilkes Riots in London in 1768 when five or six people were killed and fifteen wounded.

He says that it was in this style that Robert Peel's 'Bobbies' started their job armed only with wooden batons: 'Every recruit was taught that unarmed on the streets of London, he relied utterly on the support and approval of the public'. It is this alleged support and approval of the public[3] which has perhaps begun to ebb away from the police during recent years. We shall return to this topic in a later chapter.

The Police as Enemy of the Working Class – Bowes

Stuart Bowes in his book *The Police and Civil Liberties* writes from a political view on almost the opposite end of the spectrum to that of Clutterbuck.[4] He charts events from 1872 until the passage of the 1919 Police Act during which time the police attempted to form a trade union of their own to deal with questions of pay and conditions of service. During this period over a thousand striking policemen were dismissed. General Sir Nevil Macready was the Metropolitan Police Commissioner at the time who 'set about destroying the union'. A Police Federation was established, but this was to be 'independent of any body or person outside the police service'. Bowes sees the consequence of this isolation from organized labour as being that 'police behaviour has never been influenced by the awareness of the justification for organised working class action'. Bowes quotes W. H. Thompson noting the enormous 'readiness to baton and arrest demonstrators' during the inter-war years of widespread unemployment. This is exactly the same period which Clutterbuck describes as characterized by 'lack of bitterness and violence . . . between strikers and police'. Bowes suggests that 'police interference became most harmful and savage' and Thompson says 'the prevention, banning, and stopping of meetings finds no counterpart in the history of the working class movement before the war'.

Bowes charts the position of the police in the 1880s during colliery strikes acting clearly 'as the servants of colliery owners' and J. Keir Hardie states that in Ayrshire in 1887 police were 'riding down inoffensive children nearly to death and felling quiet old men with a blow from a baton'. Bowes shows how the Metropolitan Police were sent to Glamorganshire in 1910 to quell strikes and unrest in mining areas, and then to Hull, Salford and South Wales to help break strikes in the following year.

The police clearly did not see themselves as being part of the 'labour

---

[3] See Robert Reiner, *The Politics of the Police* (Brighton, Wheatsheaf, 1985), pp. 43–5 for a different view.
[4] The main discussion and excerpts are from Stuart Bowes, *The Police and Civil Liberties* (London, Lawrence & Wishart, 1966), pp. 23–33, 73–105.

movement' and often, as Kidd suggested, made 'a series of allegations which had not been supported by evidence during the trial and which had nothing to do with the matter before the court'. One example of this mentioned by Bowes is the case of Arthur Horner, the miners' leader, who was described by the police in court 'as an agent of a foreign power who had terrorised the population of the Welsh valley'.

The early 1920s was a period of great disillusionment after the end of the First World War and the police showed brutality to victims who were frequently the 'impoverished unemployed'. The labour leader, Wal Hannington, described a scene in October 1920 when the unemployed workers marched in support of a petition by a number of the mayors of London. The police, both on horseback and on foot, charged the marchers in circumstances in which it was impossible for the crowds to retreat.

> The police who wanted to clear Whitehall were now preventing it from being cleared. Dozens of men lay in the road and on the sidewalks groaning from pain as the blood gushed out from wounds inflicted by police batons.

Affiliation to the National Unemployed Workers Movement increased, their leaders were imprisoned and the editor of the national publication *Out of Work* was imprisoned for 3 weeks for inciting disaffection among the Metropolitan Police by appealing to them in an article not to use their batons amongst the unemployed. Marches of the unemployed were banned in Birmingham and in London. With the General Strike in 1926 the police behaviour tended more towards 'intimidation, assault and arrest'. Bowes documents 'vengeful behaviour', such as that occurring at a peaceful meeting of dockers in Poplar on 12 May 1926 after the strike.

> A lorry filled with police was driven straight through the crowd, causing injuries to several people. The lorry stopped, police got out and, after doubling back, they twice charged the crowd with batons injuring so many that 35 men had to be treated (mainly for head injuries) at a local hospital. When Father Groser, who was carrying a crucifix, approached them and attempted to explain that the meeting was peaceful, police struck him down.

Bowes documents numerous such incidents through the 1920s and 1930s, where police activity in the face of the labour movement was not orderly or sensibly reactive, but vicious, aggressive and vengeful. A particular instance between 13 and 16 September 1932 in Birkenhead brought large numbers of police into the town and 'working class areas were raided; homes entered without warrants; arrests made indiscriminately and without cause; and men, women and children beaten up. Repeated on the next two nights this terrorism caused over a hundred civilians to be taken to hospital with such severe injuries as a broken wrist, fractured ribs, broken arms and legs'.

Bowes sees this anti-unemployed worker activity as being the natural precursor of the behaviour of the police from 1935 onwards and 'the history of police protection for fascism'. The legal decision in the case of *Duncan* v. *Jones*[5] had left the police in the position of arbiters of which group could hold meetings and they used their power in accordance with their political views.

According to Bowes, the

> history of political movements shows clearly that when the police co-operate, or at least do not interfere with political demonstrations, these remain almost without exception disciplined and peaceful; but when the police seek to enforce bans, discipline is often violently destroyed and sometimes police violence is returned in kind.

Bowes gives numerous illustrations of his point. By way of example he cites the meeting at Cold-bath Fields in May 1883 when Colonel Rowan ordered an onslaught of 600 police on men, women and children, 'great numbers being seriously injured and a policeman being killed'. The inquest into the death of the policeman found a verdict of 'justifiable homicide' in view of the fact 'that the conduct of the police was ferocious, brutal and unprovoked by other people'. This is contrasted with the protest and demonstration over the sentence imposed on the Tolpuddle Martyrs in 1834 where a huge protest demonstration was not interfered with by the police and provided its own 'strict self-discipline'.

> Group after group of Labour's children marched onward to the gay green field. . . . No brawls destroyed the great assembly. No force was needed to provoke good discipline.[6]

Unlike Clutterbuck, Bowes sees the period from 1850 onward as not being an easy progress towards universal suffrage. He presents a graphic description of the Sunday trading protests in 1855 when 'the lower classes' were invited 'to see how the rich observe the Sabbath' by watching their carriages go through Hyde Park. This activity caused a ban on further meetings or assemblages in large numbers from the Metropolitan Police. Similarly, on 17 June 1866, the Metropolitan Police Commissioner banned a meeting of the Reform League due to be held in Hyde Park on 23 July. The effect of the ban and cruel police action

[5] *Duncan* v. *Jones* [1936] 1 KB 218; see ch. 6 for full details of the decision.
[6] *The Pioneer*, 26 Apr. 1834, extracted from Bowes, *The Police and Civil Liberties*, p. 79.

in enforcing it was an open fight between police and demonstrators ending with the involvement of two companies of the Grenadier Guards with fixed bayonets, and two squadrons of Life Guards fully armed and with swords drawn entering onto the scene. Interestingly, 'the soldiers were loudly cheered while the police were loudly hissed'.

Bowes traces this use of 'police brutality' in more recent times as being intended 'to intimidate and terrorise rather than to maintain public order'. One example was the demonstration on Sunday 4 November 1956 in Trafalgar Square against the invasion of Suez. After the meeting had ended and the 30,000 demonstrators were moving off in different directions the police charged a group which was 'in good humour', moving down Whitehall. 'As it was closely packed, many women and children in it became terrified and in the first and subsequent charges several people were injured.'

As usual, no announcement was made by the police and the National Council for Civil Liberties noted how the police changed a 'good natured crowd' into 'an ugly scene'. The mounted police 'used their horses in a most terrifying manner . . . galloping their horses right at the crowd . . . many of the mounted officers were enjoying the experience . . .'. 1961 saw sitdowns on behalf of the Campaign for Nuclear Disarmament and the Committee of One Hundred. Even though the protestors were all clearly peaceful the police treated them with awful brutality as if they had been involved in a violent protest. Even the *Daily Telegraph* reported, 'After midnight the police effort presented new violence. Some of those seized were making their way quietly out of the Square. When they protested they were thrown to the pavements, dragged forcibly to the vans and coaches and manhandled.'

According to Bowes, a new weapon, the motor cycle police officer, appeared in 1962 during protests against the Cuba crisis. More than 600 police dealt with 400 demonstrators, there were 126 arrests, and many people were injured and knocked senseless to the ground. 1963 brought protests against tyranny in Greece and in particular against the killing of Dr Lambrakis, a Greek peace leader. At the time of the visit of King Paul and Queen Frederika to England, the Prime Minister Harold Macmillan announced in Parliament that there would be no ban on peaceful demonstrations during the visit as 'the orderly rights of peaceful demonstration are, of course, part also of our tradition here' (Hansard, 27 June). However, the police acted vigorously to prevent any meeting or demonstration or stoppage. The *Daily Herald* reported on 10 July, according to Bowes, 'this was life in central London for some hours yesterday. A city, where one felt, even the lamp posts might be accused any moment of loitering with intent.' Such was the 'stupidity and cheerful brutality of the police' that 'an old lady of 65, a quiet and gentle-looking person of short stature' who put her hand out to stroke the head of a police horse was struck by the mounted policeman on the side of her head shattering her spectacles into her eye.

Bowes notes again the point, this time made by Flavius of the *New Statesman* on 12 July, 'there would almost certainly have been less violence and a good deal more decorum . . . if the demonstrators whose professed intentions were pacific, had been allowed to form up outside the Palace railings (where noisy demonstrations are regularly encouraged – so long as they are pro-royal)'.

In summary, therefore, Bowes' views are quite opposite to those of Clutterbuck, not only in terms of the inferences to be drawn from history, but in terms of the nature of that history in itself. Bowes seems to blame bad police organization and over-reaction to demonstrations as being the main culprit for the cause of violence on demonstrations. The underlying cause for this poor police outlook seems to him to be the splitting off of the police from their natural background of the working class.

Deciding to Prosecute – Wilcox

One of the first works attempting to explain the manner in which police discretion was used in deciding whether to prosecute (before the Crown Prosecution Service) is a book written by the former Chief Constable of Hertfordshire, Mr A. F. Wilcox.[7] In the central chapters 4 and 5 he looks at the political considerations for deciding to prosecute and some of the problems inherent in riots and demonstrations.[8] Whilst, in theory, many such decisions would now be made by different people, if not on different grounds, it is not clear whether any major policy changes have taken place as opposed to a different system of organization of prosecution. In any case, the hierarchy of the Attorney General, the Director of Public Prosecutions, Solicitor General and Treasury Counsel are still in place. It is to these that Wilcox first turns.

Wilcox chronicles the statements of numerous Attorney Generals that, even though they sit in the Cabinet and are therefore part of the executive branch of government, their decisions regarding the prosecution of offences are made completely without being affected by political influence. Such statements have been made by Sir Hartley Shawcross in 1951 regarding his decision to prosecute strikers and by Sir (as he then was) Elwyn Jones addressing the Cambridge Law Society. Wilcox

[7] A. F. Wilcox, *The Decision to Prosecute* (London, Butterworth, 1972).
[8] Ibid. The major extracts and quotations are from pp. 21–46.

also mentions the Leila Kahlid affair at which time Sir Peter Rawlinson, the then Attorney General, decided not to prosecute Leila Kahlid (an unsuccessful hi-jacker of an El Al airliner) so that she could be exchanged for some hostages then held by Palestinian guerrillas. Wilcox concludes by stating, 'it would be idle to pretend that in the past Attorneys have never been placed under political pressures; how far they succeeded in resisting such pressure is obscure'.

Wilcox recalls the Campbell affair which brought about the downfall of the Ramsey MacDonald government of 1924. The then Director of Public Prosecutions sought the advice of the Attorney General regarding an article published by Campbell headed 'The Army and Industrial Disputes: An Open Letter to the Fighting Forces', urging soldiers and sailors to have nothing to do with fighting in the event of war, but to join their comrades, the working class. Campbell was arrested for incitement to mutiny, but at the magistrates' court the Director of Public Prosecutions was said by counsel to have accepted 'representations that the intention of the newspaper article had not been to seduce men in the fighting forces from their duty'. Since no representation of this nature had come from Campbell himself, it became clear that they had come from above in the Government. The MacDonald government fell over the question of appointing a Select Committee of Inquiry to look into what had occurred.

Special political difficulties have affected the decision to prosecute offences under the Official Secrets Acts. Whereas it may be an easier question to decide whether somebody spying for another power should be prosecuted, it is more difficult to decide whether technical breaches of the Acts by protestors or demonstrators should also be prosecuted. Any charge under the Acts needs the approval of the Attorney General. When six members of the Committee of One Hundred organized a demonstration at Wethersfield aerodrome in Essex in December of 1961 they were charged with conspiracy to commit an offence against s. 1 of the Official Secrets Act 1920. This case, *Chandler v DPP*[9] reached the House of Lords where the conviction was upheld stating 'the demonstration undoubtedly constituted a purpose prejudicial to the safety and interests of the state'. This seemed to go against previous undertakings in 1911 and 1920 to use the Official Secrets Acts only in the context of espionage. Such opposing views seem to echo the problems arising from the ABC charges in 1979 and also the Campbell affair at the BBC in January 1987.[10]

Wilcox's view of the decision to prosecute in cases involving public

[9] *Chandler* v. *DPP* [1964] AC 763.
[10] See *The Times*, 26 Jan., 4 Feb. 1987.

disorder arising out of industrial disputes exhibits a measured interest in maintaining the law through a low profile:

> on the whole it would seem that if public order can be maintained by arresting the offenders and having them dealt with promptly by the magistrates it is better not to worsen the situation by bringing grave charges necessitating committal proceedings and trial before a local jury.

In dealing with the history of 'Riots and Demonstrations' Wilcox refers to the Gordon Riots of 1780 and the Peterloo Massacre of 1819, already mentioned. He describes events in Bristol in 1831 resulting from a statement by Sir Charles Wetherall in Parliament 'that the citizens of Bristol were indifferent to the cause of reform'. Sir Charles had expected his constituency to support his own opposition to universal suffrage. When, in October of that year, Sir Charles, who was also the Recorder of Bristol, was opening the Assizes he was greeted with jeering and howling crowds. A riot ensued, the prisoners were released from Bristol jail and the County jail on the outskirts of the city was burnt down as was the Bishop's Palace, numerous warehouses and the Customs House. The number of 'casualties was never ascertained, although some estimates put them as high as 500'. Eighty-one rioters were tried by the then Lord Chief Justice Tindall, four were sentenced to be hanged and the others to transportation or imprisonment. More recent events in the St Paul's area of Bristol in 1987[11] tend to pale into insignificance compared with those riots.

The civil and military authorities were blamed for 'weakness and vacillation'. The mayor and magistrates were indicted for neglect of duty, but were acquitted. The unfortunate Lieutenant Brereton who commanded the troops committed suicide while being court martialled. It was such events which brought about the Municipal Corporations Act enabling cities and boroughs to form police forces. According to Wilcox, the advent of the new organized police forces meant that from then on it was 'no longer necessary to suppress riots by calling on the troops to open fire on their fellow citizens'.

Wilcox refers to the Fascist marches of the 1930s and to the complaints that the Fascists were being favoured by the police. He records the Home Secretary's protest that 'there was no conspiracy at Scotland Yard to favour one particular party', and he notes that the Police Commissioner, Sir Philip Game did stop a march on 4 October which Sir John Simon, the Home Secretary, had refused to ban. Wilcox seems to suggest that any of the problems caused by a feeling that the police were favouring

[11] See J. Benyon and J. Solomos, *The Roots of Urban Unrest* (Oxford, Pergamon, 1987), pp. 3–5, and 61–2.

the Fascists were solved by the advent of the Public Order Act 1936. It seems equally likely that events in central Europe towards the end of the 1930s may have begun to change police reactions to Mosley and the Fascists.

Wilcox presents an interesting reaction to the thesis that it is very often the show of police strength which causes problems of violence and disorder on demonstrations through provocation. This was an argument suggested in relation to the Vietnam demonstrations of 1968 (see later) and, more generally, that if the police kept away from demonstrations they would be more orderly. Wilcox's reaction is similar to that of Clutterbuck, 'time after time the leaders of demonstrations have found themselves in the predicament of the sorcerer's apprentice who has unleashed forces he is impotent to control'.

Wilcox uses this assertion to discourse on how difficult it is to assess how many police, police vehicles and other paraphernalia of riot control will be needed to deal with any particular demonstration. The senior police officer is caught in the dilemma that 'he is likely to be criticised if he has too many police, he is certain to be condemned if he has too few'. Wilcox provides an interesting insight into how many police have been used in different demonstrations. On ten occasions in 1934 over 1000 police had to be mobilized to keep order in the face of British Union of Fascists meetings. In 1936 forces of 3000 and 4000 police were involved. Apparently, similar numbers were used for CND and the Vietnam Solidarity Campaigns in the 1960s. In April 1961 more than 3000 police were on duty in Whitehall, and in September some 4500 policed a CND march in Parliament Square. For the march on 17 March 1968 to the United States Embassy in Grosvenor Square 1275 police were on duty. Some 9000 police were kept on duty for the Vietnam March on Sunday 27 October 1968. However, Wilcox fails to mention the particular manner in which the 9000 police were maintained largely out of view of the demonstrators on the latter occasion.

Wilcox also provides a chart of the number of police used to deal with each of the events of the South African Rugby Union Team tour in 1969, together with the number of arrests which took place on each occasion. He learns from these figures that 'the display of police strength inside and outside the grounds effectively discouraged outbreaks of fighting between the rugby supporters and the demonstrators'. He attempts to use these figures to understand the relationship between disorder and the number of police present. However, this is not the only possible lesson to be learned from those figures.

It would be tempting to use information such as this provided by Wilcox in order to attempt to prove or disprove the question of whether the number of police involved in policing a demonstration will affect the amount of disorder. If there were a statistical relationship between the number of police at each of the South African Rugby Union Team tour venues and the number of arrests at that venue, then it would seem to suggest that a relationship existed between the breaking of the law and the number of police.

Such statistical adventures, however alluring, are likely to be inconclusive. If the number of arrests is larger when the number of police is greater, it could simply be that the demonstration was likely to cause more problems and therefore more police were drafted in. There is also likely to be some relationship between the number of arrests which could possibly be carried out and the number of policemen available to carry them out. With statistics covering a wider range of demonstrations than those Wilcox uses[12] covering twenty-one similar events, a statistical test might prove more conclusive, but not in such a small number of specific circumstances.

Wilcox continues his observations of the number of arrests on demonstrations, but does not attempt to draw from them further inferences. He notes that 302 people were arrested at the CND demonstration at Ruislip RAF station in 1964 and 847 marchers were arrested on 24 April 1961 when the Committee of One Hundred marched to Whitehall. On 17 September 1961, 1350 arrests were made in Trafalgar Square. He compares these numbers with the 243 people arrested in the March 1968 demonstration and only 42 in October of that year. These numbers clearly do not rank against the over 7000 demonstrators arrested in Washington on 3 May 1971 in their march against the war in Vietnam. There 'demonstrators were herded into police stations, compounds and a sports stadium and supplied with army rations and blankets'.

On the question of who selects the particular charge to be brought Wilcox points out that before the Crown Prosecution Service the charge was usually selected by the police although advice could always be sought from the Director of Public Prosecutions if they so wished. Certain offences may be charged only with the agreement of the DPP or of the Attorney General (such as the new section 1 of the Riot offence in the Public Order Act 1986, see below). Lord Windlesham, speaking in the House of Lords in 1971, explained why some offences needed such approval.

> The circumstances in which these Acts indicate the desirability of police to seek the advice of the Director of Public Prosecutions appear, for the most part, to relate to the degree of experience which the police are likely

[12] Ibid., p. 38.

to have of dealing with the offences in question, either because they are likely to occur infrequently or because the law is new or somewhat obscure and experience of its working has to be built up.

Wilcox states how in the 1960s it had been police practice to deal fairly leniently with disorder arising out of demonstrations, and the 'mods and rockers' clashes. After some comment from magistrates, judges and others, student protest began to be treated more seriously. In 1970 the Essex University undergraduates who, in a protest against apartheid, set fire to a branch of Barclays Bank were sentenced to Borstal training on a conspiracy charge. In the same year charges of riot and unlawful assembly were brought against the fifteen Cambridge students at the Garden House trial.[13] Six defendants were sentenced to imprisonment for terms ranging from 9 to 18 months and two young men under 21 were sentenced to Borstal training. Two students who used violence to invade Senate House of London University were convicted of unlawful assembly before a jury at the Old Bailey.

In charting the course of the police decision to prosecute, Wilcox explains that although an individual police officer may suggest a particular charge, it is up to the officer in charge of the police station, who would probably be a sergeant, to decide whether or not to accept the charge. In doing so the police station officer 'has to satisfy himself that there is adequate evidence of a criminal offence for which a power of arrest has been provided'. it will be interesting to see whether the police will still continue to provide this independent check on the decision to prosecute, now that the Crown Prosecution Service makes the final decision, or whether the police will attempt to encourage more prosecution by giving the decision in certain cases over to the CPS.

British Liberty in Danger – Kidd

Kidd[14] provides interesting historical background to the two major cases of 1934: *Duncan* v. *Jones*[15] and *Thomas* v. *Sawkins*.[16] In *Duncan* v. *Jones* Mrs Duncan was arrested and charged with obstructing a police officer in the exercise of his duty by insisting on addressing a public meeting outside a 'Test and Task Centre'. The effect of this case on appeal to

[13] See also below in respect of Sedley's observations.
[14] H. Kidd, *British Liberty in Danger: An Introduction to the Study of Civil Rights* (London, 1941).
[15] *Duncan* v. *Jones* [1936] 1 KB 218.
[16] *Thomas* v. *Sawkins* [1935] 2 KB 249.

Quarter Sessions and the Divisional Court was that police could decide
who could and who could not speak in the public streets.[17]

In *Thomas* v. *Sawkins* a labour meeting in a small South Wales town
was attended by the police against the wishes of the chairman of the
meeting. Although the chairman, Mr Thomas, went to the local police
station to ask Sergeant Sawkins to remove the trespassers, he refused
to do so and the sergeant committed a technical assault on Mr Thomas.
The case which finally went to the Divisional Court resulted from
Mr Thomas's summons for assault on the sergeant. The sergeant argued
that his officers could remain on private premises if they anticipated a
breach of the peace or the commission of some other offence. This was,
in fact, a quiet and peaceful meeting which ended peacefully. The Lord
Chief Justice upheld the view that the police could enter any private
premises during a meeting 'if they have reasonable grounds for
apprehending a breach of the peace or other offence', even though the
reasonable ground in this particular case may itself have been questionable. The result of these two cases was to provide the police with
enormous discretionary powers to prevent public meetings on the
highway and in meeting halls as they thought fit.

Kidd, giving the opposite view to Clutterbuck, notes the use made
by the police of *agents provocateurs* on the 1932 Hunger March. He
records how he noticed two men 'wearing knotted handkerchiefs round
their necks, cloth caps and heavy beards' who were attempting to incite
other marchers. As he watched,

> these two roughly dressed men drew two regulation police truncheons
> from their hip pockets, laid about them and arrested two other men.
> They marched their prisoners southward to the cordon. The police
> recognised them as their colleagues; the cordon was opened and the two
> men passed through with their prisoners.

Kidd and a journalist then swore affidavits giving evidence of what they
had seen of police *agents provocateurs* that day. Lord Trenchard conducted
his own inquiry at Scotland Yard which had disclosed 'that two plain
clothes officers had been employed at the very place mentioned outside
the Whitehall Theatre, and that reference was made to two arrests at
that spot during the evening'. However, Trenchard's inquiry found that
only one arrest had occurred at 9.30 and another half-an-hour later.
This, he said, discredited Kidd's entire statement. As a result of the
airing of this issue and correspondence in the press from both Kidd
and Mr A. P. Herbert, MP, substantial interest was shown in the new

[17] For details of the legal decision see ch. 6.

National Council for Civil Liberties which Kidd formed at the beginning of 1934.

The general histories have shown how easy it is for different writers to view the same facts and yet come out with directly opposite opinions based on those facts. The political undertones make for easy self-justification and malleability of conclusion. This causes difficulty to the more open researcher who has to weigh both sides constantly. Arguments seem to become circular and ideas begin to disappear like grains of sand between the fingers. However, the same issues appear repeatedly and demand attention. Concentrating on those issues through the specific facts of individual cases begins to present rather less of a moving target.

Individual Case Studies

The Campaign for Nuclear Disarmament

Christopher Driver's study of the CND provides ample detail of the amount of internal discussion, quarrelling and negotiation existing within a major protest organization and the number of different views which would finally have to be welded together or compromised to prevent a split in the protest grouping. Driver's detailed account of the antics of the numerous famous people involved first in the CND and subsequently in the Civil Disobedience Campaign of the Committee of One Hundred is a fascinating story and one of the most carefully charted accounts of the evolution of a protest movement. High ideals clashed with the practicalities of civil disobedience. The press and the media were being utilized heavily on all sides in the arguments. Numerous arrests were made in the winter of 1958.

> . . . and with the first pictures of puffing policemen hauling away limp bodies the British public now took in the fact that 37 otherwise respectable citizens were spending Christmas in gaol for being too enthusiastic about peace on earth.[18]

Driver shows the evolution of the CND through the Direct Action Committee and on to the Committee of One Hundred, Lord Bertrand Russell leaving doubters such as Canon Collins behind him. The major question of dissent in the movement was whether their activities were still to be supported by the general public so that real pressure could be brought to bear on the government, or whether the movement had

[18] C. Driver, *The Disarmers: A Study in Protest* (London, Hodder & Stoughton, 1964), p. 107.

become a vanguard too far ahead of public opinion surprised at the disorder arising out of these middle class protests. As one member of the Committee suggested, 'we had become a public spectacle, a group isolated from the general body of public opinion and feeling, a rowdy show to be televised and reported in the press for the interest and amusement of a majority who are not with us'.[19]

If this was a problem in 1961 then the events of 1963, according to Driver, made this issue much clearer. The visit of the King and Queen of Greece to England in July of 1963 brought large numbers of protestors out on the streets. These included members of the CND who were primarily protesting at the murder of the Greek MP, Gregori Lambrakis, who himself was a nuclear disarmer, and had taken part in the Aldermaston March and the Oxford Conference against Nuclear Arms that year. However,

> the Greek demonstrations as they were called damaged the Campaign more than any other incident in its history. They identified the movement more closely than ever before with the Communists who had been running a longstanding and for once not altogether unfounded campaign against the prolonged imprisonment of some members of the losing side of the Greek civil war.[20]

Of especial interest is Driver's account of the work of Detective Sergeant Harold Challoner, the proven police *agent provocateur*, who had 'planted' pieces of brick upon four people arrested during the Greek demonstrations. Substantial sums were paid out by Scotland Yard in compensation, and Challoner was found insane and unfit to plead. The enquiry caused several other prisoners who had been convicted on Challoner's evidence to be released. Driver also mentions the infamous police action on 17 September 1961.[21] He notes, as does Bowes, that it 'was officially admitted that several people had been dropped in the fountains, that a woman constable had used bad language, and that a sergeant had been too free with their fire hose.' However, a more complete insight is provided by a Mr Herb Greer in which he describes how Canon Collins and Fenner Brockway were arrested by the police and taken away from Trafalgar Square just before midnight.

> After midnight the reason for the summary removal of prominent people became suddenly and shockingly obvious. Ranked policemen, surly and foul tempered at the long hours of struggling and having weekend leaves cancelled, launched a deliberate and vicious attack against the scattered

[19] Ibid., p. 125.
[20] Ibid., p. 156.
[21] See above p. 31 under Bowes, *The Police and Civil Liberties*.

remnants of the crowd. Cameramen were told abruptly that if they filmed another foot they would be arrested. Demonstrators, onlookers, passers-by – it made no difference – were punched, knocked down, kicked. Scores of constables threw struggling civilians into the icy water of the fountain basin. Middle-aged women were slammed down and dragged by one leg through puddles, face down against the concrete pavement.[22]

This seemed to show that the police attack, and the carting away of 'prominent figures' beforehand, was an operation which must have been planned by people above the ranks of the junior police officers there.

Events such as this brought public attention to a changing vision of the police. The Royal Commission on the Police did not find 'evidence of deteriorating relations between police and public'. Driver, however, notes:

> a growth of scepticism among magistrates and others about police methods and veracity would not necessarily strike at the roots of British society, or prevent us from continuing to think, even though less romantically and whole-heartedly than before, that our policemen are better than anyone else's. On the face of it, it would be surprising if the comparatively small scale CND demonstrations had done a quarter as much as the swelling volume of motoring cases or the occasional scandal like the Sheffield 'rhino whip' enquiry of 1963, to convince the middle classes that policemen had their share of human faults as well as superhuman virtues. Thus in one particular age group, the eighteens to twenty-fives, where the Royal Commission itself found there was cause for concern, CND and the Committee of One Hundred formed a natural focus for the general crisis of authority. Within the Campaign itself, despite its overall middle class character, young people of widely differing background met on equal terms. Interpreting the police simply as the incarnation of authority and also as the extension of the Government, to be used for any purpose the Home Secretary thought fit, Campaigners lent a ready ear to stories of police violence or duplicity.[23]

With this background of a changing view of the police on the part of more of the general public, we can now turn to the case studies of the Vietnam demonstrations of 1968.

The Anti-Vietnam Demonstrations of March and October 1968

Whilst events in Paris brought students and workers out on the streets together in defiance of the government, and the freedom marches of the early 1960s in the south of the USA had turned into a student movement

[22] Ibid., pp. 158–9.
[23] Ibid., pp. 161–2.

in the late 1960s, the streets of London were also affected by protest. In the USA a large movement made up of numerous disparate groups was forming:

> The entire movement, however, including its vanguard, is intelligible only as an amalgamation of individuals who share a mood, a cultural division without the structure and linear direction of a political ideology. One may discern Marxists, Neo-Trotskyites, pacifists, Democratic Socialists, Yippie (politicians of joy), Americans for Democratic Action, and a host of traditional ideologues, but when one looks for a common political denominator, it is nowhere to be found. The answer lies in the ambience of a generation born after the failure and death of ideology.[24]

It has been suggested by some that a similar movement existed over here (see *The Trouble at LSE?*).[25] Student protest at this time was challenging university authority and authority generally, and the Anti-Vietnam marches of 1968 were the most visible signs of a more general movement.

17 March 1968 According to Jeremy Bugler,[26] some demonstrators marched on 17 March to Grosvenor Square after a meeting in Trafalgar Square. The protest seemed to him to be more in favour of victory for the NLF, the North Vietnamese communists, than a compromise solution. Speakers in Trafalgar Square showed 'how rent rises and wage freezes in Britain were linked with the war in Vietnam, because the higher interest rates in the United States which had arisen because of the war had led to a shift of money from Britain to the United States'. There were other 'direct attacks on capital economics' and the 'imperialistic neo-colonialist functions of the United States' were often mentioned. The major distinction, for Bugler, between this march and previous CND marches was the lack of organization. Whereas CND marches had been 'highly organised, efficient and much staffed' so as not to present too much of a problem to the police, traffic and the rest of the public concerned, this demonstration was clearly organized to be disorganized. Those who had organized the demonstration specifically intended not to be in charge of what occurred on the route because their idea was more 'to seize the area, not march on one side of the road, tidily so the traffic can get through'. Bugler experienced the fear

---

[24] Gary R. Weaver, 'Introduction' in *The University and Revolution*, ed. G. R. Weaver and J. H. Weaver (New Jersey, Prentice-Hall, 1969), p. 24.
[25] See H. Kidd, *The Trouble at LSE, 1966–1967* (London, Oxford University Press, 1969) and T. Blackstone, K. Gales, R. Hadley and W. Lewis, *Students in Conflict* (London, Weidenfeld & Nicolson, 1970).
[26] J. Bugler, 'Solidarity with Violence', *New Society*, 21 Mar. 1968.

of being charged by police horses and of 'listening to good natured remarks by these police and watching, just behind them, a demonstrator getting a fearful beating'. At the same time he reacted strongly against the group of demonstrators who shouted 'Traitor' at a West Indian bus driver in Charing Cross Road who declined to leave his bus (and thereby his job) to join the march. Bugler doubted whether further marches would be able to contain the ceiling of violence he experienced on the demonstration.

The report by the National Council for Civil Liberties on the same demonstration, based on the views of 26 accredited observers who were present throughout, tends in many respects to uphold Bugler's view. From their report, it appears that the organizers had evaded their responsibilities for communicating their objectives both to the participants and to the police. The NCCL also complains of the use of police horses and dogs in relation to crowd control, and the drawing of truncheons, the use of which was widespread on that day. From the NCCL account it appears that 'a small minority of demonstrators came prepared for violence', but 'marbles, bags of paint, flour, smoke bombs are annoying but cannot be considered serious weapons. The most dangerous weapons on the scene were police truncheons'. The police tactics were scathingly criticized. What they were attempting to do was unclear to all except the police themselves. By setting up cordons in particular places around Grosvenor Square to prevent people moving in particular directions the police provided useful targets for missiles thrown by the demonstrators who were caught in each area and prevented from going where they had intended, without any clear reason.

Like Bugler, the NCCL say that the outbreaks of violence were individual rather than organized. 'Some officers may have been so hard pressed as to be forced to draw their truncheons but the violent attacks which a small minority made on demonstrators could not be justified under any circumstances'. The individual accredited observers show that, although there was some violence caused by elements in the crowd, it was certainly not called for by any of the organizers and that 'the vast majority of both the demonstrators and of the police acted throughout the afternoon with great restraint under very tense circumstances'. However, the police were to blame for very poor organization and control of the crowds in sealing off too many of the entrances to the square and causing so much pressure to build up that violence of some sort was likely to occur.

In short, the March 1968 procession was seen as a badly organized and badly policed protest that allowed violence to occur. The public reaction was enormous. Although the demonstrators got their wish to be noticed the media portrayed little public support for their cause.

27 October 1968 A great deal has been written about the second
Vietnam demonstration that year. It was given massive coverage
beforehand by all the media, expecting similar violence to that
experienced in March, or much greater violence. It was also made the
subject of a specific study into *Demonstrations and Communications*[27]
looking at the effects of the media on that march. The research team
could not presume what the march would have been like if there had
not been such massive media attention. It was difficult, therefore, to
draw any major conclusions. However, the study does serve as a useful
summary of what occurred and a careful map of lead up events in the
media. This was to be a perennial topic returned to by Lord Scarman
at the Brixton Inquiry with a suggestion that 'copycat riots' were
engendered by the media reporting of disorder elsewhere.[28]

Detailed reports of protests, protest movements and demonstrations
provide very different views from the generalized mythologies that go
into the general account histories. Perhaps this is because the sorts of
people who research and write up such detail on this subject area have
a particular political persuasion sympathetic to the movements they
study or a greater desire to understand. Whatever the reason, accounts
of the October demonstration present a fascinating study on which most
commentators seem to agree.

The first result of the massive publicity in the media and the threat
of violence was that a great deal of security precautions were taken in
relation to buildings on or near the route. Iron gates had been drawn
across the entrance to Australia House (Australian troops were present
in Vietnam), windows along Fleet Street were boarded up by the national
newspapers and policemen surrounded the BBC studios at Broadcasting
House in Portland Place. A duplicate tape of the afternoon's programmes
was sent up to the BBC studios in Birmingham in case there was 'an
occupation of the London studios' by the protestors.

Great tension built up on the roads into London where police stopped
coaches and private cars and searched for offensive weapons. There was
also tension among the 2000 protestors who had spent the weekend at
the London School of Economics in Houghton Street, occupied by the
protestors against the order of the new Director, Dr Walter Adams.[29]

Internal tension existed on the march with rival briefing sheets being
handed out by the 'ad hoc committee' and the 'Committee for Solidarity
with Vietnam', the latter urging the march to go to the Embassy, the

[27] James D. Halloran, Philip Elliott and M. Murdock, *Demonstrations and Communications: A
Case Study* (London, Penguin, 1970).
[28] See Howard Tumber *Television and the Riots* (London, British Film Institute, 1982) for a
completely opposite view.
[29] Halloran et al., *Demonstrations and Communications* p. 34.

former asking marchers 'to go the whole route' of the intended march to Hyde Park Corner and not Grosvenor Square. The massive build-up of police could not be seen by most of the demonstrators as this time the police were parked in vans in side streets out of view. Their presence there could not of itself provoke antagonism. As soon as the march began and it became clear that the police would be restrained the tension eased and the main march went ahead without trouble. The NCCL estimated the numbers on the march as some 60,000 people. Symbolic protests were made outside Australia House, at Downing Street and the Cenotaph, and speeches were finally given in Hyde Park to the main marchers. The group led by Mr Abhimanya Manchanda broke away from the main march at Trafalgar Square and went up to the Embassy in Grosvenor Square. There the police had set up a fairly restrained show of force that was able to control any attempt to reach the Embassy. At all times individual incidents were tolerated by the police, without allowing any particular incident to get out of hand. Thus, when the American flag was burned by demonstrators outside the US Embassy they allowed it to burn for several minutes before removing it and stamping out the flames. Mr Manchanda then asked his group to disperse peacefully and return to Hyde Park, but after this appeal at 4.45 p.m. a number of demonstrators still remained.

As more demonstrators crowded up to the cordons near the Embassy the police used 'pincer movement' tactics which allowed a number of demonstrators past the cordon and then siphoned them off into side streets. These prevented the problems of attempting both 'containment' and 'dispersal' at the same time which were later a problem for the police at Red Lion Square. Such tactics as these continued on into the evening with some use of the mounted police at one point to reinforce the cordon in front of the Embassy. Most of the 3000 or so demonstrators in the square 'simply stood and watched' and 'there were also over 1000 spectators bystanders, observers and reporters'.[30] Only a small group was 'involved in the attempts to break the cordon'[31] and vehicles were able to move through the square at a slow speed.

There was a small amount of pressure and a few skirmishes occurred in the side streets, but the demonstration began to quieten down towards 8.00 p.m. At that point the police began to clear those remaining in the square by moving slowly along 'appealing through a megaphone to everyone to disperse, allowing people plenty of time to withdraw'.[32] Interestingly, 'a group of about 200 marchers who had started an

[30] Ibid., p. 45.
[31] Ibid., p. 45.
[32] Ibid., p. 46.

impromptu but orderly political discussion on the south east corner of the square were allowed to continue without interference'.[33] It was at about 8.30 p.m. when the famous ending to this day's protest occurred 'and the police and marchers who remained signalled the end of the day by singing "Auld Lang Syne", linking arms together'.[34] It is perhaps, as Clutterbuck suggests, something that could have occurred only in England.

Forty-three people were arrested and charged with offences arising out of incidents connected with the march over the whole weekend. Eleven of these were arrested during the course of the marches. Only twenty-five of those arrested were monitored by the Halloran study, including the eleven arrested during the march and those charged with assault on police officers in Grosvenor Square and South Audley Street. Fourteen out of the twenty-five monitored were in the 17–20 age group. Six of those arrested were unemployed, eight were from the lower non-manual social grouping and four were students. Although students composed 75 per cent of the marchers they were only 16 per cent of those arrested. It was not clear whether people arrested were actually involved in the march or were among other groups attempting to taunt the marchers and cause violence. Some seventy-four police, and ninety-six marchers and bystanders were injured on the march, with only one policeman detained in hospital for observation overnight. This was PC Derek Rogers who was featured in a photograph on the front page of six daily national newspapers on the morning of Monday 28 October being kicked by a bearded man wearing sports shoes.

In examining 'the political and historical context' of the demonstrations Halloran et al.[35] show how the new groupings differed considerably from the older CND movements, although many of them had their schooling and background in those movements. The position of the London School of Economics as a focus for anti-Vietnam activity and in the forefront of student political action had begun in 1967 with student reaction to the appointment of a new Director of LSE, Dr Walter Adams, who had previously been the Principal of the multi-racial University College of Rhodesia. Some of the 'New Left' ideas and movements that had become popular in the USA were beginning to appear in Britain, including the Radical Students' Alliance and the Revolutionary Socialist Students' Federation.

Halloran et al. attempted to discover whether these were affected by ideas arising out of the work of Herbert Marcuse, a Berkeley professor.

[33] Ibid.
[34] Ibid. and P. Barker, H. Taylor, E. de Kadt and Earl Hopper, 'Portrait of a Protest', *New Society*, 31 Oct. 1968, pp. 61–4.
[35] Halloran et al., *Demonstrations and Communications*, ch. 3.

His theory of 'confrontation' suggests the 'police are a visible symbol of the generally repressive nature of the capitalist system and that confrontation with the police is therefore a valid symbol of the struggle of oppressed peoples everywhere to liberate themselves'.[36] These views were aided by the new image given to the police (and portrayed above in Bowes) resulting from bad police behaviour at previous demonstrations and the Challoner affair. Halloran et al. feel that the evidence from both the Vietnam demonstrations in 1968 shows that 'the Marcusian idea of seeking a violent confrontation instead of political tactics does not seem to have fathered many adherents[37] in England. Even the breakaway group of Mr Manchanda appealed to his supporters after staying in the Square 'we have achieved our object, we have burned the American flag', 'don't let us be provoked into violence, let us leave'.

If then, Halloran et al. point out, active confrontation was sought, it was not sought by either of the groups of organizers. The authors argue persuasively that the arguments and theories of the press, and seemingly the police, that confrontation was sought on the streets of Paris and Chicago, and would therefore be sought on the streets of London ignores 'a critical factor in its genesis, i.e. the behaviour of the police'. Where the police expect confrontation and react to any incident as if it is an example of such determined confrontation, violence is likely to be caused. This it appears is what may have happened in Paris and Chicago, and it certainly happened in London in March of 1968. Thus, the different policies employed by the British police in October showed how it was possible to withdraw from any 'confrontation' on both sides. This tended, according to Halloran, to disprove the argument that the (then) current movement and demonstrations were based on Marcuse's ideas.

The Report of the National Council of Civil Liberties on the demonstration enquires less into the ideology of the protesters and more into events on the march. It does echo the same general feeling that 'the change of police tactics was wholly successful as far as the main march was concerned'.[38] Largely, it states, the demonstration went off well with good humour on the part of demonstrators and 'exemplary behaviour' by individual police officers. The Report also notes the amount of tension generated by the press and by two newspapers in particular before the march. It also voices some disquiet about the general searching of motor vehicles without apparent legal authority and the use of plain clothes police officers on the demonstration.

---

[36] Ibid., p. 71 and H. Marcuse, *An Essay on Liberation* (London, Penguin, 1969).
[37] Halloran et al., *Demonstrations and Communications*, p. 127.
[38] NCCL Report.

The Garden House Demonstration and Subsequent Trial

The visit of the Greek King and Queen in July 1963 and the protests resulting from that visit have been mentioned above.[39] On 13 February 1970, the festivities involved in a 'Greek Week' in Cambridge and particularly a 'Greek dinner' to be held at The Garden House Hotel caused a demonstration by Cambridge students which prevented the holding of the event and rattled some of those attempting to attend it. The charge of riotous assembly (under the old common law) and its use against a certain number of students with a background of political activity either personally or in their family seemed to Stephen Sedley[40] to show an extremely disturbing trend. Defendants were charged with 'riotous assembly' without any evidence of violent action (or even specific activity in some cases) other than being at the assembly, and in some cases shouting and in another case 'pushing'. Although damage occurred to some property in the hotel, none of the defendants were accused of being involved directly in causing this.

What seemed especially disturbing was that the defendants 'were selected largely from lists of demonstrators handed by the Proctors to the police'. The defendants were not arrested at the time. Sedley shows how a similar system operated in relation to the Hilton Hotel trial, and the trial of some who besieged and damaged South Africa House in 1969. Although the defendants protested against their selection in this manner (a selection which could only have been carried out based on police files of their, or their relatives' previous political behaviour), the Court of Appeal rejected the 'why pick on me?' argument as they called it.

Sedley explains how political views are used in such trials. Although the prosecution and the judge are at great pains to point out how the trials have 'nothing to do with politics but only with the preservation of law and order',[41] political information is available to be used only against the defendants and not in their favour. Much is made in such trials by the prosecution of evidence of political slogans, banners of political groups and statements or writings of political groups. Where defendants are prepared to go into the witness box the prosecution will often put political statements to them and ask them to either agree or disagree with them. Where a defendant wishes to explain in more detail his or her political view the judge will immediately stop the defendant, saying that a trial is not a political platform. Even where defendants

---

[39] See pp.31 and 40 above.
[40] Stephen Sedley, *The Listener*, 6 Oct. 1970.
[41] Ibid.

have disagreed with views put to them, the jury will have heard those views and they may well be remembered as the views of the defendants.

Swingeing sentences were meted out in the 'Garden House Case'[42] to those defendants found guilty,[43] with imprisonment ranging from 9 to 18 months[44] for being actively involved in a demonstration. Lord Justice Sachs in the Court of Appeal spoke of 'the freedom of citizens who assemble peacefully in a permissible place to express their views in a lawful manner' as being 'a right which the courts have always safeguarded'.[45] However, this supposed right was not proved in this case, or in any of the other cases where its existence is so fondly and, therefore, so misleadingly, stated.

A dilemma concerning the conduct of protest is faced by the police and powers of authority as shown by the Garden House Trial. If a protest is banned beforehand, further disorder than was expected may be caused by the existence of the authoritarian ban. Certainly, any supposed 'freedom of speech' will be prevented. If, on the other hand, the demonstration is allowed to occur and demonstrators are singled out on the day or charged subsequently as a result of lists prepared by others the police will be accused of victimization of those after the event. Those prosecuted will be tainted by what occurred if there was violence, whether or not they were part of it.

Sunday 30 January 1972 – 'Bloody Sunday'

Lord Widgery was appointed to conduct a Tribunal of Inquiry into the events of 'Bloody Sunday' in Londonderry in Northern Ireland when a number of people were killed and many wounded as a result of troops opening fire after a march of the Northern Ireland Civil Rights Association. The Inquiry shows in detail the preparations made before such a march, the operational orders and the chain of command in making decisions within the army brigade involved.[46]

A number of lessons may be learned from reading between the lines of the Report although some of these were not faced as issues in the Inquiry. First of all, it seems that it was the very presence of the law enforcement agency, the army, which provoked the immediate violence on that day. It is of course not possible to tell what would have happened

---

[42] See *R. v. Caird* [1970] 54 Crim. App. Rep. 499 (CA).
[43] Seven out of fifteen defendants were acquitted on all charges.
[44] *R. v. Caird*, 504.
[45] Ibid., 510–11.
[46] 'Report of the Tribunal Appointed to Inquire into the Events on Sunday 30th January 1972, which Led to Loss of Life in Connection with the Procession in Londonderry on that day' by The Rt. Hon. Lord Widgery, OBE, TD.

in their absence. Much more disorder may have occurred and perhaps more lives lost among people who held opposing views or who came from a different religious background. Nevertheless, it should be noted that the immediate occasions of violence were the show of force by the army.

Secondly, the difficulty in assessing after the event exactly what occurred is shown in remarkable detail by this inquiry. Although there were numerous witnesses who stated that the Army had shot first near the Rossville Flats the view expressed by the Army evidence was preferred by Lord Widgery. It might be imagined that such definite behaviour as would necessitate the use of firearms and the deadly consequences that could result from their use, would provide a scenario of much more clarity than in an ordinary demonstration with more minor disorder. It appears from this author's reading of the Report that similar problems occur, and that the forces of inquiry and adjudication will lean towards favouring the view of the law enforcement authorities, whatever the preponderance of evidence.

It is interesting to see exactly how this occurs. The Inquiry actually sets out 'a representative sample of the civilian evidence'[47] in great detail. The reader is therefore given the appearance of objectivity and fairness on the part of the adjudicator, whilst the actual adjudication goes the opposite way. This seems to this author to be the same form of result as is achieved by appellate court judges paying lip service to 'freedom of speech' and 'freedom of protest' whilst confirming the guilt of protestors. In this sense, adjudication or inquiry may be seen as an important part of a symbolic process manufactured and worked by government and state in the symbolism of the democratic theory and process.

The court and the tribunal are almost cynically used as a theatrical format for dispensing the idea of 'justice' whilst really underlining the force of their own power. This use of ostensibly just and fair process and venue for these objectives can have harsh and deleterious effects on the working of the social system. If those who have some disagreement or protest to voice find that there is nowhere within the system that they can obtain a real sense of fairness or justice, they will be forced further back into irregular political activity and into harsher forms of political violence in order to obtain their objectives. Therefore, the short-term effect of a trial or inquiry providing the image of fairness to the public may not be worthwhile if in the long term it brings not only the police, but also the courts, and the law and legal system of the country into disrepute.

[47] Ibid., para. 50.

Red Lion Square, 15 June 1974

Disturbances at Red Lion Square on 15 June 1974 arose out of competing demonstrations involving two opposing marches and meetings. One was organized by the right-wing National Front and the other organized by an anti-racist umbrella group, Liberation. Events on the day brought the opposing demonstrations closer together than the police would have wished. This seems to have precipitated unwise police reaction in a set of uncoordinated attempts at what they referred to as 'dispersal' and 'containment' all at the same time. As a result a number of people were injured and Kevin Gately, a student from Warwick University, died from a blow to the head. Many items of interest can be learned from the Inquiry instituted under the Police Act 1964 with the chairmanship of Lord Scarman.[48] These include the chain of police command, the use of police communication network radios and the particular uses of what was then known as the Special Patrol Group and of mounted police in dealing with demonstrations.

Police uncertainty, indecision and confusion about what was happening, and what they intended to do on the day seemed to pervade the evidence of Chief Superintendent Adams, Chief Superintendent Cracknell, Inspector Finch and others.[49] In one major instance standing cordons and mounted police pushed forwards against a group of demonstrators who had nowhere to move because they were confined within one street and behind them another cordon of police prevented their dispersal. This was an example of the process described by the police both as 'dispersal' and 'containment', terms which would seem to be entirely contradictory.

Much blame for the violence and disorder which occurred was placed on the International Marxist Group, a small splinter group who broke away from the main Liberation march and carried on (in the direction which the march had originally intended to go) and which took them closer to the National Front meeting. However, careful cross-examination of police witnesses in the inquiry seemed to suggest that there had been a good deal of rationalization after the event. There had also been among the police a certain amount of concoction of mythology beforehand in relation to the likely disorder to be caused by the entire demonstration itself, and the specific IMG group had not figured greatly in that mythology.

[48] 'Report of the Inquiry into Events at Red Lion Square on 15th June 1974 before Lord Justice Scarman', HMSO, Cmnd 5919.
[49] See Tony Gilbert, *Only One Died: an Account of the Scarman Inquiry into the Events of 15th June 1974, in Red Lion Square* (London, Kay Beauchamp, 1975) and transcript of evidence before the tribunal (on file with author).

The inquiry shows how easy it is for police and demonstrators to hold different views of each other's likely conduct, and how the holding of such views may in itself produce the result most feared. The lessons of restrained police activity which might have been learned from October 1968 seemed to be diminishing. As soon as the police found that they were out of control of the marchers, they reacted in a manner which seemed to cause more problems than the initial situation itself.

Any inquiry held afterwards will suffer from the viewpoint of the 'armchair' protagonist and is therefore likely to favour a view of events which will not taint too closely the activities of those enforcing 'law and order'.[50]

The Inquiry lasted some 28 days. The Report of the Inquiry does not vindicate the actions of the police, but nor does it condemn them. It is only in Part II in the suggestions for what should occur in the future that one can find a criticism of what did occur in the past. None of the suggestions made by the police and others for the tightening of the law relating to public order, or the need for legislating that demonstrators should give 7 days notice of a demonstration to the police was taken up by (then) Lord Justice Scarman. The notice element has since been overtaken by the passage of the Public Order Act 1986. Lord Justice Scarman called for 'a radical amendment of section 6 of the Race Relations Act'. Amendment did take place, but the Act to a great extent still provides similar problems to those which were outlined then.

Among other insights allowed to the Tribunal was a copy of the report of Mr Gerard, the senior police officer from Scotland Yard in charge of the demonstration on that day, to the Home Secretary. The report was shown to be full of inaccuracies and errors and the whole tenor of the report was misleading, as David Turner Samuels QC said in his summing up speech:

> This is the first Tribunal of its kind to have been held, this is the first occasion . . . on which the report of the officer in charge to the Home Secretary has been available to the public. It is unhappy that on this sole occasion such a report should be seen to be so misleading, and one can only wonder what sort of information the Home Secretary has received on other occasions.[51]

The Notting Hill Caribbean Carnival, August Bank Holiday 1976

In 1975, the West Indian Carnival that had begun to take place on the Summer Bank Holiday weekend a few years previously on the streets

---

[50] See A. Sherr, 'The Scarman Report on "The Brixton Disorders 10–12 April 1981": A Retrospective Review', *Urban Law and Policy* 7 (1985), 227–41.
[51] Transcript of evidence, and Gilbert, *Only One Died*, p. 34.

of Notting Hill in London had caused major problems of crowd control for the police. With this background, the police had decided to be more involved in arrangements for the 1976 carnival and to assist in its organization. There had also been crime problems the previous year. Four hundred empty purses and wallets had been found and 140 complaints about pick-pockets recorded, according to the report by a *Sunday Times* Enquiry Team.[52]

The desire of the police to be involved in the organization of the carnival precipitated a clash of interests and culture. The police force was 'bent, for the best of motives, on transforming two days of cheerful anarchy into a neat and tidy Black people's version of the Lord Mayor's Show'.[53] The essential spontaneity of the occasion was quite out of order with the way the police wished to proceed. They tried to obtain the agreement of the carnival organizing committee to hold the carnival first at the White City and then at Chelsea football club. However, the committee spent a long time in not making any decision, at least in terms of moving the carnival off the streets of Notting Hill. For them it was a street event and a demonstration (if not a protest) of Caribbean culture. As all other possible venues became booked up and the day drew closer it became clear that the carnival was once again going to be held on the streets.

A total of 1398 policemen were detailed to deal with the expected crowd and the groups, bands and floats. On some occasions sixteen policemen and two senior officers were to be seen looking after thirty revellers, and one witness told the researchers that there had been sixty-three policemen around one band of twelve people. Subsequently, it was said that 'the massive police presence was a self-fulfilling prophecy of trouble'.

Police reaction to this criticism was that they had been frustrated in 1975 to see pick-pockets at work, but had been unable to reach them in the crush, and that they could not agree that certain parts of London should be seen as 'Black territory' or no-go areas for the police. They suggested that they had tried to allow 'Black people [to] look after their own events – notably some fairs in south London'. However, the police claimed that it did not work, and they had often to move in to protect people and property when it was too late.

In order to deal with the thieves the police deployed some forty-eight plain clothes CID men in groups of four among the crowd. However,

[52] David Blundy, Peter Gilman, Derek Humphy and Philip Knightley, *Sunday Times*, 5 Sept. 1976.
[53] Ibid.

by the Sunday, thieves were operating in groups of up to 12, and simply holding up their victims. If the police tried to chase or arrest the pick-pockets the crowd would impede them – or even attack them. On Sunday evening a police sergeant who tried to arrest a thief needed 31 stitches after his left arm was slashed with a broken bottle. The constable with him needed 5 head stitches after a brick was thrown with such force it actually penetrated his helmet. A detective constable who tried to arrest another thief was stabbed in the groin.[54]

The climax of the carnival was on the Monday (Bank Holiday) when some 150,000 attended the carnival, many of them tourists carrying large sums of money. The incident which sparked off major rioting in which nearly 300 people were injured, 150 of them seriously enough to warrant hospital attention, occurred at about 4.45 p.m. near the end of Acklam Road. At this point there was a general play area underneath the enormous concrete arches of the raised Westway motorway, which had carved its alien path through Notting Hill some years before. Traffic to and from the West of London makes its way along this motorway by day and night, not a pleasant aspect for any neighbourhood. Under the arches at Acklam Road a number of teenage Black groups had gathered to play Jamaican reggae music from loudspeakers. The organizers had agreed with the police that such gatherings would not take place that year, but when they saw the loudspeakers set up they decided that it was best to ignore this breach of agreement. This area apparently became a static meeting place for groups of disaffected youth who were not part of the main carnival which was moving all the time. At about 4.45 p.m.,

> a white woman was robbed of her handbag. When she tried to chase the youth who had snatched it, some dozen youths surrounded her. She was punched and kicked.
> Two policemen rushed to her rescue. She managed to break away; the youths promptly set upon the police. One fell under the blows. 'I thought the boys were kicking cans or something' a young Black onlooker recalled. 'Then I saw it was a policeman'. Six more policemen plunged in to help. They too were attacked. Six more policemen joined the fray. Suddenly a volley of stones, bottles and cans was thrown at them. Police withdrew in disorder, carrying their wounded.[55]

When the police, remarshalled with reinforcements, started to make their way back to the area they were greeted with volleys of missiles. General rioting began which did not die down until 10.00 that evening.

---

54 Ibid.
55 Ibid.

With the hindsight of disorders in the 1980s in Brixton and Birmingham and on the Broadwater Farm Estate, one can suggest that what was at issue here was not just a clash of lifestyles, but also a deeply felt antagonism towards the police as a result of previous police activity.[56] Events on that day did not help this and many witnesses talked of 'police beating peaceful residents on the steps of their houses' as the police roamed, uncertain of who were their enemies.

The Summer of 1977

The summer of 1977 brought the National Front in strength on the streets of Lewisham,[57] Streatham, Birmingham and Manchester.[58] They were opposed by numerous groups and especially by the Socialist Workers Party. There were calls for each of the National Front marches to be banned and major disorder occurred at all except for the march in Manchester in October 1977. No trouble occurred at the latter march because the Chief Constable of Manchester, Mr James Anderton, made a secret agreement with Martin Webster, the National Front National Activities organizer, not to announce 'the venue, assembly point or route' of Martin Webster's march. Some 2000 police kept the 700–1000 National Front supporters away from the counter demonstrators. Many suggested, however, that the collusion between the police and the National Front was a poor precedent to set and left the National Front with a publicity victory.

In the same year the Notting Hill Carnival went off with little crime and disorder. The new Metropolitan Police Commissioner, Mr David McNee had announced that police 'will be unobtrusive' at the Notting Hill Carnival that year.[59]

Summary

From the general and specific case histories set out in this chapter a variety of political viewpoints regarding demonstration and protest will have emerged, as well as the great variety among the forms of protest, protesters and matters forming the subject of protests. In addition to

---

[56] See J. Benyon, *Scarman and After* (Oxford, Pergamon, 1984); M. Kettle and L. Hodges, *Uprising* (London, Pan, 1982), especially pp. 64–97. See also recent Carnival experiences – *The Times* 1, 2, 3 and 9 Sept. 1987 – the Carnival has become almost a barometer of black feelings.
[57] *The Times*, 15–18 Aug. 1977.
[58] *The Times*, 8, 10 Oct. 1977.
[59] *The Times*, 25 Aug. 1977.

the problems associated with protests and demonstrations, the case histories have shown the manner in which other forms of street usage such as the Notting Hill Caribbean Carnival can easily become a public order problem. We have also noted how protest activity in circumstances of high tension can, if mis-managed, end up with the events of 'Bloody Sunday' as in Northern Ireland.

None of the case studies, however, shows the general form of demonstration which occurs regularly on the streets of our major cities, without much disturbance, or any violence to the police or others. These numerous marches and protests do not make the headlines because of their normality. They are, though, extremely important to note in understanding the full picture of public order. They also are seen by some as a drain on the public purse as shown by the reports of the Metropolitan Police Commissioners during the last few years. Similarly, they give rise to problems of traffic control, use of police forces from elsewhere, and difficulties of overtime and shortage of staff. Their existence calls into question what exactly it is that changes a particular demonstration from the humdrum to the category of those we have looked at in these case studies.

One thing is clear. Violence or other extraordinary behaviour is what engenders media interest and, therefore, public knowledge of a particular protest. It is a more complex question to ask whether only protests which gain media acknowledgement, and therefore publicity, are effective. In many cases, as we have seen, people may be protesting partly for their own psychological benefit, as much as in the realistic belief that they will succeed in changing attitudes or events in the manner expressed. In this sense demonstrations may for certain parties be a ritual and for others they may be an unprecedented step taken as a last resort in order to try to right wrongs.

There is another element of ritual in terms of the confrontation between police and protestors on demonstrations. Actions and reactions seem to form part of a ritualistic game with each 'side' testing out the other in a demonstration. These moves seem to be recognized each by the other side and give a fair warning by each to the other of what will be tolerated on the demonstration. Something akin to the children's game of paper, stone and scissors operates in such moves. Only when one party does not understand the intentions of the other, or behaviour is contemplated by either side outside of the usual tolerated game behaviour, does violence seem to occur.

This seems to be the only possible explanation for scenes such as the joining of arms between police and demonstrators, and singing Auld Lang Syne at the end of a demonstration.[60] Neither is that example

---

[60] Halloran et al., *Demonstrations and Communications* (October 1968 Vietnam Demonstration).

unique. Outside the London School of Economics in the early 1970s students were trying to close Houghton Street to traffic. This was a one-way street running in between the main buildings of the London School of Economics and Political Science. Newspaper vans and taxis frequently came down this street at great speed and a student had been knocked over. The students blocked the road in protest, police were called and formed a cordon, clearing student barricades and pushing students out of the way. In between the bouts of pushing and shoving the police would relax and stand about talking to students. Then, as if a bell had sounded to begin the next 'round', the fighting started again. The psychological impact of being on a demonstration and the nature of these inter-party games warrants more careful study. It will have to be sufficient for our purpose simply to note their existence.

A further interesting distinction which may be made on the basis of the case studies above concerns what has subsequently been referred to as 'hard' and 'soft' policing approaches.[61] When the police have turned out for demonstrations with a big show of force this is a product of the 'hard' policing image, and when they have come out in low profile, whether or not in large numbers this could certainly be seen as a 'soft' policing approach. The soft approach aims at obtaining the consent of the general public leading to obedience and political isolation of offenders. The hard approach aims at coercion by taking the initiative and attacking criminal behaviour head-on.

Both approaches can be seen in the case histories enumerated above and the consequences of each approach are also visible. The question of which approach to take lies at the heart of the debate on modern policing in England and it does not seem to have been effectively answered by Lord Scarman's report on the Brixton Disorders.[62] This distinction raises two further issues on which this chapter will close: the need for a 'Third Force' and the function of the police in handling a demonstration.

If the hard approach is necessary to avoid disorder and violence on demonstrations then perhaps a specially trained and armed third force (in between the police and the army) is necessary, as can be seen in other countries.[63] As Reiner points out[64] police behaviour on occasions of public disorder can destroy their legitimacy in other police work, and if police are not properly trained and equipped for 'riot control' they can cause more injury to themselves and others thereby. Perhaps

---

[61] See, e.g., Reiner, *The Politics of the Police*, pp. 18–19 and 203–4; S. Jones and M. Levy, 'The Police and the Majority: The Neglect of the Obvious', *Police Journal*, LV, 1, 4 and P. Boateng, K. Oxford and M. Simey in Benyon, *Scarman and After*, chs 9, 11 and 13.
[62] The Scarman Report: 'The Brixton Disorders', Cmnd. 8427 (London, HMSO, 1981), reprinted London, Penguin, 1982. See also A. Sherr, 'The Scarman Report'.
[63] E.g. the National Guard in the USA, the CRS in France and the Kidotai in Japan.
[64] Reiner, *Politics of the Police*, p. 204.

it has become too difficult for one force to carry the burden of the need for both approaches.

More fundamentally, the proper role and function of the police in relation to demonstration and protest are unclear. That they have an obligation, within certain limits of discretion, to ensure that crimes are not committed is obvious. Whether they also have an obligation to try to defend some notion of 'freedom of speech' or the 'right of protest' is not clear. If such obligation existed, as seems to be suggested by some police rhetoric, it would have no legal base and what power the police have to arrogate to themselves this obligation is not certain.[65] Where crime prevention and control were in conflict with defending free speech, crime prevention and control might take precedence. Neither would the enactment of a constitutional set of 'rights' such as the European Convention clarify this enigma, since the police function would not change as a result.[66]

With the background of the general and specific case histories and these concluding thoughts in mind we turn to see how the legal regulation fits into this picture.

[65] See further in ch. 8.
[66] See further in ch. 9.

3

Meetings and Processions: the Public Highway and the Public Place

This is the first of five chapters which form the central core of the book and which deal in detail with the legal regulation of protest and demonstration. In this chapter the use of the public highway is considered in relation to our subject of demonstrations. The public highway is compared with the wider concept 'public place' and some common law specific to the highway is examined. The chapter then sets out sections 11–14 of the Public Order Act 1986 which legislates for control over processions and meetings, and the possibility of banning processions. It goes on to consider what has been a major defining characteristic of the law: the distinction between static assemblies and meetings, and moving processions. The conduct of people on such processions or during such meetings is left to subsequent chapters, and here the legality of the meeting or procession itself is explored.

Public Place and Public Highway

Supperstone suggests that 'the modern concept of a "public place" is of a place to which in fact the public have access, not necessarily as of right'.[1] He points out that the emphasis is 'on access rather than on the ownership, possession or control of the land'. He sets out a formidable list of possible public places mentioned in a large number of cases, from dance halls and skating rinks to car parks and zoos.[2] Some provisions such as section 54 of the Metropolitan Police Act 1839 do not include a definition of a public place, whereas others, such as the old Race Relations Acts included a rather more 'elaborate definition'.[3]

[1] Michael Supperstone, *Brownlie's Law of Public Order and National Security*, 2nd edn (London, Butterworth, 1981), pp. 32–4.
[2] Ibid., p. 34.
[3] Ibid.

The statutory definition of a 'public place' in the Public Order Act 1986, section 16, as it applies to England and Wales, is,

(a) any highway . . . and (b) any place to which at the material time the public or any section of the public has access, on payment or otherwise, as of right or by virtue of express or implied permission.[4]

The concept of a public place is therefore wider than, and will include, the public highway; and some of the legislation to be dealt with in this chapter refers to 'public place' rather than 'public highway'. However, there is an important area of common law relating only to the highway and not to public places in general, and this law will be considered first.

The Importance and Use of the Public Highway

All public roads, streets and the walkways on either side of them form public highways. This means that all public processions are likely to be held on a highway. Many public meetings, held outside in the open air, will also by their nature be held on the public highway. The law relating to the highway is therefore important in deciding the rights of protesters and demonstrators. The hotch-potch of modern statutes regulating, but not giving the right, of procession and the old cases of trespass to property in neighbouring land comprise this strange, but interesting area of the law.

The common law element also provides a useful introduction to the evolution of the law of public order in the United Kingdom. Much of the effective law has grown out of historical usage intended for purposes quite different from the controlling of demonstration and protest. Much of the law also includes such vague concepts as 'the right to pass and re-pass' with discretion to construe these concepts in particular cases left firmly in the hands of the courts.

It is the right of the public to use the public highway, but not exactly as they wish. It may be used only for 'passing or re-passing'. As a result, a static assembly on the public highway is almost certain to be an unlawful usage of the highway, whereas a moving procession may well be equivalent to a 'passing or re-passing'[5] and, therefore, an

---

[4] Similar definitions occur in the Prevention of Terrorism (Temporary Provisions) Act 1984, s. 2 (but including 'premises') and in the Northern Ireland (Emergency Provisions) Act 1978, s. 31; but see the Indecent Displays (Control) Act 1981, s. 1 for a definition specific to that offence.

[5] See Supperstone's somewhat optimistic view on this (Supperstone, *Brownlie*, pp. 26, 27, 30, 44) and the discussion between A. L. Goodhart in 'Public Meetings and Processions' [1936] 6 CLJ 161, H. R. Wade in 'The Law of Public Meeting' [1938] 2 MLR 177 and E. R. H. Ivamy in 'The Right of Public Meeting' [1949], *Current Legal Problems* 183. Even the academics seem to allow the judges two opinions to choose from – to keep judicial discretion at its optimum.

authorized use. This bold statement conceals the complication of the competing rights of highway users, highway owners and owners of land adjacent to a highway. The definition of a highway, as set out in Halsbury's Laws[6] is somewhat circular, as is the concept itself,

> A highway is a way over which all members of the public are entitled to pass and re-pass; and conversely, every piece of land which is subject to that public right of passage is a highway or part of a highway.

A 'highway' can therefore include a 'cul-de-sac',[7] a bridge or a tunnel[8] and a village square[9] as well as the more obvious conceptions of a highway.

A specific and rather curious form of private property right has been created in relation to the highway. Although the public have a right 'to pass and re-pass' over the highway, it is, in fact, not 'public' land in the sense of ownership. Even highways are owned by the highway authority, being central or local government. Maintenance of highways is carried out as the responsibility of the Department of Transport, and by County Councils, Metropolitan District Councils and London Boroughs.[10] Where a highway is not 'maintainable' at the public expense as to its surface and sub-soil the legal estate up to the mid-point vests in the owners of adjoining land on either side of the highway.[11]

Highways are the most probable places for outdoor protests to be held, and a large amount of legislation deals with them and their use, including the creation of the offence of 'obstruction of the highway'.[12] In addition, the cases concerning use of the highway present an enlightening view of the way in which our legal system handles the confrontation between property right and civil liberty.

The Common Law

One has to look closely at the older cases of *Harrison* and *Hickman* in order to trace the property right and its effect, but these two old chestnuts are rewarding for the expenditure of such effort.

---

[6] *Halsbury's Laws*, 3rd edn, p. 9.
[7] See Supperstone, *Brownlie*, p. 39.
[8] Section 294 of the Highways Act 1959, now Highways Act 1980, Section 328.
[9] In Stow-on-the-Wold, see *Gloucestershire County Council* v. *Farrow* [1983] 2 All ER 1031.
[10] See ss. 1, 263, 265–7 of the Highways Act 1980.
[11] *The Mattin Brothers' Liberty & Co. Ltd* [1903] 1 Ch 118 at 1266.
[12] Section 137 Highways Act 1980, Metropolitan Police Act 1839 s. 54 (6), Town Police Clauses Act 1847 s. 48, Regulation 103 of the Road Vehicles (Construction and Use) Regulations 1986 (SI 1986 No. 1078) and at common law for nuisance, see chapter 6.

Harrison v. *Duke of Rutland*[13]   The Duke of Rutland owned moors which were crossed by a highway. Since the land on both sides of the highway belonged to the Duke the soil of the highway was vested in him.[14] Harrison used the highway in question to scare the grouse away from the Duke and his guests who were trying to shoot the grouse. Lest one should jump to the conclusion that Harrison was an early anti-blood sports protestor, the judgment of Lord Justice Lopes should be noted,

> the vision of the grouse is signally acute, and very little will induce them to shy away from the butts and follow a course which would be out of reach of the guns of the sportsmen occupying the butts. The plaintiff, knowing this and believing that he had cause of annoyance with the Duke or with his predecessor in title, placed himself, avowedly and admittedly, on the highway in such a position and so acted as to prevent the grouse from approaching the butts. The plaintiff had done this on former occasions, and had threatened to continue so to act whenever the Duke drove his moors. Some years before the moors had been let to a tenant. During that time the plaintiff, who had been paid by the tenant, had desisted from any interference with the shooting on the moors; but so soon as the Duke resumed the shooting on his moors, so soon did the plaintiff resume his interference with the sport.[15]

The case, therefore, considered the question of what was allowable on a public highway. Lord Justice Lopes considered it to be 'a case of great importance',[16] contrary to what one might expect from such a trivial set of circumstances. The nature of the case was such that the rights of the public in using the highway were effectively confined only to 'the right of passage'.[17] Anyone using the highway for any other purpose than the 'right to pass and re-pass' is a trespasser. As Lord Justice Kay points out even an artist setting up his easel by the side of the highway might be a trespasser, 'but no-one in his senses would bring an action against him for an occasional trespass of that kind'.[18] The Master of the Rolls, Lord Esher took this rather further:

> Highways are, no doubt, dedicated prima facie for the purpose of passage; but things are done upon them by everybody which are recognised as being rightly done, and as constituting a reasonable and usual mode of using a highway as such. If a person on a highway does not transgress

[13] *Harrison* v. *Duke of Rutland* [1893] QB 142 CA.
[14] Ibid., 143.
[15] Ibid., 150.
[16] Ibid., 149.
[17] Ibid., 152.
[18] Ibid., 156.

such reasonable and usual mode of using it, I do not think that he will be a trespasser.[19]

Lord Esher therefore allowed a way out of the narrow path advocated by the other judges, but left to succeeding cases what might be considered to be a 'reasonable and usual mode' of using the highway. As far as Mr Harrison was concerned it was clear that he was using the highway not for passage, but in order to interfere with the property rights of the owner of the adjacent land and indeed the owner of the soil on which Mr Harrison was standing.

Hickman v. *Maisey*[20] Eight years later the Court of Appeal were served up with a case so close to *Harrison*, that it is surprising that it went to them on appeal. In this case the plaintiffs owned land used for training race horses, which was crossed by a highway. The surface and subsoil of the highway similarly vested in this landowner as in the previous case. The defendant was a 'racing tout', one of the owners of a publication which published accounts of race horses in training and he watched the race horses in training on the plaintiff's land from the highway. The plaintiff contended that the defendant was not using the highway for the purpose to which the public was entitled, and was using the highway to the detriment of the landowner and was, therefore, a trespasser on it. Lord Justice Collins accepted that

> it is not very easy to draw an exact line between the legitimate user of a highway as a highway and user which goes beyond the right conferred upon the public by its dedication. But, as in many other cases, it is not difficult to put cases well on one side of the line or the other.[21]

The case in question fell outside the line of 'legitimate and reasonable user of a highway as a highway' and therefore the defendant was found to be a trespasser.

Once again we are left with a fairly vague conception, allowing succeeding courts to make their own decisions on the basis of whatever new facts occur. The system is being manipulated to provide an appearance quite different from the reality. A vague openness is portrayed in the formal, written legal regulation. However, there is much more certainty than appears from the cases. Succeeding judges are to be relied upon to come down strongly on the same side as the judges in these two cases. It is therefore necessary to read between the

[19] Ibid., 146.
[20] *Hickman* v. *Massey* [1900] 1 QB 754 CA.
[21] Ibid., 757.

lines of the cases, in order to see how much further they go than a strict construction of their wording suggests.

It is upon such cases as these that the right of a demonstrator to use the highway for the purposes of protest or demonstration is queried and often rejected. One further modern case needs to be looked at together with these older cases in order to complete the picture.

Hubbard v. *Pitt*[22]   In 1974 parts of Islington in Central London were being 'gentrified'. Houses in multi-occupation by poorer families were being purchased by developers, restructured and redecorated, and sold to 'single families who are well-to-do'.[23] In the course of this process many tenants had been 'persuaded' to leave. Such persuasion, it was alleged by the Islington Tenants Campaign, included harassment of the tenants and a 'winkling' out of the tenants by offering an inducement to leave or using other means to exert pressure on them to do so. The Islington Tenants Campaign set up a picket outside the shop of the major estate agents practising in the area, Prebble & Co., who were the plaintiffs in the action. After a number of Saturday mornings during which the defendants, who were members of the campaign, had picketed the offices, the plaintiffs took action to obtain an interim injunction against the defendants in order to prevent their protest picket.

This case must first be differentiated from cases of industrial picketing where pickets involved in trade disputes would be specifically permitted by the Trade Disputes Act 1906 to picket premises.[24] This was a non-industrial protest and involved a static assembly immediately outside the Prebbles shop. Placards were held and placed against windows stating 'Tenants watch out Prebbles about' and 'If Prebbles in – your out!'. Leaflets were also handed out to passers by, explaining the reasons for the picket.

The Court of Appeal, including Master of the Rolls, Lord Denning, were asked to decide whether the interlocutory injunction granted to the plaintiffs by Mr. Justice Forbes should stand.

In essence the case decides whether it will be easy for any person or organization to prevent a protest outside their premises by means of an interlocutory injunction pending a trial which is most likely never to occur.[25] This point and issue were understood by Lord Denning, who in a dissenting judgment affirmed,

---

[22] *Hubbard* v. *Pitt* [1976] QB 142, [1975] 3 All ER 1.
[23] [1975] 3 All ER 4.
[24] For picketing in residential areas in the USA see *Carey* v. *Brown* [1980] 447 US 455.
[25] For a fuller discussion of this case see Wallington, 'Injunctions and the Right to Demonstrate' [1976] 35 CLJ 82.

"the undoubted right of Englishmen to assemble together for the purpose
of deliberating upon public grievances". Such is the right of assembly.
So also is the right to meet together, to go in procession, to demonstrate
and to protest on matters of public concern.[26]

He also repeated Lord Scarman's statement in the report on the
inquiry into Red Lion Square that 'a positive right to demonstrate
exists, subject only to limits required by the need for good order and
the passage of traffic'. Lord Denning went on to say that it is time for
the courts to recognize that

> they should not interfere by interlocutory injunction with the right to
> demonstrate and to protest any more than they interfere with the right
> of free speech; provided everything is done peaceably and in good order.
> That is the case here.[27]

Such words, within a judgment in dissent, unfortunately pay only lip
service to the creation of such positive rights or freedoms.[28]

It is therefore necessary to look at the judgments which decided that
it would be easy in almost all such circumstances to prevent by an
interlocutory injunction any such protest. The judgments of Lord
Justices Stamp and Orr are based on the (then) recent case of *American
Cyanamid Company* v. *Ethicon Ltd*,[29] in which Lord Diplock gave the
leading speech in the House of Lords on a totally different issue, an
action for infringement of a patent, but which set out guidance rules
for interlocutory injunctions. As stated by Lord Justice Orr the test set
out by Lord Diplock has four stages. The first stage is 'whether there
was a serious question to be tried in the sense that the claim was not
frivolous or vexatious'.[30] This was taken to be a lesser burden than a

[26] [1975] 3 All ER 10.
[27] Ibid., 11.
[28] In his defence one should also state that Lord Denning has made similar statements when
not in dissent, including his comment in *Verrall* v. *Great Yarmouth Borough Council* [1980] 1
All ER 839. There he said the judge at the trial court had made an order 'because of the
importance of freedom of speech and freedom of assembly. These are among our most precious
freedoms. Freedom of speech means not only freedom for the views of which you approve,
but also freedom for the views of which you most heartily disapprove. This is a land, in the
words of the poet, where
"A man may speak the thing he will.
A land of settled government.
A land of just and old renown,
Where Freedom slowly broadens down
From precedent to precedent" (Tennyson).'
Unfortunately, the particular case involved a decision to allow the neo-Nazi National Front
to hold their annual conference at premises owned by the defendants. See the effect of the
quotation of this case in *Kent* v. *MPC*, *The Times*, 13 May 1981 and Association transcript.
[29] *American Cyanamid Co.* v. *Ethicon Ltd* [1975] 1 All ER 504.
[30] Ibid., 19.

prima facie case, simply that if there was any possibility at all of a case succeeding it would pass this first stage.

Stage two was to ask 'whether, if the plaintiffs were to succeed at the trial, they would be adequately compensated for the interim continuance of the defendants' activities'.[31] The answer was, and must always be in the circumstances of a protest, that there would be no real likelihood that those protested against could be adequately compensated by the protesters for such possible results of a protest.

The next question is to put the situation vice versa: 'whether if the defendants were to succeed at the trial they would be adequately compensated for the interim restriction on their activities which the grant of an interlocutory injunction would have imposed'. The learned judge answers that the demonstrators would be adequately compensated since 'the disadvantage involved would be minimal, and in any event I see no reason to suppose that the plaintiffs would be unable to pay any damages properly recoverable'.[32]

Finally, according to *Cyanamid*, the judge must consider 'the balance of convenience' in deciding whether to grant an interlocutory injunction on the basis of the answers to the three previous questions. The balance of convenience was found here to be 'heavily weighted in favour of the grant of the injunction'[33] because the defendants could not pay for the serious damage to the plaintiffs' business if an injunction were to be granted. The plaintiffs on the other hand could pay the inconsequential damages involved in loss of their protest to the defendants if the injunction were granted.

There was no trial of the issue and therefore the entire decision regarding the legal viability of this form of peaceful protest was made on the question of the interlocutory injunction. This will almost always be the case and the reasoning of the 'balance of convenience' will always be against the protesters and in favour of those who are the subject of the protest. This case and the possibilities it permits for prevention of protest are therefore serious incursions into any liberty or right to demonstrate.[34]

Seen in context against the older cases, *Hubbard* once again seems to view the rights of the public in using the highway as being restricted by the competing and superordinate rights of neighbouring landowners to use their property without being affected by users of the highway. The more intangible liberty of the subject to speak and protest freely is therefore subservient to property rights and the commercial interest

---

[31] Ibid., 20.
[32] Ibid.
[33] Ibid.
[34] These issues were not addressed or accepted by the majority judges in the Court of Appeal.

therein, and there is no effective means of balancing or even taking into account this conflict of interests in English law.

Statutory Restrictions

Highway Obstruction This particular issue, because it is one of the crimes most often charged against protestors, is dealt with in detail in chapter 6. For present purposes it is necessary to mention only that obstruction of the highway is an offence. It should also be remembered that there is a common law offence of public nuisance entailing an unreasonable user of the highway, causing obstruction or excessive noise. This crime will also be dealt with in chapter 6.[35]

Town Police Clauses Act 1847 section 28 and Metropolitan Police Act 1839 section 54 (6) These substantially similar sections create an offence by any 'person who, by means of any cart, carriage, sledge, truck or barrow, or any animal or other means wilfully interrupts any public crossing or wilfully causes any obstruction in any public footpath or other public thoroughfare'.

Road Vehicles (Construction and Use) Regulations 1986, Regulation 103 Since vehicles have often been used as road blocks in demonstrations, and protesting taxi drivers, etc., have driven around parts of central London and then stopped *en masse* in the middle of the road in order to block traffic, this particular regulation may also be important. 'No person in charge of a vehicle or trailer shall cause or permit the vehicle or trailer to stand on a road so as to cause any unnecessary obstruction thereof'.

Although these statutes and statutory instruments seem not to be intended so directly to deal with protesters and demonstrations, sections 11–13 of the Public Order Act 1986 are aimed more clearly in their direction, and it is to these that we now turn.

Control of Public Processions and Public Meetings

Prior to the 1986 Public Order Act a major distinction existed between the powers of the police in relation to the control of public processions and control of public meetings. It was possible under section 3 of the

[35] See, e.g., *R.* v. *Clarke* [1964] 2 QB 315.

old Public Order Act 1936 to impose conditions on public processions and even to ban them.[36]

The ban was a form of prior restraint which appears to have been considered necessary in relation to processions because of the possible effects on traffic as well as the more serious problems of disorder related to a moving, rather than a stationary crowd.

The Public Order Act 1986 has removed part of this distinction by allowing a similar imposition of conditions relating to public assemblies (s. 14) as exists for public processions (s. 12). A 'public assembly' is defined as 'an assembly of 20 or more persons in a public place which is wholly or partly open to the air'.[37] Previously, public meetings could take place and the police would have to wait to see whether any breach of the peace or obstruction of the highway had occurred before they could intervene. Now a prior assessment can be made and if necessary a meeting can have conditions imposed on it under section 14 of the Public Order Act 1986 by a senior police officer. However, it is not possible for the police to ban assemblies as opposed to processions under the 1986 Act.

It will also be difficult for the police to ascertain or assess effectively the circumstances of a public assembly or meeting since there will be no obligation on organizers of a public meeting to give advance notice of a public meeting to the police, as is now the case for processions under section 11 of the 1986 Act.

Advance Notice of Public Processions.

In 1980 a spate of local statutes were enacted making it mandatory for 'organizers' of processions to give written notice to the police beforehand. Such provisions[38] made it compulsory for the police to be given a certain amount of notice (usually between 3 and 7 days) of a procession so they could exercise their power under section 3 of the Public Order Act 1936 to impose conditions or to ban the prospective procession.[39]

---

[36] Section 3 (2) and (3) of the Public Order Act 1936.
[37] See Public Order Act 1986 s. 16. For further details of this and other aspects of the Public Order Act 1986, see R. Card, *Public Order: The New Law* (London, Butterworth, 1987); J. Marston, *Public Order: A Guide to the 1986 Public Order Act* (London, Fourmat, 1987); A. T. H. Smith, *Offences Against Public Order, Including the Public Order Act 1986* (London, Sweet & Maxwell, *Police Review*, 1987) and P. Thornton, *Public Order Law – Including the Public Order Act 1986* (London, Financial Training, 1987).
[38] As were to be found in County of Merseyside Act 1980, s. 31, West Midlands County Council Act 1980, s. 38, Cheshire County Council Act 1980, s. 28, Isle of Wight Act 1980, s. 26, Greater Manchester Act 1981, s. 56 and East Sussex Act 1981, s. 29.
[39] According to Lord Denning, then Master of the Rolls, in *Kent* v. *MPC*, *The Times* 13 May 1981, discussing s. 3 of the 1936 Act, 'it may "have been implicit" in the statute – that those who are arranging a procession of this kind should notify the Commissioner of Police of the

These sundry bye-laws have now been repealed, and replaced by section 11. The types of public procession which are included in the need for advance notice seem to include a wide group involving those

(a) to demonstrate support for or opposition to the views or actions of any person or body of persons,
(b) to publicise a cause or campaign, or
(c) to mark or commemorate an event.

It is not clear why it was necessary to specify in this way the intentions of the public processions considering how few exclusions arise from this wording. Notice must be given 'of *any proposal* to hold a public procession' (s. 11 (1) my emphasis) – of this sort, which seems to suggest that early consultation is required at the beginning of the planning stage. It is difficult, however, to see how this could be enforced.

Processions 'commonly or customarily held' or funeral processions are excluded from the necessity for advanced notice (s. 11 (2)), as are those processions where it is 'not reasonably practicable' to give any advance notice.

The notice must specify the date, starting time, route, and name and address of an organizer of the demonstration (s. 11 (3)). The notice must be delivered to a police station in the area in which the procession will start (s. 11 (4)) and must be delivered more than six clear days before the procession is intended to be held (s. 11 (5)) or 'if that is not reasonably practicable, as soon as delivery is reasonably practicable (s. 11 (6)). An offence is committed by 'each of the persons organizing' a public procession if either notice is not given, or the date, time or route of the actual procession differ from those actually specified in the notice (s. 11 (7)).

There are defences for those who can prove that they did not know of any such failure to comply or that they neither suspected nor had any reason to suspect such failure (s. 11. (8)). Similarly, it would be a defence under section 11 (9) for a defendant to prove that any difference in date, time or route of the actual procession 'arose from circumstances beyond his control' or from something done 'with the agreement of a police officer or by his direction'. Offences under this section are liable to a maximum fine on summary conviction at level 3 on the standard scale.

No definition is given of what is involved in 'organizing' a

---

date, the time, the route and the numbers which it is estimated will assemble'. For general criticism of advance notice and its 'chilling effect' see *The Control of Protest – the New Public Order Bill – the Response of the GLC* December 1985, pp. 27–32.

demonstration. In the case of *Flockhart* v. *Robinson*[40] under section 3 of the Public Order Act 1936 the defendant was found guilty of 'organizing' a public procession which had been banned. 'Organizing' was there taken to include activity in which the defendant, walking in front of a banned procession, signalled with hand movements to other people in the procession when to stop and when to move, and which direction to take. It may be more difficult to prove 'organizing' of a procession without such direct and obvious physical involvement. In view of this case being the only authority on 'organizing' a procession it might have been more sensible to have provided a wider definition in the Act of what 'organizing' might mean. By remaining silent on this issue it could be argued that the case limits the meaning of this word.

Imposing Conditions on Public Processions

Table 3.1 sets out a comparison between section 12 of the 1986 Act and section 3 (1) and (4) of the Public Order Act 1936. As will be seen, the main structure of the provisions remains the same. The senior police officer must have 'regard to the time or place at which and the circumstances in which any public procession is being held or is intended to be held and to its route and proposed route'. There are minor variations in the wording, but the same issues are to be taken into account by the senior police officer under both old and new statutes. The new Act, however, has a second dimension, having regard to those issues, in terms of the senior police officer's assessment of the situation. Under the old legislation, where the chief police officer (CPO) had 'reasonable ground for apprehending that the procession may occasion serious public disorder' the CPO could impose conditions on the procession. Under the new Act conditions may be imposed if the CPO reasonably believes *either* that

(a) it may result in serious public disorder, serious damage to property or serious disruption to the life of the community, *or*
(b) the purpose of the persons organising it is the intimidation of others with a view to compelling them not to do an act they have a right to do, or to do an act they have a right not to do (s. 12 (1)).

The new legislation therefore allows the senior police officer to make conditions not only where that police officer 'reasonably believes' that serious public disorder may occur, but also where serious damage to

---

[40] *Flockhart* v. *Robinson* [1950] 2KB 498 (NB a Mr Leslie Scarman was counsel for the defendant) 31.

property may result or 'serious disruption to the life of the community'. The latter could conceivably include any long term closing of a major road to traffic because of a public procession. To these are added the police officer's reasonable belief in section 12 (1) (b) that the organizer's purpose is 'intimidation'. It is not clear what intimidation would mean in this context, since it is possible for any large public procession to be regarded as intimidatory, and the line between urging or persuading and 'the intimidation of others with a view to compelling them' may be quite thin at times in the eyes of a senior police officer.

It would seem that this intimidation section may have been included originally as a result of trade union activity in the miners' strike of 1984–5[41] and subsequently gained credence as a result of activity in support of trade union action in relation to *The Times*' move to the Wapping site in 1986. If these are, in fact, the motives or reasoning behind the inclusion of this clause, then such motives might have been better served by dealing specifically with such issues in relation to industrial disputes than importing such words into an Act aiming to deal with all public protest. The wording of the section and its specificity in relation to 'an act they have a right to do', or 'an act they have a right not to do' seems likely to cause more difficulties than it would solve. The police have often asked for clear guidance to be given to them in relation to such issues which have strong political overtones and effects.[42]

The remainder of sub-section 1 carries on in similar style to the old section 3 (1) of the 1936 Act with minor adjustments for what may now be prevented. The proviso regarding 'the display of flags, banners or emblems', which in any case always seemed somewhat strange in the old Act, is removed.

Formality The directions given for a future procession need now to be set down in writing (s. 12 (3)), which should help clarify any dispute as to what the directions said.

Offences and Defences Separate offences are created for a person 'who organizes' (s. 12 (4)), 'who takes part' (s. 12 (5)), or 'who incites another' to take part (s. 12 (6)) in a public procession knowingly failing to comply with a condition imposed under section 12.

It is a defence for someone accused of organizing or taking part to

[41] See *The Times* 16 Sept. 1987, comments of Mr Ronald Cowles, Legal Adviser to British Coal at the International Bar Association Conference: 'The Public Order Act 1986 resulted largely from the strike' etc.
[42] See also Peter Thornton, 'We Protest' (London, NCCL, 1985), pp. 54–8.

Table 3.1 Imposing conditions on public processions

New POA 1986 s. 12	Old POA 1936 s. 3 (1) and (4)
(1) If the *senior police officer*, having regard to the time or place at which and the circumstances in which any public procession is *being held* or is intended to *be held* and to its route or proposed route, reasonably *believes* that:	(1) If the *chief officer of police*, having regard to the time or place at which and the circumstances in which any public procession is *taking place* or is intended to *take place* and to the route taken or proposed to be taken by the procession, has reasonable *ground for apprehending* that the procession may occasion serious public disorder,
(a) it may result in serious public disorder, serious damage to property or serious disruption to the life of the community, or	
(b) the purpose of the persons organizing it is the intimidation of others with a view to compelling them not to do an act they have a right to do, or to do an act they have a right not to do,	
he may give directions imposing on the persons organizing or taking part in the procession such conditions as appear to him necessary to *prevent such disorder, damage, disruption or intimidation*,	he may give directions imposing upon the persons organizing or taking part in the procession such conditions as appear to him necessary *for the preservation of public order*.
including conditions as to the route of the procession or prohibiting it from entering any public place specified in the directions	including conditions prescribing the route to be taken by the procession and conditions prohibiting the procession from entering any public place specified in the directions: provided that no conditions restricting the display of flags, banners or emblems shall be imposed under this subsection except such as are reasonably necessary to prevent risk of a breach of the peace.

Table 3.1 Imposing conditions on public processions (*continued*)

New POA 1986 s. 12	Old POA 1936 s. 3 (1) and (4)
(4) A person who *organizes* a public procession and knowingly fails to comply with a condition imposed under this section is guilty of an offence, but it is a *defence* for him to prove that the failure arose from circumstances beyond his control.	(4) Any person who knowingly fails to comply with any *directions given* or conditions imposed under this section . . . shall be guilty of an offence.
(5) A person who *takes part* in a public procession and knowingly fails to comply with a condition imposed under this section is guilty of an offence, but it is a defence for him to prove that the failure arose from circumstances beyond his control.	
(6) A person who incites another to commit an offence under subsection (5) is guilty of an offence.	

(N.B. The italics are the author's and are intended to show up differences between old and new law which may not be evident from a linear comparison.)

prove that such failure 'arose from circumstances beyond his control' (s. 12 (5)).

Arrest and Penalty A constable in uniform is given powers of arrest without warrant for anyone the constable reasonably suspects of committing any of these offences (s. 12 (7)).

Punishment for organizers or inciters is a maximum on summary conviction of 3 months imprisonment or a fine not exceeding level 4 or both (s. 12 (10)). Ordinary demonstrators in contravention would be liable on summary conviction to a maximum level 3 fine (s. 12 (9)).

Delegation The chief officer of police may delegate the chief officer's functions as to impending processions to a deputy or assistant chief constable or an assistant commissioner of police, as relevant (s. 15).

Imposing Conditions on Public Assemblies

Section 14 of the Public Order Act 1986 provides for the possibility of imposing conditions on public assemblies, in very much the same way as section 12 deals with public processions. As we have seen above a 'public assembly' means 'an assembly of 20 or more persons in a public place which is wholly or partly open to the air' (s. 16).

The wording of the two sections is almost entirely the same, including the reasonable belief of the senior police officer which allows the section to come into play.

The only material difference relates to the character of the 'directions' which may be imposed 'on the persons organising or taking part in the assembly'. The conditions which may be imposed are within the discretion of the senior police officer, 'as appear to him necessary to prevent . . . disorder, damage, disruption or intimidation'. The directions imposed by the senior police officer may apply to

the place at which the assembly may be (or continue to be) held, its maximum duration, or the maximum number of persons who may constitute it (s. 14 (1)).

In one of the first cases under this section the exact location of a demonstration in 'Trafalgar Square' or 'Trafalgar Square East' was important in deciding whether there were still 20 people in that area for the purposes of judging the force of a Chief Inspector's directions[43] under section 14.

The conditions under this section would appear to be the *only* directions, i.e. place, duration and maximum number, which may be imposed. Conditions under section 12 were stated to be '*including* conditions as to the route of the procession or prohibiting it from entering any public place specified in the directions'. This would suggest that directions under section 12 might *include* other elements relating to the procession, but that directions under section 14 could apply *only* to the elements there mentioned.

Similar offences are created as in section 12 with similar penalties and similar powers of arrest granted to a constable in uniform. The directions given by a chief officer of police relating to 'an assembly intended to be held' have to be given in writing in the same way as such directions regarding a procession 'intended to be held'. Similar

---

[43] Brickley, States and Kitson, *Legal Action*, Sept. 1987, p. 15. In a further case arising out of the South African Embassy picket the Bow Street Magistrate found that 'intimidation' under S. 14(1)(b) did not include 'causing discomfort' to visitors to the Embassy, *Police* v. *Reid (Lorna)* [1987] Crim. LR 702.

powers of delegation from the chief officer of police to a deputy or assistant also apply to this section as they did in section 12 above.

Banning Orders for Public Processions

The wording of sections 2 and 3 of the Public Order Act 1936 have been substantially repeated and re-enacted in section 13 of the 1986 Public Order Act. The only major distinction in the main part of the provision is in the broadening of its effect from 'any Borough or Urban District' to 'any district or part of a district'.

Orders prohibiting public processions were only available under the old Act for urban processions. In theory, therefore, it was possible to march all over the countryside, providing the procession did not enter a borough or urban district. Under the new legislation it is possible to ban a public procession wherever it is to be held. One wonders whether this is the result of recent campaigns in favour of nuclear disarmament whose effects have often been seen outside of towns.

The new section 13 does, however, set out the steps in the banning procedure more clearly. If the chief officer of police 'reasonably believes' that (the old wording was 'is of opinion that') his powers to impose conditions are not sufficient to prevent serious public disorder he '*shall*' (my emphasis) apply to the local council for an order prohibiting all public processions or of any class of public procession in that area.

The council, on receiving the application, *may* 'with the consent of the Secretary of State' make an order along the lines of the application or with modifications approved by the Secretary of State.

A slightly different procedure is set out, as was the case in the 1936 legislation, for the City of London and the Metropolitan Police district. In these cases there is no intervening local authority with powers to control the police and, therefore, the Commissioner of Police for the City of London and the Metropolitan Police Commissioner do not make application to the local authority, but '*may* with the consent of the Secretary of State make' a banning order in similar circumstances to those mentioned above. Supperstone[44] makes much of the difference between the word 'shall' for a Chief Constable outside London and 'may' for the Metropolitan Police Commissioner. However, in view of the above the distinction does not seem as important as he suggests.

Formality The new legislation formalizes the procedure of passing prohibition orders, allowing them to be revoked or varied (s. 13 (5)) and legislating for all such orders either to be 'made in writing' or to 'be recorded in writing as soon as practicable' (s. 13 (6)).

Offences, Penalties and Powers of Arrest Once again separate offences

[44] Ibid., p. 53.

are enacted for those organizing (s. 13 (9)), taking part in (s. 13 (8)), or inciting another to take part in (s. 13 (9)), a banned procession. Taking part in a banned procession was not a crime under the 1936 Act and this is, therefore, a significant change from the previous position in which only organizers and inciters were guilty. This particular addition will obviate the need to prove 'organizing' or 'inciting' and enable the police to break up a banned procession by arresting all those on it.

Organizers and inciters have a maximum penalty on summary conviction of 3 months imprisonment or a fine at level 4 or both (s. 13 (1) (13)), whereas demonstrators in contravention are liable to a maximum level 3 fine on summary conviction (s. 13 (12)).

A constable in uniform is once again given power to arrest, without warrant, anyone reasonably suspected of organizing, inciting or taking part in a banned demonstration (s. 13 (10)).

Problems Relating to the Prohibition of Processions

The power to ban processions has caused a number of difficulties, both legal and practical, which merit study.

Specificity Section 13 has continued the same wording as in the previous section 3 legislation for the types of procession which may be banned. What may be prohibited is 'the holding of all public processions (or of any class of public procession so specified)'. This does not seem to allow for the banning of a particular march, but only of either all processions or a complete class of processions. This was a matter which concerned the Home Affairs Committee in their report.[45] The problem appears to be that it may be impractical and invidious to ban a particular demonstration. It would be invidious because if (say) a left wing demonstration were banned and a right wing demonstration allowed to proceed, the police would be accused of favouring one against another. Then, if a demonstration by the X group were to be banned, they could easily form themselves into the Y group to hold the demonstration. The rationale, therefore, behind a blanket form of ban is clear.

On the other hand, a blanket ban, especially for a long period, may well affect a large number of processions and demonstrations which are innocuous or unrelated to the target procession. It is thought that the particular order could be specific enough as to time and place that it would only affect the target procession. Forms of words can surely be found which would allow those processions considered not to be target processions to proceed.[46]

---

[45] Law Relating to Public Order, Vol. I, Home Affairs Committee 5th Report. Session 79–80.
[46] Supperstone, *Brownlie*, pp. 52–3 at fn. 11 sets out possible formulas used in Ilford North in 1977 and in Glasgow in 1980.

This was the view held by the European Commission of Human Rights in the one public order case to come before them questioning the Metropolitan Police Commissioner's discretion.[47] Christians against Racism and Fascism (CARAF) queried a blanket ban in Ilford which was aimed at preventing a procession by the racist National Front. The Commission said that a general ban can only be justified 'if there is a real danger of demonstrations resulting in disorder which cannot be prevented by other less stringest measures'.[48] The Commission thought the 2-month ban was not unreasonable considering the current atmosphere in Britain resulting from National Front and opposing marches. Article 11 of the European Convention can then be seen in its true colours. It would be very difficult to prove a contravention of article 11 (2).[49]

Questioning Discretion In August 1977 the Metropolitan Police Commissioner refused to ask for the consent of the Home Secretary to ban a march by the National Front although the local authority wanted him to do so.[50] The London Borough of Lewisham tried to obtain an order of mandamus against the Commissioner directing him to seek the Home Secretary's consent to ban the march. Although Mr Justice Slynn observed that he did have 'power to grant mandamus' and that 'circumstances could arise in which I could make an order' he refused to do so in the particular case.[51]

Aiming to stop a ban, Mgr Bruce Kent, then General Secretary of the Campaign for Nuclear Disarmament applied for judicial review of an order made by the same Metropolitan Police Commissioner, Sir David McNee, prohibiting all public processions within the Metropolitan Police district 'except those traditionally held on May 1st to celebrate Mayday and those of a religious character customarily held'.

Mgr Kent said that the order was geographically too wide and 'ranged from a fair at Chislehurst to a carnival at Fulham and a student march to the House of Commons'. Mgr Kent suggested 'that there were no reasonable grounds on which he (the Metropolitan Police Commissioner) could come to the conclusion that the CND marches would be likely to be of a kind to cause 'serious public disorder''.' However, the three judges in the Court of Appeal were unanimous in deciding that the Commissioner's order was valid. Lord Denning, Master of the Rolls, said

[47] *CARAF* v. *UK* (Application 8440/78) 21D and R. of E.C. H.R. 138 p. 150; and see D. Kretzmer, 'Demonstrations and the Law' [1984] Isr. LR pp. 82–3.
[48] R. of E. C. H. R. at p. 138.
[49] See further in chs 8 and 9.
[50] See *The Times*, 30 Jul. 1977.
[51] *The Times*, 12 Aug. 1977 and Supperstone, *Brownlie*, p. 52.

It was a matter of the judgment of the Commissioner who might well say that there was a 'risk of serious public disorder'.

The Court could not say that the Commissioner was at fault or that the order made was ultra vires, especially when the Home Secretary had agreed with it.[52]

Lord Justice Ackner said that:

On the face of the order the Commissioner had proper regard to the circumstances in the area. . . . Parliament has entrusted to him the power to make decisions regarding public processions subject to the concurrence of the Home Secretary and not to us. There was nothing to suggest that he had acted outside his power or capriciously. He had defined 'class' by exclusion: 'all public processions except' traditional Mayday processions and those of a religious character.

Near the end of April there was clear evidence of a highly volatile, 'tinder box' situation throughout all the Commissioner's area and that a month's respite from all marches in London was necessary to prevent serious public disorder. It was hooligans the police were trying to control, not the members of peaceful marches. Violence was the object of hooligans who were not concerned with the philosophy of the marchers. The march was a target for their viciousness. It was ironic that the ban protected the CND from the violence which the Commissioner had anticipated.
. . .
The Commissioner thought that there was a real risk, otherwise he would not have made his order. His Lordship accepted that the CND regretted the loss of publicity from their march and said that the report of the appeal might give them more coverage in the media.[53]

Sir Dennis Buckley concurred, but had a slightly different view:

In a case such as the present the order making authority should put clearly before the court the considerations which led to the making of the order. Here the Commissioner's reasons for his order seem meagre.

But it was for the applicants to demonstrate that there were no or no reasonable grounds on which the Commissioner could have held that the CND marches would be likely to cause 'serious public disorder'.

Although the courts suggest that there may be a possible occasion on which the Metropolitan Police Commissioner's discretion either to ask for a ban or not to ask for a ban can be questioned they have steadily refused to contravene the MPC's exercise of that discretion either way. This can be seen as a further example of the English system of

[52] *The Times*, 15 May 1981 and the Association transcript.
[53] *The Times*, 15 May 1981, with additions from the Association transcript.

determining legal rights by asserting that they exist at the same time as denying them in practice.

To Ban or Not to Ban – Suppression or Victimization The existence of the executive possibility of ordering a prohibition on a public procession presents a dilemma for any Chief Officer of Police. A Chief Officer who decides to prohibit the procession will be accused of the suppression of free speech by those intending to march and by civil libertarians generally.[54] If the Chief Officer decides not to ban a procession, and public disorder does occur, as was the case in Lewisham on 15 August 1977,[55] the Chief Officer is accused of causing the disorder by those affected and is accused of victimization by those who are arrested and prosecuted for offences arising out of such disorder.

The Chief Officer is therefore placed in a difficult position and any decision is likely to be criticized by one side or the other. Some have suggested that it is unwise for the police to be involved in 'making political decision' of this nature.[56] Chief Officers see the decision as a policing decision and the political aspects can be dealt with by the Home Secretary or the Local Authority.[57] The Home Secretary, and the Local Authority outside of London, provide a political screen for police action and there does not seem to be much evidence that the police decision has been more politically motivated than any other police decision. It is also not absolutely clear whether one would prefer a directly political authority to take the decision or an authority who is at least in theory independent such as the police. The problem seems to be the more general problem of police accountability to which we will return in chapter 8. It is difficult to see how the police could be removed from being involved in the decision to ban a procession, but they should be subject to much more control than the courts currently allow.[58]

The Problem of the Rival Group – Beatty v. Gillbanks and the Prohibition of Meetings and Processions at Common Law The 1880s brought a test to public order which was not specifically mentioned in the general case histories in chapter 2. The Salvation Army and its frequent marches against alcohol and in favour of 'salvation' were causing an interesting

[54] See *Kent* v. *Metropolitan Police Commissioner, The Times*, 13 May 1981.
[55] Supperstone, *Brownlie*, p. 51.
[56] L. Lustgarten, *The Governance of Police* (London, Sweet & Maxwell, 1986), pp. 12–22 and Supperstone, *Brownlie*, p. 52.
[57] On 'operational' decisions see Lustgarten, *The Governance of Police*, pp. 20–2, 172–3.
[58] See D. Kretzmer, 'Demonstrations and the Law', p. 47 for a comparative overview of bans and permits reviews in the UK, USA and Israel.

moral dilemma to the police and public authorities. Increasingly frequently, when they marched, they were met by an opposing group, calling themselves the Skeleton Army, holding a banner inscribed with a skull and crossbones. The two 'armies' would clash, and fights and general disorder would ensue. The problem was the moral worth of the salvationists compared with their antagonists, who were described as 'miserable creatures, haunters of public houses and loiterers at street corners'.[59] On the other hand, if the Salvation Army would not take to the streets then they would not provoke the Skeleton Army into confronting them and causing disorder. Hence, the difficult dilemma of who to stop, the Skeletonists or the Salvationists.

Williams[60] recounts how Sir William Harcourt, the Home Secretary in 1881 responded to questions from the Magistrates of Stamford as to how to deal with the problem. Pointing out that 'processions as such are not illegal', he said that 'if the police can convince them (the Magistrates) that they will lead to "riotous collisions" with antagonists then they should issue proclamations to forbid such gatherings'.

On 24 March 1882 two Magistrates at Weston-super-Mare signed a Public Notice which purported to 'require, order and direct' all persons to abstain from assembling to the disturbance of the public peace'. The Salvation Army leaders defied this ban on the next Sunday, 26 March, by processing through the streets. The march leaders, Beatty, Mullins and Bowden were arrested, and subsequently ordered by the Magistrates' Court to be bound over to keep the peace for 12 months. They refused to be bound over and appealed to the Divisional Court of the Queen's Bench Division which ruled in their favour. The binding over order was discharged and the judges specifically denied 'that a man may punished for acting lawfully because he knows that his so doing may induce another man to act unlawfully'.[61] The Salvation Army by its lawful action of processing through the streets could not be taken to have acted unlawfully simply because the Skeleton Army was induced by the Salvation Army's appearance to come out and attack. The Court also gave no suggestion that the Magistrates' proclamation or the advice of the Home Secretary had any legal force.

This case is important in a number of respects. It affirmed that there was no common law right to ban meetings (they were actually charged with unlawful assembly) or processions. The case also seemed to suggest that there was some right of lawful procession or protest. Finally, the case seemed to advocate that whoever was 'first in the field' was correct.

[59] David Williams, *Keeping the Peace: the Police and Public Order* (London, Hutchinson, 1967), p. 51.
[60] Williams, *Keeping the Peace*, p. 51.
[61] *Beatty* v. *Gillbanks* [1882] 9 QBD 308.

This seemed to be the natural result of their ruling. However, if the Skeleton Army decided in another town to march and as a result the Salvation Army decided to march against it and violence ensued, *Beatty* v. *Gillbanks* seemed to suggest that the Skeletonists could not be charged with unlawful assembly or be bound over. One wonders how the Court would really have decided in those circumstances.

This particular issue has been treated in a different manner in further public order cases. In *Wise* v. *Dunning*,[62] a Protestant pastor who went out into the Catholic area of Liverpool to make inflammatory speeches against Catholicism was found guilty of unlawful assembly under a local by-law because his speeches offended his audience. This particular case seems to suggest that a speaker must 'take his audience as he finds it', and that if what the speaker says is going to annoy people such that they may cause violence as a result the speaker will be guilty of a public order offence. This is in direct contrast to the view expressed in *Beatty* v. *Gillbanks*. If it is lawful for the Salvationists to march, even though they know this will inflame and annoy another group, why is it not lawful for Pastor Wise to make statements which he knows may inflame and annoy another group? The particular point is taken further in the case of *Jordan* v. *Burgoyne* in which Colin Jordan addressed a public meeting in Trafalgar Square with the words,

> more and more people every day are opening their eyes and coming to say with us Hitler was right. They are coming to say that our real enemies, the people we should have fought, were not Hitler and the National Socialists of Germany but world Jewry and its associates in this country.[63]

Jordan was charged with using insulting words whereby a breach of the peace was likely to be occasioned under section 5 of the Public Order Act 1936. Although this section has been repealed by the new Act the principle enunciated in the case may still be important. Lord Chief Justice Parker, with some curious wording, stated,

> I cannot myself, having read the speech, imagine any reasonable citizen, certainly one who was a Jew, not being provoked beyond endurance and not only a Jew but a coloured man, and quite a number of people of this country, who were told that they were merely tools of the Jews and that they had fought in the war on the wrong side, and matters of that sort.[64]

He stated that the test was that of taking one's particular audience

[62] *Wise* v. *Dunning* [1902] 1 KB 167.
[63] *Jordan* v. *Burgoyne* [1963] 2 QB 744. See also ch. 9 for a comparison with the position in the USA.
[64] Ibid., 748.

as one found it; once again quite contrary to the view expressed in *Beatty* and *Gillbanks*.

This seems to be but one further example of the vague and discretionary nature of this area of the law. One court can come to a definitive legal view based on that court's view of the particular parties, i.e. the Salvation Army as opposed to the Skeleton Army. This does not appear to stop the next court making a decision in entirely the opposite way where it happens to prefer the views of the audience (in one case the defamed Catholics of Liverpool in *Wise* v. *Dunning*, and in another the slated Jews and CND supporters of *Jordan* v. *Burgoyne*) to those of the speaker. Jordan was 'first in the field' in having obtained the platform in Trafalgar Square by organizing a public meeting there; but since the views he expressed were unpopular to both his audience and the Divisional Court he was criminally liable. Whilst one might not wish to query the essential wisdom of backing the Salvationists and not backing Colin Jordan, the lack of a meaningful peg on which to hang such decisions in a less discretionary manner becomes obvious. The antics which these contradictory cases have caused writers to go through in order to justify the cases are perhaps instructive in understanding how law evolves[65] but do nothing to clarify the law or promote its respect.

'Bans' under the Metropolitan Police Act 1839, Sections 52 and 54, and Town Police Clauses Act 1847   According to Williams[66] section 52 of the Metropolitan Police Act was used to ban a counter-procession and counter-meeting within half a mile of the Albert Hall during the period of a fascist meeting held there. Similarly under this section, the famous 'Trenchard Ban' was issued in which the then Commissioner of the Metropolitan Police, Lord Trenchard, banned all public meetings in the vicinity of a Labour Exchange.[67]

In *Papworth* v. *Coventry*[68] the Metropolitan Police Commissioner had made directions by virtue of section 52 of the Metropolitan Police Act, known as 'Sessional Orders', directing police constables to disperse assemblies or processions of people in the vicinity of Parliament during the period that Parliament was sitting.

Papworth and some others held a vigil in Whitehall opposite the end of Downing Street against the Vietnam war from noon to 1.00 p.m. on 26 April 1966. The vigilants remained stationary in the gutter or on the curb and were spaced out so that nobody was obstructed. Three of

[65] See, e.g., Supperstone, *Brownlie*, pp. 125–30.
[66] Williams, *Keeping the Peace*, p. 68.
[67] Ibid.
[68] *Papworth* v. *Coventry* [1967] 2 All. ER 41.

them were arrested and charged under section 54 (9). Although there was no evidence that anyone was obstructed in obtaining access to the Houses of Parliament and the conduct of the group 'was good mannered, restrained and gentlemanly' they were convicted and each fined £2.

Papworth appealed by way of case stated to the Divisional Court contending that the directions contained in the Sessional Orders were *ultra vires* section 52 of the Act. The court was not prepared to state that the directions were *ultra vires*, but sent the case back to the Magistrate asking her to find whether the persons concerned 'constituted an assembly which was capable of giving rise to an obstruction . . . or to disorder or annoyance likely to lead to a breach of the peace'.[69] Papworth was in the event acquitted[70] and an important public right to be able to protest near parliament was safeguarded, and could not simply be banned by police order, provided such protest was peaceful.

Orders made under section 52 were also used against protesters picketing outside South Africa House in Trafalgar Square on 7 May 1987, this time coupled with a reliance on the Vienna Convention and the duties of a host state towards a foreign mission. Although the Metropolitan Police Commissioner's directions were not *ultra vires*, it was held that insufficient information was given to the accused to make them acquainted with the directions. The Metropolitan Stipendiary Magistrate, Sir David Hopkin said:

> If the waving of banners and placards and chanting done day after day by larger groups than two did not impair the mission's dignity, I do not see why such action should, when done by the two defendants on this occasion.[71]

Regulation of Public Use of Particular Public Places

There are particular regulations for the use of public parks, forests, military areas, public libraries and other public places.[72] The use of Trafalgar Square for meetings is governed by the Trafalgar Square Regulations 1952[73] and permission must be obtained for assemblies, parades, processions, public speeches and addresses from the Minister for the Environment. Cox reports the Department of the Environment's announcement in 1972 that they would not allow the Square to be used

---

[69] Ibid., 48 and see Supperstone, *Brownlie*, p. 61.
[70] Ibid.
[71] *Police* v. *Perry and Markovich* [1987], *Legal Action*, Sept., p. 15.
[72] See Supperstone, *Brownlie*, pp. 35–8.
[73] SI 1952 No. 776, see Supperstone, *Brownlie*, pp. 35–6 and 348–9.

for demonstrations relating to Northern Ireland.[74] The Department's policy is stated as being to keep the Square 'as a major national setting for serious public meetings based on the making of speeches', and songs and other such presentations are not encouraged.[75] The use of the nation's most prestigious venue for large open-air meetings is therefore covered by executive discretion,[76] unfettered by the courts.[77] When the Square was to be closed for 2 years for renovation in February 1987, it was suggested this was an attempt to stifle expression.[78]

Conclusion

There is no specific direct body of law enabling meetings and processions. What we see instead is a group of statutory provisions coupled with some other areas of 'no-right' emanating from the common law. The law of meetings and processions on the public highway and in public places is therefore a construct which needs quite an imaginative artist to draw the lines between the unconnected dots of existing law and tradition.

The resulting, charming, antique framework to be found in this chapter should be seen as separate from what has become the more important law on public order to which we will now turn. These are the sets of individual offences against public order which will be dealt with in succeeding chapters.

---

[74] B. Cox, *Civil Liberties in Britain* (London, Penguin, 1975), pp. 56–7.
[75] Supperstone, *Brownlie*, p. 36.
[76] See also Williams, *Keeping the Peace*, pp. 72–86.
[77] For cases considering the Greenham Common and Bulford Ranges By-Laws, see Ex p. Hutchinson and Ex p. LCC, *The Times* LR 27 Aug. 1987, Ex P. Hutchinson [1988] 1All ER333 and Cohen, B. 'Byelaws under the MLA1892', *Legal Action*, April 1988 p. 14.
[78] *The Times*, 21 Feb. 1987.

4

From Threats and Insults to Riot: the Frightening Gradation

This chapter looks at some specific areas of public order law which deal with violence used collectively or individually, and other behaviour amounting to offensive conduct which might cause violence, harassment, alarm, distress or racial hatred.

Charting this area of the law has been made easier by the enactment of sections 1 to 5, and 17 and 18 of the Public Order Act 1986, which has created new offences of riot, unlawful assembly/violent disorder, affray, and using threatening, abusive or insulting words or behaviour and disorderly behaviour. The old common law offences with similar names have been repealed as have sections 5 and 5A of the Public Order Act 1936. These offences may appear to start with a clean slate, but issues which arose in relation to the old offences remain important at least until specific rulings have been made on the new offences.

This chapter first examines the new array of offences and then looks at three offences originally associated with the violence of protest which have not been affected by the new legislation: incitement, sedition and treason. Through these one can see historically the state's view of political opposition and also perceive the current position regarding the armed services and police personnel.

Fear is the Key – The Range of Offences

The 1986 Public Order Act sets out a sequence of steps for five offences from 'riot' at the top of the scale down to 'harassment, alarm or distress' at the bottom. Although the five offences are linked, there is a clear distinction between the three more serious offences of riot, violent disorder and affray, and the two less serious offences contained in sections 4 and 5, as shown below.

Trial on indictment	**S. 1. Riot** 12 people 10 years DPP consent		
Trial either way	**S. 2 Violent Disorder** 3 people 5 years/6 months		
		S. 3 Affray 1 person 3 years/6 months	
Summary trial		**S. 4 Threats, etc. – violence** 1 person 6 months	
			S. 5 Threats, etc. – distress 1 person Fine only

The list shows how each of the offences is differentiated by the level of violence used or caused, the number of people involved in the behaviour causing the offence, the seriousness of the penalty involved and whether or not the consent of the Director of Public Prosecutions is necessary for the offence to be charged. A more complete picture can be obtained from Table 4.1 (pp. 100–3) which sets out a comparison of the ingredients of all the offences against each other and their common law or statutory precursors.

The key to all of the offences is the possibility of the causing of fear or alarm for their personal safety to others. The three offences of Riot (s. 1), Violent Disorder (s. 2) and Affray (s. 3) all contain the common core that the conduct of the offender(s), 'is such as would cause a person of reasonable firmness present at the scene to fear for his personal safety'. The lesser offences 'Fear or Provocation of Violence' (s. 4) and 'Harassment, Alarm or Distress' (s. 5) involve causing a more direct fear of violence, or violence itself, to or by a specific person (s. 4), and behaviour which might cause 'harassment, alarm or distress' (s. 5) to another within that person's sight or hearing.

At the top end of the scale (see list above), Riot needs twelve or more people acting for a common purpose and carries a maximum penalty of 10 years' imprisonment or a fine (or both). One step down, Violent Disorder needs at least three people and is punishable on conviction on indictment with a maximum term of 5 years' imprisonment or a fine (or both) and on summary conviction with 6 months or a fine (or both).[1] Affray needs only one person and is punishable on conviction or indictment with a maximum of 3 years or a fine (or both) and 6 months on a summary conviction or fine (or both).[2]

Fear or Provocation of Violence needs one person only and is punishable on summary conviction with 6 months or a level five fine or both. At the bottom end of the scale, 'Harassment, Alarm or Distress' needs one person only and is punishable on summary conviction with a fine not exceeding level three.

Ingredients of the More Serious Offences: Riot, Violent Disorder and Affray

Violence

Section 1, 2 and 3 offences all involve either the 'use' or 'threat' of 'unlawful violence' by the required number of persons for the offence to be committed. The use or threat of unlawful violence in Affray must be 'towards another' person, which does not appear to be necessary for the commission of Violent Disorder or Riot. The latter offences may, therefore, be committed by using or threatening violence against property as well as people.[3] It is a little surprising that the two more serious offences may involve violence to property whereas the lesser offence only includes people. A similar philosophy percolates down to the section 4 and 5 offences which also involve people present.

A major distinction exists between the offence of riot and the other two serious offences of violent disorder and affray. Although twelve or more persons present together must '*use or threaten* unlawful violence for a common purpose' it is only those persons 'using unlawful violence for a common purpose' who are guilty of riot. In this case, therefore, it is not enough for a person to threaten unlawful violence. Unlawful violence actually has to be *used* by one or more of the twelve for that

---

[1] Note that its predecessor unlawful assembly probably did need a common purpose as with riot. See table 4.1 and Supperstone, *Brownlie*, p. 120. For further details, see also R. Card, *Public Order: The New Law* (London, Butterworth, 1987), pp. 24–8; J. Marston, *Public Order: A Guide to the 1986 Public Order Act* (London, Fourmat, 1987), pp. 68–73; A. T. H. Smith, *Offences Against Public Order, Including the Public Order Act 1986* (London, Sweet & Maxwell, *Police Review*, 1987), ch. 3, and P. Thornton, *Public Order Law – Including the Public Order Act 1986* (London, Financial Training, 1987).
[2] Riot, violent disorder and affray are also excluded from the early release provisions of the Criminal Justice Act 1982, Schedule 2.4, Public Order Act 1986.
[3] See s. 8 and its 'extended' definition of 'violence'. See also Smith, *Offences Against Public Order*, pp. 55–7.

person, or those persons, to be guilty of riot. Such unlawful violence seemingly could be used against property as much as against persons since no person need actually be present at the scene (see below). In violent disorder and affray a *threat* of unlawful violence is enough to make a person guilty of the crime.

Presence – the Victimless Crime

In all three cases, riot, violent disorder and affray 'no person of reasonable firmness need actually be, or be likely to be present at the scene'. This suggests that riot and violent disorder might be committed as 'victimless crimes' in that it is possible for them to be committed without anybody (or even any property except in the case of riot) being affected. Even affray could conceivably be 'victimless' if the 'another' is not present and would not otherwise know about the threat (see Table 4.1, pp. 100–3).[4]

This particular provision that 'no person of reasonable firmness need actually be, or be likely to be present at the scene' seems to have been included to avoid the problems found in a number of cases dealing with the previous common law. In *Kamara* v. *DPP*[5] it was stated 'that the essential requisite in both (affray and unlawful assembly) is the presence or likely presence of innocent third parties, members of the public not participating in the illegal activities in question'. In *Munday* v. *Metropolitan Police District*[6] a case involving a finding of riot under the Riot (Damages) Act 1886, Mr. Justice Pritchard felt it necessary to find that 'force or violence' had been 'displayed in such a manner as to alarm at least one person of reasonable firmness and courage'.[7] In that case a house neighbouring Chelsea Football Ground was being invaded by crowds who had been unable to get into a match against the Moscow Dynamos. The gardener who was present at the house at the time was not prepared to say that he was alarmed,

> Mr. Green's evidence proved every one of the elements about which I have to be satisfied, except, possibly, the putting in fear of a person of reasonable firmness and courage. Mr. Green says he was not afraid, but I am rather disposed to think he was possessed of firmness and courage in a degree which other witnesses did not possess, and I find here that

---

[4] I am indebted to Debi Gould for pointing out this factor.
[5] *Kamara* v. *DPP* [1973] 2 All ER 1242.
[6] *Munday* v. *Metropolitan Police District* [1949] 1 All ER 337.
[7] Thus, following the case of *Field* v. *Metropolitan Police Receiver* [1907] 2 KB 853.

other people were afraid. I am quite satisfied from the evidence of the plaintiff's daughter, Miss Munday, that she was afraid.

In the case of *R.* v. *Taylor (Vincent)*[8] a fight between the appellant and some police officers in a club left only one person charged with affray even though the only persons in court were police officers attempting to question the appellant. The holding was that the ingredients of affray included 'the spectacle of fighting to the peril of persons who were or might be present'.[9] Similarly, in the Garden House trial (*Caird and others*)[10] Sachs said that

> the moment when persons in a crowd, however peaceful their original intention, commence to act with some shared common purpose supporting each other and in such a way that reasonable citizens fear a breach of the peace, the assembly becomes unlawful.

It was probably necessary, therefore, in all three of the common law offences to prove either the causing of fear or the possibility or likelihood of causing fear to people present. It is now not necessary for the prosecutor to prove that anybody that might have been affected was present, or even 'be likely to be' present at the time. Although one can see how this might make the prosecutor's job easier in proving the elements of each of these crimes, the absence of this barrier seems almost to have created the effect of a crime in a vacuum without any necessity for outsiders to be involved or affected. This once again leaves the police with wide discretion to decide how to deal with activity which they may have witnessed, but which need not have been seen by and need not involve any member of the public.

Place – the 'Privatization' of Public Order Offences

Each of the offences may be committed in private as well as in public places.

This position is a confirmation of a trend in public order cases which has enabled offences originally intended to be used only against bad behaviour in public to be charged in relation to behaviour in private places as well. The arguments in *Button* v. *DPP* and *Swain* v. *DPP*[11] and in *Kamara* v. *DPP*[12] were that both affray and unlawful assembly

---

[8] *R.* v. *Taylor (Vincent)* [1972] 3 WLR 961.
[9] In *Attorney-General's Ref. (No. 3 of 1983)* [1985] 1 QB 242 it was held that it was not necessary for there to be, or even be likely to be, a bystander if the affray took place in public.
[10] *Caird* (1970) 54 Crim. App. Rep. 499.
[11] *Swain* v. *DPP* [1965] 3 All ER 587.
[12] *Kamara* v. *DPP* [1973] 2 All ER 1242.

were intended to 'uphold public order and to protect the public generally'.[13] The public peace could be 'endangered by a rowdy, disorderly meeting just as much if it is held inside a building as outside'. As a result, offences which had previously only been available for public behaviour could now be used even regarding a self-contained inside meeting or events inside the embassy or high commission of a foreign power. As clarified in the Act, the situation probably does not represent a change from the immediately preceding law.

That it became necessary for the courts to widen the sphere of public order offences in this manner seems to be evidence of the increasing formality of demonstration and protest in modern times, as well as the range of forms of behaviour with which public order offences are intended to deal. Many more protest meetings are held now in meeting halls or other semi-private places, and the streets are less used than they might have been. This suggests more planning for protests and a more formal approach to the way they are managed, as opposed to the sort of views that were expressed by John Berger in chapter 1.[14] The use of public order offences such as affray in relation to late night brawls at public houses and dance halls, as well as in relation to activity on demonstrations, shows how wide is the ambit of behaviour such offences are intended to cover. It also shows how free of background morality or political intention the commission of such offences need be, where such disparate forms of activity as angry protest and public house brawl may both fall foul of the same offence.

Intent

A person will be guilty of riot only 'if he intends *to use* violence or is aware that his conduct may be violent'.[15] A person will only be guilty of violent disorder or affray 'if he intends *to use or threaten* violence or is aware that his conduct may be violent *or threaten* violence' (my emphasis).

With respect to Riot and Violent Disorder such intent 'does not affect the determination of the number of persons who use or threaten violence' and it therefore seems that the intention or *mens rea*, as apart from the *actus reus*, will not be important for computing the numbers for section 1 and 2 offences.

It is not clear what purpose this will serve other than to assist prosecutors by limiting the number of items they need to prove. Riot

[13] *Kamara* v. *DPP* [1972] 3 All ER 1007 CA (affirmed in HOL at [1973] 2 All ER 1248).
[14] See p. 15 above.
[15] For a discussion of 'awareness' and 'recklessness' see Smith, *Offences Against Public Order*, pp. 68–71.

also needs 'a common purpose' and only those 'using unlawful violence for the common purpose' are guilty of riot, although the common purpose may be inferred from conduct.[16]

Consent

A prosecution for the offence of Riot also needs the consent of the Director of Public Prosecutions.

Defences

No specific possible defences are set out for these offences, but one is specifically disallowed by section 6 (5). Non-medically prescribed self-induced intoxication will not be a defence to any of these crimes.[17]

Ingredients of the Less Serious Offences: Fear or Provocation of Violence and Harassment, Alarm or Distress

The lesser offences in sections 4 and 5 (which seem to be intended to replace section 5 of the Public Order Act 1936) are somewhat different in character. They are linked in to the more serious offences of sections 2 and 3 by the section 7 (3) statement that:

> If on the trial on indictment of a person charged with Violent Disorder or Affray the jury find him not guilty of the offence charged, they may . . . find him guilty of an offence under section 4.

Behaviour

The section 4 offence of 'Fear or Provocation of Violence' uses the familiar formula of 'threatening, abusive or insulting words or behaviour' and the distribution or display of 'any writing, sign or other visible representation which is threatening, abusive or insulting'. However, such words or behaviour or distribution or display must be 'towards another person' for this offence to be committed.

Where 'threatening, abusive or insulting words or behaviour, *or disorderly behaviour*', or a display (but not distribution) of 'any writing, sign or any other visible representation which is threatening, abusive or

---

[16] For a discussion of 'common purpose' see Smith, *Offences Against Public Order*, pp. 81–3.
[17] For the general position regarding intoxication as a defence see A. Dashwood, 'Logic and the Lords in Majewski', [1977] Crim. LR 532 and D. Farrier, *Drugs and Intoxication* (London, Sweet & Maxwell, 1980).

insulting', occurs 'within the hearing or sight of a person likely to be caused harassment, alarm or distress thereby' then a section 5 offence is committed. Whereas section 4 is designed to prevent violence, section 5 aims at preventing a lower order of fear: harassment, alarm or distress.[18]

It seems certain that definitions given in cases under section 5 of the Public Order Act 1936 to words such as 'threatening', 'abusive', and 'insulting' will be carried over to the new Act. These words in particular are to be given their ordinary meaning as Lord Reid declared in *Brutus* v. *Cozens*,[19] 'An ordinary sensible man knows an insult when he sees or hears it'.

As Supperstone points out,[20] the gestalt or ordinary meaning approach is not very helpful in deciding whether any particular words or behaviour are in fact threatening, abusive or insulting. Lord Chief Justice Parker stated in *Jordan* v. *Burgoyne* that all of these words should be regarded as 'very strong words'. This view was upheld in *Brutus* v. *Cozens*[21] where the appellant had interrupted play during the course of a tennis match at Wimbledon and was charged with insulting behaviour. Viscount Dilhorne pointed out that the behaviour was probably 'annoying' but more was needed for the behaviour to become 'insulting'. Since the magistrates had found as a question of fact that the appellant's behaviour was not insulting, this was not a matter which could be reversed by a decision of a higher court.[22]

Supperstone[23] notes a number of cases of demonstration and protest where 'considerable variation in prosecution policy' may be observed. He suggests that 'some police officers, prosecutors and magistrates appear to take the view that political assertions or slogans chanted in a public place are ipso facto insulting'.[24] He uses as examples actions such as holding a match under a large American flag outside the United States Embassy, or handing out leaflets opposing the war in Vietnam

---

[18] According to the White Paper Cmnd 9510 (1985) para 3.22, s. 5 was intended to deal with hooliganism on housing estates, and rowdy and loutish behaviour at bus and cinema queues or late at night in the streets. A test case at Horseferry Road Magistrates Court in December 1987 showed, however, that displays would not too easily breach the section. Three artists were prosecuted under s. 5 for displaying a poster depicting the Prime Minister in fishnet stockings, suspenders and wielding a whip just before the general election. Two police witnesses admitted the poster was 'amusing' and the stipendiary magistrate ruled there was no case to answer.

[19] *Brutus* v. *Cozens* [1973] AC 854.

[20] Supperstone, *Brownlie*, p. 6.

[21] *Brutus* v. *Cozens* [1973] AC 854.

[22] See Glanville Williams, *Criminal Law: The General Part*, 2nd edn (London, Sweet & Maxwell, 1961), for the distinction between fact and law.

[23] Supperstone, *Brownlie*, p. 10.

[24] Ibid.

and inviting American soldiers to desert outside a club for United States servicemen.

Intent

The old formula from section 5 of the 1936 Public Order Act that the words or behaviour or distribution or display should be made 'with intent to provoke a breach of the peace or whereby a breach of the peace is likely to be occasioned' does not exist in the new section 4. Instead, similar *mens rea* sub-sections apply as with sections 1 to 4 above. Two possible intents are available:

> with intent to cause that person to believe that immediate unlawful violence will be used against him or another by any person[25]
> or to provoke the immediate use of unlawful violence by that person or another.[26]

If those two intents are not provable then it is also possible to commit the offence where the use of words, behaviour, distribution or display to another person is made

> whereby that person is likely to believe that such violence will be used or it is likely that such violence will be provoked.

In terms of general intent a person will only be guilty of a section 4 or 5 offence if 'he intends his words or behaviour or the writing, sign or other visible representation, to be threatening, abusive or insulting, or is aware that it may be threatening, abusive or insulting'.[27] In relation to section 5 he may alternatively 'intend his behaviour to be or is aware that it may be disorderly'.[28] This is a slightly different general intent than the one related to section 4 of the Public Order Act 1936[29] where it needed to be proved:

(a) that the person using the particular words or behaving in a particular manner intended to use the words or behave in that manner; and

(b) in addition, that it was intended that the words or behaviour should

---

[25] This is an extraordinarily obtuse expression of a mixed objective/subjective test. Smith, *Offences Against Public Order*, discusses it at length at pp. 106–9, but we will have to wait for some early cases to discover with any clarity how it will be used.

[26] Section 4 (1). Smith, *Offences Against Public Order*, p. 95, suggests that there are really two entirely different types of behaviour covered here and they should therefore be treated as two different offences. Section 7 (2) prevents this.

[27] Section 6 (3) and (4).

[28] Section 6 (4).

[29] See Supperstone, *Brownlie*, p. 11.

be threatening, abusive or insulting to the audience or that he was reckless as a reasonable person as to whether they were so.[30]

The *mens rea* of section 5 of the 1986 Act does not include recklessness, but needs either intention or awareness that the words or behaviour might have the effect necessary, for the commission of the offence. This results in a rather different mental element than 'the same objective test that currently exists in relation to section 5' of the 1936 Act which the Government White Paper[31] had promised.

As was mentioned in chapter 3, in the case of *Jordan* v. *Burgoyne*[32], Lord Chief Justice Parker suggested two tests for intention under section 5 of the 1936 Public Order Act. One of these tests appeared to be objective, when he used the words,

> I cannot myself, having read the speech, imagine any reasonable citizen, certainly if he was a Jew, not being provoked beyond endurance, and not only a Jew but a coloured man, and quite a number of people of this country who were told that they were merely tools of the Jews, and that they had fought in the War on the wrong side, and matters of that sort.

The second test, if it is in fact any different from the first, appears to be more subjective, when he uses the following formula,

> If in fact it is apparent that a body of persons are present – and let me assume in the defendant's favour that they are a body of hooligans – yet if words are used which threaten, abuse or insult – all very strong words – then that person must take his audience as he finds them, and if those words to that audience or that part of the audience are likely to provoke a breach of the peace, then the speaker is guilty of an offence.

It is not clear whether the new 'intention' set out in section 6 (3) and (4) is meant to convey an objective or a subjective test. It is also not clear whether having now moved away from the 'with intent to provoke a breach or the peace or whereby a breach of the peace is likely to be occasioned' parts of the old section 5, cases such as *Jordan* v. *Burgoyne* are still important.

In relation to the new section 5 offence, the need for the offence to occur 'within the hearing or sight of a person likely to be caused harassment, alarm or distress thereby' seems to turn this offence into more of a subjective context, and the defence set out in (c)[33] seems to create a subjective element at least in relation to the new section 5

---

[30] Ibid., p. 16.
[31] 'Review of Public Order Law' Cmnd. 9510 (1985), para 3.11.
[32] *Jordan* v. *Burgoyne* [1963] 2 QB 744.
[33] Section 5 (3) (c), pp. 100–3 and see 'Defences' section below.

offence. The specificity in the new section 4 offence of 'another person' and intent 'to cause *that person* to believe' or to provoke the use of unlawful violence 'by *that person*' or 'whereby *that person* is likely to believe' may also connote a subjective test in relation to a particular audience. It may, however, need a few cases to go up on appeal before a definite sense can be obtained of how these sections will be understood.

In particular, the problem of the police officer[34] and the good-natured, law-abiding bystander (both of whom were unlikely to breach the peace under the old law, however insulting, etc. the words or behaviour of a defendant) does not necessarily seem to be affected by the new law. The Law Commission had specifically recommended a change.[35] It is submitted that no change is necessary regarding police officers, who may in any event provoke some of the reactions they witness, by officiousness or unnecessary involvement.[36] The 'likely' elements of section 4 (1) and 5 (1) should allow a sensible use of objectivity in relation to bystanders appropriate to the behaviour involved.

Place

Once again the new policy of 'privatization' of public order offences leaves sections 4 and 5 of the 1986 Act capable of being committed either in a public or a private place unlike the 1936 Act section 5 which could be committed only 'in any public place or at any public meeting'. Incidents during the miners' dispute in which pickets were on private property, and protesters present at military bases or on private farm land encouraged the Government White Paper to suggest opening up the venue for such offences.[37]

No offence can however be committed under the new sections 4 and 5 where the offending behaviour is carried out 'by a person inside a dwelling and the other person (*to whom the action is addressed*) is also inside that or another dwelling'. This appears to be aimed at the *Wilson* v. *Skeock*[38] type of case in which two neighbours quarrelled with each other and it was said by Mr. Justice Cassels: 'I do not think that the Act of 1936 provides a proper procedure to apply to the well known custom of the passing of unpleasantries from one neighbour to another on their own premises'.[39]

[34] Smith, *Offences Against Public Order*, p. 96, 'the policeman defect'.
[35] 'Offences relating to Public Order' Law Com. No. 123 [1983] paras 5.15–16.
[36] See, e.g., *Marsh* v. *Arscott* (1982) 75 Crim. App. Rep. 211, and *G* v. *Chief Constable for Stroud* [1987] Crim. LR 269; *R.* v. *Howell* [1982] QB 416 and *Albert* v. *Lavin* [1982] AC 546. But see *DPP* v. *Orum* [1988] *Times LR*, 25th July and *Nawrot and Shaler* v. *DDP* [1988] Crim. LR. 107.
[37] Cmnd. 9510 [1985] para. 3.8.
[38] *Wilson* v. *Skeock* (1949) 113 JP 294.
[39] Ibid., p. 296. In fact, in the *Wilson* case one neighbour was standing in the 'back yard' and one was inside a flat, and it is therefore interesting that they would therefore not seem

Defences

Under the new section 5, 'harassment, alarm or distress' offence there
are three possible defences available in the alternative:

(a) that he had no reason to believe that there was any person within
hearing or sight who was likely to be caused Harassment, Alarm or
Distress, or
(b) that he was inside a dwelling and had no reason to believe that the
words or behaviour used, or the writing, sign or other visible
representation displayed, would be heard or seen by a person outside
that or any other dwelling, or
(c) that his conduct was reasonable.

It will be interesting to see how the (c) defence will be used in
practice. Although it appears quite open and vague and seems to throw
entire reliance onto the court to construe, there may be very few
occasions on which it can usefully be employed.

As with the section 1, 2 and 3 offences, intoxication which is self-
induced and not as a result of medical prescription will not be allowed
as a defence to a charge under these sections.

Powers of Arrest

As both riot and violent disorder are punishable by a maximum term
of imprisonment of 5 years or more, they both constitute 'arrestable
offences' under section 24 (1) of the Police and Criminal Evidence Act
1984. The new offences of affray (s. 3 (6)), fear or provocation of
violence (s. 4 (3)) and harassment, alarm or distress (s. 5 (4)) are all
specifically made into arrestable offences by statutory designation. A
constable may therefore 'arrest without warrant anyone he reasonably
suspects is committing' an offence under section 3 or section 4.

Where the section 5 offence is concerned,

(4) A constable may arrest a person without warrant if –
(a) he engages in 'offensive conduct' which the constable warns him
to stop, and
(b) he engages in further offensive conduct immediately or shortly
after the warning.
(5) In subsection (4) 'offensive conduct' means the conduct the constable
reasonably suspects to constitute an offence under this section, and

---

to have come under the exception provided by s. 4 (2) and s. 5 (2) of the new Act since one
of them was not actually 'inside' a dwelling.

the conduct mentioned in paragraph (a) and the further conduct need not be of the same nature.

A constable could arrest without warrant any person reasonably suspected by him of committing an offence under section 5 of the Public Order Act 1936.[40] However, in relation to section 5 of the 1986 Act it appears to be necessary for a constable to warn a suspected offender to stop the 'offensive conduct' and for that offender to engage in 'further offensive conduct immediately or shortly after the warning' before a constable may arrest without warrant. This seems to presuppose a situation where a constable is close to the offender such as at a demonstration where the constable is already present in order to police the demonstration. Alternatively, the constable may be brought in to warn the offender as a result of a complaint by someone else who has been caused 'harassment, alarm or distress'. This section tends to leave a great deal of subjectivity and discretion to a complainant and an attending officer. Behaviour which may cause 'harassment, alarm or distress' near, e.g. a home for the aged, may be quite different from what may do so at a pop concert, and both of these may be quite different from what may cause reactions in a political meeting, demonstration or protest. This once again calls into question the tension in the law between being first in the field and taking one's audience as one finds it.[41] We will return to this issue and the problem of the 'hecklers veto' in a later chapter.

The philosophy of the 1986 Act is obscure in providing the necessity for a warning by a police officer before arrest without warrant for the most minor offence; while allowing a police officer to arrest without warrant and without warning for offences which carry much heavier penalties. It should also be noted that a constable need not be in uniform or even on duty when effecting such arrest. This may cause the problems seen already in such cases as *Albert* v. *Lavin*[42] and *Kenlin* v. *Gardiner*[43] where a police officer laying hold of another may be reacted to as if the officer were any other lout.[44]

---

[40] Public Order Act 1936 s. 7 as amended under the Public Order Act 1963 s. 1 (2), Race Relations Act 1976 s. 70 and the Criminal Law Act 1977 s. 28, Schedule 6.
[41] See ch. 3.
[42] *Albert* v. *Lavin* [1982] AC 546.
[43] *Kenlin* v. *Gardiner* [1967] 2 QB 510.
[44] See, e.g., Smith, *Offences Against Public Order*, p. 125.

The Tables and the Old Law

Having provided an overview of sections 1 to 5 of the Public Order Act 1986 it is necessary to provide a short comparison with the position under the previous legislation and common law which have been repealed by the new Act. Table 4.1 is provided to allow the comparison to be made more easily. The specific headings in Table 4.1 (which are of the author's construction and not in the Act) are intended to highlight the relevant differences between the new and old law. Such comparisons are important for an understanding of the current state of the law because it is not at present clear how much of the old public order law will still be relevant for cases under the new legislation, as a result of similar expressions used or forms of words used or not used in the new Act. This means that some of the old cases may still be relevant, either in order to understand the meaning of similar words used in the new Act or to understand the situations excluded from the new Act intended to overrule the effects of previous cases.

Setting out all of the 'Fear' sections in this way is intended to portray the graduated nature of the new offences as well as to pose the questions whether such a detailed set of steps was actually necessary, and whether such individualized steps will raise more difficulties for the development and proof of a prosecution case than is necessary for the control of the behaviour intended.

Steps or Trip Wires – The Workings of Sections 1–5 of the 1986 Act

The 1986 Act has attempted to provide a clear system of gradation of the seriousness of public order offences. The Law Commission had suggested the need to clarify the common law vagueness of the legal situation[45] and the Government must have wanted to show the public that it was trying to deal with disorder. It is not certain, however, whether the new range of offences will actually make the law clearer and life simpler for the prosecution and the courts. It is conceivable that the new steps in seriousness of offence may prove a tricky flight to tackle.

As noted above, a link is made between section 4 and section 2 and 3 offences by section 7 (3) of the Act. This allows a jury on the trial of a person charged with violent disorder or affray who find the defendant

---

[45] Law Commission Working Paper No. 82, 'Offences Against Public Order' (1982) and Law Commission Report, 'Offences Relating to Public Order' (1983) Law Com. No. 123.

not guilty of the offence charged, to find him guilty of an offence under section 4'. This would seem to assist the prosecution case where they have not been able to prove the major offence, but may have been able to prove the section 4 offence. However, it may not be of great assistance to a judge in needing on a trial on indictment for section 2 and 3 offences, also to have to go through the ingredients of the section 4 offence with the jury, in case they decide to find the defendant guilty of section 4 behaviour instead. The other possibility is that on any finding by a jury of 'not guilty' to a charge under section 2 or 3, the judge may then have to go through the evidence again this time in relation to a charge under section 4. Although it seems like a good fail-safe mechanism, it may in the event turn out to be somewhat difficult to negotiate.

The range of penalties available and the degree of seriousness of each offence has certainly been clarified. However, under the common law system which previously dealt with the offences of riot, unlawful assembly and affray the penalties were 'at large' which meant that it was up to the individual court to set whatever penalty it thought was necessary for the particular activity in question. The current position moves the discretion in relation to penalty away from the court and into the hands of the prosecutor deciding which offence to charge.

The ingredients of the most serious offence, riot, are now very much narrower than riot had been at common law. Even at common law only 26 people were found guilty of riot in 1985 and this was not therefore a widely used offence.[46] Twelve persons are needed as opposed to the original three, the consent of the Director of Public Prosecutions is necessary for a charge, and only those shown to have actually used unlawful violence for the common purpose will be guilty of riot. Under the common law position as shown in *Caird*[47] it does not appear to have been necessary to have actually been involved in using force or violence to have been found guilty of riot,

> it is the law – and, indeed, in common sense it should be the case – that any person who actively encourages or promotes an unlawful assembly or riot, whether by words, by signs, or by actions, or who participates in it, is guilty of an offence which derives its great gravity from the simple fact that the persons concerned were acting in numbers and using those numbers to achieve their purpose.[48]

The older offence of riot was therefore wider and more vague.[49]

[46] Home Office figures.
[47] *Caird* (1970) 54 Crim. App. Rep. 499.
[48] Ibid., 505.
[49] Although incitement to s. 1 offence of riot specifically needs the consent of the DPP (see s. 7(1)) conspiracy to riot seems not to, which might allow some vagueness to creep back into the law.

Table 4.1

	Riot P.O.A. 1986 s.1.	Riot at Common Law now repealed	Violent Disorder P.O.A. 1986 s. 2	Unlawful Assembly at Common Law now repealed
Number	Where 12 or more persons who are present together	Three or more persons	Where three or more persons who are present together	Three or more persons gathered together
Act	Use or threaten unlawful violence for a common purpose	using force or violence with a common purpose	Use or threaten unlawful violence	with a common purpose *Either* to commit a crime of violence *or* to achieve some other object lawful or unlawful
Fear Level	and the conduct of them (taken together) is such as would cause a person of reasonable firmness present at the scene to fear for his personal safety	execution or inception of the common purpose not merely in and about the common purpose, but displayed in such a manner as to alarm at least one person of reasonable firmness and courage	and the conduct of them (taken together) is such as would cause a person of reasonable firmness present at the scene to fear for his personal safety	in a manner which is calculated to give firm and courageous persons in the neighbourhood reason to fear a breach of the peace
	each of the persons using unlawful violence		each of the persons using or threatening unlawful violence	
	for the common purpose is guilty of riot		is guilty of violent disorder	
	It is immaterial whether or not the 12 or more use or threaten unlawful violence simultaneously		It is immaterial whether or not the three or more use or threaten unlawful violence simultaneously	
Arresta-bility		The common purpose may be inferred from conduct		
Presence	No person of reasonable firmness need actually be, or be likely to be, present at the scene		No person of reasonable firmness need actually be, or be likely to be, present at the scene	
Place	Riot may be committed in private as well as in public places	In a public or private place	Violent disorder may be committed in private as well as in public places	In a public or private place

Affray P.O.A. 1986 s.3.	Fear of Provocation of Violence P.O.A. 1986 s.4	Harassment, Alarm or Distress P.O.A. 1986 s.5	Old s.5 P.O.A. 1936
(1) A person is guilty of affray if he	(1) A person is guilty of an offence if he	(1) A person is guilty of an offence if he	Any person who
uses or threatens unlawful violence towards another	(a) Uses *towards another person* threatening, abusive or insulting words or behaviour, or (b) *distributes* or displays to another person any writing, sign or other visible representation which is threatening, abusive or insulting	(a) uses threatening, abusive or insulting words or behaviour, or *disorderly behaviour.* or (b) displays any writing, sign or other visible representation which is threatening, abusive or insulting	Uses threatening, abusive or insulting words or behaviour, or distributes or displays any writing, sign or visible representation which is threatening, abusive or insulting
and his conduct is such as would cause a person of reasonable firmness present at the scene to fear for his personal safety		within the hearing or sight of a person likely to be caused harassment, alarm or distress thereby	with intent to provoke a breach of the peace or whereby a breach of the peace is likely to be occasioned
(2) Where two or more persons use or threaten the unlawful violence, it is the conduct of them taken together that must be considered for purposes of subsection (1) (3) For the purposes of this section a threat cannot be made by the use of words alone	with intent to cause *that person* to believe that *immediate* unlawful violence will be used against him or another by any person or to *provoke* the *immediate* use of unlawful violence *by that* person or another or whereby *that person* is likely to believe that such violence will be used or it is likely that such violence will be provoked		shall be guilty of an offence
(6) A constable may arrest without warrant anyone he reasonably suspects is committing affray	(3) A constable may arrest without warrant anyone he reasonably suspects is committing an offence under this section	(4) A constable may arrest a person without warrant if (a) he engages in 'offensive conduct' which the constable warns him to stop, *and* (b) he engages in further offensive conduct immediately or shortly after the warning (5) In sub-section (4) 'offensive conduct' means conduct the constable reasonably suspects to constitute an offence under this section, and the conduct mentioned in para (a) and the further conduct need not be of the same nature	
(4) No person of reasonable firmness need actually be, or be likely to be, present at the scene			
(5) Affray may be committed in private as well as public places	(2) An offence under this section may be committed in a public *or a private place*, except that no offence is committed where the words or behaviour are used, or the writing, sign or other visible representation is *distributed or* displayed, by a person inside a dwelling and the other person is also inside that or another dwelling	(2) An offence under this section may be committed in a public *or a private place*, except that no offence is committed where the words or behaviour are used or the writing, sign or other visible representation is displayed, by a person inside a dwelling and the other person is also inside that or another dwelling	in any *public place* or at any *public meeting*

Table 4.1 *continued*.

	Riot P.O.A. 1986 s.1.	Riot at Common Law now repealed	Violent Disorder P.O.A. 1986 s.2	Unlawful Assembly at Common Law now repealed
Penalty	A person guilty of riot is liable on conviction to imprisonment for a term not exceeding 10 years or a fine or both	Penalty at large	A person guilty of violent disorder is liable on conviction on *indictment* to imprisonment for a term not exceeding 5 years or a fine or both, or on *summary* conviction to imprisonment for a term not exceeding 6 months or a fine not exceeding the statutory maximum or both	Penalty at large
Intent	A person is guilty of riot only if he intends to use violence or is aware that his conduct may be violent (6 (1)) – this does not affect the determination of the number of persons who use or threaten violence (6(7))	Intent on the part of the persons in question to help one another, by force if necessary, against any person who may oppose them in the execution of that common purpose	A person is guilty of violent disorder only if he intends to use or threaten violence or is aware that his conduct may be violent or threaten violence (6(2)) – this does not affect the determination of the number of persons who use or threaten violence (6(7))	
Defence	By or with consent of DPP Non-medical self-induced intoxication, no defence		Non-medical, self-induced intoxication, no defence	

Affray P.O.A. 1986 s.3.	Fear or Provocation of Violence P.O.A. 1986 S.4	Harassment, Alarm or Distress P.O.A. 1986 s.5	Old s.5 P.O.A. 1936
(7) A person guilty of affray is liable on conviction on *indictment* to imprisonment for a term not exceeding 3 years or a fine or both, or on *summary* conviction to imprisonment for a term not exceeding the statutory maximum or both A person is guilty of affray only if he intends to use or threaten violence or is aware that his conduct maybe violent or threaten violence (6(2))	(4) A person guilty of an offence under this section is liable on *summary conviction* to imprisonment for a term not exceeding *6 months* or a fine not exceeding *level 5* on the standard scale or both A person is guilty of an offence under section 4 only if he *intends* his words or behaviour, or the writing, sign or other visible representation, to be threatening, abusive or insulting, or is *aware* that it may be threatening, abusive or insulting (s. 6 (3))	(6) A person guilty of an offence under this section is liable on *summary convicion* to a fine not exceeding *level 3* on the standard scale A person is guilty of an offence under section 5 only if he *intends* his words or behaviour, or the writing, sign or other visible representation, to be threatening, abusive, or insulting, or is *aware* that it may be threatening, abusive or insulting or (as the case may be) he intends his behaviour to be or is aware that it may be *disorderly* (s. 6 (4))	and shall on *summary conviction* be liable to imprisonment for a term not exceeding 6 months or to a fine not exceeding *£1000* or both
Non-medical self-induced intoxication, no defence	Non-medical self-induced intoxication, no defence N.B. If on the trial on indictment of a person charged with violent disorder or affray the jury find him not guilty of the offence charged, they may (without prejudice to section 6 (3) of the Criminal Law Act 1967) find him guilty of an offence under section 4 (s. 7 (3)) The Crown Court has the same powers and duties in relation to a person who is by virtue of (s. 7 (3)) convicted before it of an offence under section 4 as a magistrates court would have on convicting him of the offence (s. 7 (4))	(3) Non-medical self-induced intoxication, no defence It is a defence for the accused to prove (a) that he had no reason to believe that there was any person within hearing or sight who was likely to be caused harassment, alarm or distress, or (b) that he was inside a dwelling and had no reason to believe that the words or behaviour used, or the writing, sign or other visible representation displayed, would be heard or seen by a person outside that or any other dwelling, or (c) that his conduct was reasonable	

Notes: (i) Only the wording of the new legislation is included in the tables, therefore the text must also be considered in order to ascertain the complete picture.

   (ii) For reasons of space the old common law affray has not been included, but the new s. 3 is compared with the other sections, and the old law appears in the text (p. 104).

   (iii) Emphasis is the author's and is used to highlight comparisons which might not otherwise appear from the table.

The new offence of violent disorder is also a little narrower than the old offence of unlawful assembly since it needs the use or threat of unlawful violence, whereas the offence of unlawful assembly at common law did not necessarily need a crime of violence provided there was a common purpose and the activities were carried on 'in a manner which is calculated to give firm and courageous persons in the neighbourhood reason to fear a breach of the peace'. This was a more commonly used offence with 333 guilty verdicts in 1985.[50] It is not necessary to show a common purpose with the new law.

Affray at common law needed

(1) unlawful fighting by one or more persons or a display of force by one or more persons without actual violence;
(2) in such a manner that a person of reasonably firm character might be expected to be terrified.[51]

Lord Reid had stressed the vague nature of the offence with the words 'I would not seek a rigid definition of a common law offence . . . if a new point arises the question should always be whether it is within the mischief aimed at and within the principles established by the authorities'.[52] The offence might even have been committed where 'a man arms himself with dangerous and unusual weapons in such a way as will naturally cause terror to the people'.[53] The element of causing 'terror' seems to have been watered down in the new offence to causing 'fear for . . . personal safety'. Lord Hailsham had said in *Taylor* v. *DPP*[54] 'it is essential to stress that the degree of violence required to constitute the offence of affray must be such as to be calculated to terrify a person of reasonably firm character. This should not be watered down.' However, it may well be that the ingredient of terror had, in fact, become weakened before the new law was enacted.[55] Some 955 people were found guilty of affray in 1985.[56]

The concept of a breach of the peace, which will be looked at more closely in a succeeding chapter, had been important in relation to the common law crime of unlawful assembly and in relation to the statutory offence of section 5 of the Public Order Act 1936. The vagueness of the breach of the peace concept had appeared to be useful to the courts.

---

[50] Home Office figures.
[51] See Supperstone, *Brownlie*, p. 141.
[52] *Taylor* v. *DPP* [1973] 2 All ER 1108.
[53] See Supperstone, *Brownlie*, p. 142, and *R.* v. *Sharpe, R.* v. *Johnson* [1957] 1 QB at 559.
[54] *Taylor* v. *DPP* [1973] 2 All ER 1112.
[55] See Supperstone, *Brownlie*, p. 143.
[56] Home Office figures.

The new concepts are fear for personal safety, fear of violence or violence itself, or the likely cause of harassment, alarm or distress. It will be interesting to see the different effect of these tests as opposed to the old breach of the peace test.

Stirring Up Racial Hatred

The 1986 Act has brought into line with the new section 4 and 5 offences an offence of stirring up racial hatred which replaces section 5A of the Public Order Act 1937.[57] Since many of its aspects and procedures for dealing with its commission are similar to sections 4 and 5, it is convenient to include it at this point. The Act also includes a range of new racial hatred offences dealing with publishing or distributing written material; public performance of a play; distribution, showing or playing a recording; broadcasting and possession of racially inflammatory material. These are not enumerated here since they do not form part of the main subject area of this work. The different rationale behind offences of this nature should also be noted.[58]

'Racial hatred' is described in section 17 as 'hatred against a group of persons in Great Britain defined by reference to colour, race, nationality (including citizenship) or ethnic or national origins'. This is similar to the previous formulation.

Section 18 (i) legislates that:

A person who uses threatening, abusive or insulting words or behaviour, or displays any written material which is threatening, abusive or insulting, is guilty of an offence if
(a) he intends thereby to stir up racial hatred, or
(b) having regard to all the circumstances racial hatred is likely to be stirred up thereby.

This is a rather more serious offence than that under section 4 with a maximum penalty of 2 years imprisonment, although many of its features are the same. 'Behaviour' is added for the first time to this offence which previously only included 'words'. All the new racial hatred offences, including this one, require the Attorney-General's consent for prosecution, and it is therefore unlikely that minor infractions will be visited with prosecution of this offence. It will, however, now include, in common with sections 1–5 of the Act, actions in private as well as

[57] Introduced by s. 70 of the Race Relations Act 1976.
[58] See L. Lustgarten, *Legal Control of Racial Discrimination* (Macmillan, London, 1980).

in public (s. 18 (2)) subject to the similar exemption of being inside a private dwelling as was enacted in relation to sections 4 and 5 above,[59] together with the specific defence in relation to being inside a dwelling similar to the one in section 5 (3) (b) above.[60]

It is not clear why the legislation needs to strive at this amount of similarity, considering the very different nature of the mischief aimed at by sections 4 and 5 on the one hand, and section 18 on the other. The particular elements of the dwelling exemption and defence seem to be totally inapplicable to section 18. Either those exemptions cover domestic disputes within a family, in which case stirring up racial hatred is unlikely; or the exemption and defence covers neighbour disputes in which stirring up racial hatred in (say) public housing estates might actually be a real problem.

In common with the section 4 offence, 'a constable may arrest without warrant anyone he reasonably suspects is committing an offence under this section (s. 18 (3)), which seems to suggest that such an arrest cannot take place if the constable is called well after the offence has been committed and it is unlikely to be repeated immediately.

Unlike the previous section 5A which used only the section 18 (1) (b) formulation,[61] the new section 18 (1) (a) adds a specific *mens rea* possibility to the offence. Where intention is evident the prosecutor may try to prove the offence with section 18 (1) (a), and where this is difficult the objective formulation in section 18 (1) (b) will be used. However, in the latter case sub-section 5 allows such a person the defence of proving that 'he did not intend his words or behaviour, or the written material, to be, and was not aware that it might be, threatening, abusive or insulting'. Therefore, the objective test of section 18 (1) (b) is substantially watered down by the possible defence of section 18 (5). If there is no proof of intent to stir up racial hatred and no proof of intent or awareness of being threatening, abusive or insulting, even if racial hatred is likely to be stirred up, no offence has been committed.

Since proof of intention had been a major problem under section 6 of the 1965 Race Relations Act, it is surprising that the movement away from an objective test has been so strong in section 18. The considerable difficulties that have existed in relation to previous legislation covering this area are unlikely to be helped by such massive swings of the pendulum from objectivity on one side to specific intent on the other.

From the 1986 Public Order Act offences, we turn to some older common law and legislation dealing with organized disorder.

[59] See s. 4 (2) and s. 5 (2).
[60] See p. 96 and 103.
[61] Using the words 'in a case where, having regard to all the circumstances hatred is likely to be stirred up against any racial group in Great Britain by the matter or words in question'.

Incitement to Disaffection, Sedition and Treason

Two offences of incitement to disaffection regarding members of the armed forces and members of the police force are important in relation to demonstrations and protests. Both the armed forces and the police are used, and have been used to police demonstrations. Historically, the armed forces have been involved at times of great civil commotion and the result has sometimes been the death of protesters.[62] As a result protesters have often attempted to dissuade members of the armed forces from being involved in protests. Similarly, on occasions when the armed forces have been involved in military action which itself was the subject of protest, those with views against such action have protested against British military involvement by attempting to dissuade members of the armed forces from being so involved. The Incitement to Disaffection Act 1934 states in section 1:

> If any person maliciously and advisedly endeavours to seduce any members of His Majesty's Forces from his duty or allegiance to His Majesty he shall be guilty of an offence under this Act.

Section 2 (1) enacts

> If any person with intent to commit or to aid, abet, counsel, or procure the commission of an offence under section one of this Act has in his possession or under his control any document of such a nature that the dissemination of copies thereof among members of Her Majesty's Forces would constitute such an offence, he shall be guilty of an offence under this Act.

Recent prosecutions of some of those campaigning for the withdrawal of British troops from Northern Ireland have concerned the possession and distribution of leaflets to army barracks, and towns where army barracks exist, suggesting that the soldiers not be involved in activity in Northern Ireland.[63] One particular prosecution of Pat Arrowsmith, a well known pacifist and the leader of the campaign, went to the Court of Appeal.[64] Ms Arrowsmith contended that since the Director of Public Prosecutions had informed her solicitors that he would not consent to a prosecution regarding similar literature distributed earlier in the year by Pat Arrowsmith, this had given her the impression that no offence

[62] David Williams, *Keeping the Peace: the Police and Public Order* (London, Hutchinson 1967), pp. 179–92.
[63] See *The Times*, 7 and 20 Oct. 1975.
[64] *Arrowsmith* v. *DPP* [1975] QB 678.

was committed by distributing that literature in similar circumstances. Although this argument was not accepted as a defence to a charge under the Act, it was used in order to reduce her sentence. In 1975 the *Times* reported[65] that the Director of Public Prosecutions had not consented to a prosecution under the Act against Professor Adam Curle of Bradford University Peace Studies Department and five others who had delivered leaflets at the Army Careers Office in Bradford. Later in the year fourteen defendants charged with similar offences under the Act to those in *Arrowsmith* v. *DPP* were acquitted by a jury.[66]

These offences are fairly specific in their operation, but historically the range of protest which might be seen as incitement to disaffection is quite wide. The Act has a very clear effect on preventing protest of a particular kind and in relation to a large range of international military involvement. Conceivably, the Act might also be used against campaigners for nuclear disarmament who invite members of the Armed Forces not to be involved in dealing with nuclear weapons or with American forces who are themselves dealing with nuclear weaponry.

Disaffection in the Police

According to section 53 of the Police Act 1964,

> (1) Any person who causes, or attempts to cause, or does any act calculated to cause, disaffection amongst the members of any police force or induces or attempts to induce, or does any act calculated to induce any member of the police force to withhold his services or to commit breaches of discipline, shall be guilty of an offence . . .

There do not appear to have been any recent prosecutions. Prosecutions under the previous enactment rose out of the activities of the unemployed in the 1920s involving speeches such as 'Policemen! You fought for us in France. Don't help the capitalists now'.[67] The offence seems to have been used often in relation to attempts by demonstrators to call for working class solidarity from the police.[68]

Although this offence has rarely been used its existence must have a chilling effect on certain types of protest.

---

[65] *The Times*, 23 Aug. 1975.
[66] *R.* v. *Williams*, *The Times*, 11 Dec. 1975. See also Supperstone, *Brownlie*, p. 243.
[67] See Williams, *Keeping the Peace*, p. 193.
[68] One possible modern day use for the offence might involve the activity of some black journalists calling upon black policemen and women to dissociate themselves from racism in the force; see, e.g., *Caribbean Times*. See also Stuart Bowes, *The Police and Civil Liberties* (London, Lawrence & Wishart, 1966) on its use against police unionization activity.

Sedition and Treason

For the sake of completeness these two offences, which are not considered particularly important in modern times, but are still part of the common law, are mentioned here.

Sedition had a fairly wide definition according to *Stephen's Digest*:[69]

> An intention to bring into hatred or contempt or to excite disaffection against the person of Her Majesty, her heirs and successors, or the government and constitution of the United Kingdom, as by law established, or either House or Parliament, or the administration of justice, or to excite Her Majesty's subjects to attempt, otherwise than by lawful means, the alteration of any matter in Church or State by law established, or to raise discontent or disaffection among Her Majesty's subjects or to promote feelings of ill-will and hostility between different classes of such subjects.

This wide definition seemed to include almost any comment aimed at authority. It seems to have become more narrowed by the cases of *R*. v. *Burns*,[70] *R*. v. *Aldred*[71] and *R*. v. *Caunt*.[72] These seem to suggest that 'it is not enough to provoke hostility or ill-will . . . sedition has always had implicit in the word, public order, tumult, insurrections or matters of that kind'. The prosecutions of *Leese*[73] and *Caunt*[74] were both made regarding antisemitic articles. It is possible that such publications may now constitute offences under the Public Order Act (see above).

Treason, which still carries the death penalty,[75] includes 'levying war against the King in his realm' which now may involve 'the use or display of force' by large and even small numbers of persons with an intention to reform matters concerning national policy, to alter the established law or religion, or to usurp the government in matters of a public or general nature.[76] It does not, however, seem likely that prosecutions today on this basis would be well treated by the courts, unless they would in any case be illegal for other reasons.

The most recent uses of treason relate to 'adhering to the King's enemies in his realm, giving them aid or comfort in the realm or

---

[69] *Stephens Digest*, 9th edn, art. 114.
[70] *R*. v. *Burns* (1886) 16 Cox 355.
[71] *R*. v. *Aldred* (1909) 74 JP 55.
[72] *R*. v. *Caunt* (1948) 64 Law QR 203.
[73] *The Times*, 19 and 22 Sept. 1936.
[74] *R*. v. *Caunt* (1948) 64 Law QR 203.
[75] Treason Act 1814, s. 1.
[76] See Supperstone, *Brownlie*, p. 231 and sources quoted *in extenso* there.

elsewhere' even where the treason is committed out of the realm. This was the case in the prosecutions of *Casement*[77] and *Joyce*[78] and seems to be really applicable only in time of war. However, situations such as the current problems in Northern Ireland might conceivably give rise to such prosecutions.[79]

Summary

This chapter has looked at a spectrum of offences including the new range of causing fear offences in the Public Order Act 1986 and more vague common law offences dealing with the general stirring up of discontent and disaffection among armed forces, police or among other people in society against the state. It reveals a wide armoury of possibilities for the state to use against organized opposition.

However, the major use of many of these offences will be in dealing with small outbreaks of violence or fighting which have very little to do with protest or demonstration. This wide spread of different forms of behaviour covered by the same offences, without any possibility for a court to take such differences into account[80] leaves demonstrators in the same category as more purposeless perpetrators of unrest.

---

[77] *Casement* [1917] 1 KB 98.
[78] *Joyce* v. *DPP* [1946] AC 347.
[79] Fuller statements and discussion of these offences can be found in J.C. Smith and C. Hogan, *Criminal Law*, 5th edn (Butterworth, London, 1983), pp. 796–804; C. S. Kenny, *Outlines of Criminal Law* 19th edn (Cambridge, CUP, 1966), p. 295, W. O. Russell, *Russell on Crime*, vol. 1 (Sweet & Maxwell, London, 1964), pp. 297ff and Supperstone, *Brownlie*, pp. 230–40.
[80] Except perhaps as regards sentence.

5

The Peace and its Breach: a Prior Restraint Approach

This chapter continues the theme of outlining offences relating to public order which may be used against demonstrators by looking at the concept of the Queen's peace, and at offences and circumstances which involve the use of that concept. These range from the common law offence of conduct likely to cause a breach of the peace, to circumstances in which the police may arrest someone without a warrant if they suspect the likelihood of a breach of the peace, and further, to the power of the courts to bind over an offender to be of good conduct and to keep the peace. Many of these offences and the binding over power have been used extensively in relation to protesters and demonstrators especially in curtailing the activities of organizers of protests. We will also look at how specific conditions of bail have been used to prevent demonstrations or the organization of protest even before a defendant has been convicted.

These will be considered in terms of their preventive ('prior restraint' in American terminology) nature. These offences and powers are aimed at catching behaviour 'which is likely to cause a breach of the peace', rather than aiming at the breach of the peace itself. It will be seen that use of the concept in this manner creates an effective, subjective criterion for the use of preventive power.

Breach of the Peace

A breach of the peace is a substantive offence in Scotland,[1] but it is

---

[1] But, even there, the 'inchoate' offence is used – *The Times*, 2 Nov. 1987 reported that 'three Scottish Premier Division football players were charged . . . with conduct likely to cause a breach of the peace after incidents on the field during the Rangers/Celtic match on October 17.' A Chelsea player had previously been fined in 1983 for using threatening behaviour during a match at Brighton.

not absolutely clear that it is such an offence in the jurisdiction of England and Wales. Its importance as a concept has, however, been far greater than one would imagine for an offence of uncertain existence. Firstly, there does appear to be an offence of 'conduct likely to cause a breach of the peace'. Secondly, such conduct has been important as part of the definition of other crimes. Thirdly, both the possibility of a 'breach of the peace' and 'conduct likely to cause a breach of the peace' have become important in defining the powers of arrest without warrant of a Police Constable and the powers of arrest of ordinary citizens.

Conduct Likely to Cause a Breach of the Peace

It seems that there is an offence of this name with a somewhat vague definition, covering all sorts of behaviour which may be thought to be undesirable, but are not specifically forbidden by the criminal law. A case mentioned in *The Times* on 10 September 1975 provides a good example

> Mr Neil McElligott, the Marlborough Street magistrate, stopped proceedings yesterday against David Andrew Jones aged 46, described as a doctor of medicine, of High Road, Hambleton. He was brought before the court as a person whose conduct was likely to provoke a disturbance of the peace.
>
> It was alleged that Dr Jones kept looking up a woman's skirt as she lay asleep, sunbathing in Hyde Park.
>
> Stopping the proceedings without calling on Dr Jones, Mr McElligott said: 'I suppose she was a pretty girl. He denied what is alleged, but I think he had a look, probably on more than one occasion. But I cannot conceive that that was likely to cause a breach of the peace. Maybe if she had woken up she would have been flattered'.
>
> Police constable Leonard Hare said the woman had pulled her skirt up to mid thigh. Dr Jones had sat four or five feet away with his back to her, but then turned and faced her and kept looking up her skirt.
>
> Mr McElligott said the constable had been right to take action, but he thought the matter should go no further.[2]

On the one hand, this sort of 'catch-all' offence is useful to the police to deal with minor problems as they arise. On the other hand, it gives an enormous power of discretion to police and to courts to change, or widen, the law to fit each circumstance. Whether or not, as in the above case, the court decides to go along with a policeman's view, simply being charged and prosecuted can itself destroy a person's character.

---

[2] The name and address of the doctor have been changed from the original report so as not to cause any unnecessary distress by this publication.

If the offence can be used in such less obvious circumstances then the discretion of the police to use it in circumstances such as public protest or at public meetings will also be clear. Many of the specific circumstances written up in recent years relating to public meetings and possible breaches of the peace have involved offences fitting better in the next section. These have included insulting, etc., behaviour likely to cause a breach of the peace by blowing a nose at a public meeting.[3] The 1839 case of *Woodding* v. *Oxley*[4] holds that disturbance by noise at a meeting by cries of 'Hear, Hear' and interjections would not be a breach of the peace. As also noted by Supperstone,[5] the concept seems to have flowed over into the power of binding over in relation to the breach of the peace which will be dealt with at part 3 of this chapter, and it is not clear whether conduct caught in that manner is to be seen as different from conduct which might otherwise fall under this heading.

'Breach of the Peace' as Part of the Definition of Other Offences

Two offences which included the fear of a breach of the peace and 'with intent to provoke a breach of the peace or whereby a breach of the peace is likely to be occasioned', have now disappeared as a result of the Public Order Act 1986. It is not clear, therefore, whether the decisions made in relation to an understanding of the concept within those contexts will still be important.

Unlawful assembly at common law included the need for three or more persons gathered together with a common purpose either to commit a crime of violence or to achieve some other object lawful or unlawful in a manner which was calculated to give firm and courageous persons in the neighbourhood reason to fear a breach of the peace. This offence has now been repealed and substituted by section 2 of the Public Order Act (Violent Disorder) which uses the different test,

> and the conduct of them (taken together) is such as would cause a person of reasonable firmness present at the scene to fear for his personal safety.

It seems clear that fearing for one's 'personal safety' may differ from fearing a breach of the peace in that a breach of the peace might also include violence to property whereas 'personal safety' does not. 'Firm and courageous' persons has also been watered down to a 'person of reasonable firmness' and no such person as we have seen in chapter 4 above need actually be, or be likely to be, present at the scene.

[3] R. Kidd, *British Liberty in Danger* (London, Lawrence & Wishart, 1940), p. 134.
[4] *Woodding* v. *Oxley* [1839] 9 C & P 1.
[5] Supperstone, *Brownlie*, p. 3.

Section 5 of the Public Order Act 1936, which has now been repealed by the 1986 Act[6] used the concept in the following way

> any person who in any public place or at any public meeting – a) uses threatening, abusive or insulting words or behaviour; or
> – b) distributes or displays any writing, sign or visible representation which is threatening, abusive or insulting with intent to provoke a breach of the peace or whereby a breach of the peace is likely to be occasioned will be guilty of an offence.

This offence as we have seen above has been overtaken by the new sections 4 and 5 of the Public Order Act 1986. Each of those new offences uses a different sort of test from the breach of the peace test in the old section 5. Section 4 uses a test involving causing a belief that violence will be used, or provoking violence or making it likely that a recipient will believe that violence will be used or provoked. The violence in question will once again be against a person rather than against property. The new section 5 uses a test in which the threatening, abusive or insulting words, etc., are used 'within the hearing or sight of a person likely to be caused harassment, alarm or distress thereby'. It would seem that this test in the new section 5 reaches a much lower level of 'fear arousal' than would have been necessary for the likely occasioning of the breach of the peace. Contrasting the new legislation with the previous law shows more specific formulations replacing the concept of breach of the peace. The pressure from the Law Commission has been to move away from vague concepts, and if these particular changes are successful, then we may see a further limitation of the use of 'breach of the peace' in the future.

One particular case under this heading is worth noting since it demonstrates the use of the old formula, ties in with a problem raised in the previous chapter, and leads onto later themes relating to the policing of demonstrations. In *Marsh* v. *Arscott*[7], Mr Justice McCullough and Lord Justice Donaldson held that a breach of the peace was not likely to be caused by a defendant where only the defendant and police officers were present. This was a prosecution under section 5 of the Public Order Act 1936. The defendant was found slumped over the bonnet of his car at 11.30 one night, in a drunken state in a car park owned by the defendant's 'Tregadillett Mini Stores' in Launceston, Cornwall. On being questioned by the police, he informed them that he was the owner of the property and asked them to leave. At some stage his wife appeared on the scene and was recognized by the police. When the police still did not leave the defendant 'removed his coat,

---

[6] See Schedule 3.
[7] *Marsh* v. *Arscott* (1982) 75 Crim. App. Rep. 211; *The Times LR*, 3 March 1982.

became aggressive in manner and speech and threatened the police officers'. According to Mr Justice McCullough since it was the duty of the police officers to keep the peace, and only they and the defendant were present, the defendant's behaviour 'could not be said to be likely to bring about any breach of the peace'. This seems to set up a special 'unprovocable' status for police officers which may not accord with reality, but certainly seems to be theoretically correct. Since the reactions of citizens, including protesters, are clearly affected by police behaviour, the courts should recognize this in maintaining the balance between individuals and the police. The 'unprovocable' status reflects this need well.[8] It will be interesting to see whether a defence along these lines will prove useful and continue to be upheld in succeeding cases.

Breach of the Peace as an Element in the Power of Arrest

Many of the cases which have looked more specifically at the ingredient of a 'breach of the peace' have come under this heading.

The situation seems to arise in the following way. A police officer dealing with a disturbance or even with the day to day running of police work[9] finds some difficulty in obtaining the acquiescence of the individual or individuals encountered to do what the police officer asks. The situation becomes tense and the police officer is forced to make a decision either to withdraw, or to arrest the individual or individuals concerned. Under such circumstances police officers do not always consider clearly whether they have a power of arrest.

In some cases, the person arrested then strikes the officer and is accused of assault on a police officer in the exercise of his duty. In other cases the 'arrestee' sues the officer for assault, false arrest, false imprisonment or malicious prosecution. Police officers seem to believe that there is a power of arrest for the alleged offence of obstructing a police officer in the exercise of his/her duty under section 51 (3) of the Police Act 1964. However, no such power exists, and case after case decides that the power does not exist at the same time as they show historic proof that police officers still seem to arrest on that basis. Where, however, a police officer has made such an arrest and the legality of that arrest is questioned in court either on a prosecution of the 'arrestee' or in civil suit against the police, the police officer has to attempt to show that there was a power of arrest without warrant. Such

---

[8] For a contrary view see A. H. T. Smith, *Offences Against Public Order; including the Public Order Act 1986* (London, Sweet & Maxwell, *Police Review*, 1987), p. 96, and see the first case under S.5(1) of the 1986 Act *DPP* v. *Orum The Times LR* 25th July 1988 saying the constable was capable of being subject to 'harassment, alarm or distress'. Cf. *Nawrot and Shaler* v. *DPP* [1988] Crim. LR 107.

[9] See, e.g., *Wershof* v. *Commissioner of Police* [1978] 3 All ER 540.

a common law power does exist, it seems, where a police officer reasonably apprehends a breach of the peace.

A closer look at the cases will be helpful. In the most recent test of *R.* v. *Howell*[10] two almost totally conflicting sets of evidence were presented to the trial judge in relation to events after a party in Coventry. The police said they were attempting to clear the streets whilst party goers accused them of harassing some of the black people who had attended the party. The Court of Appeal (Criminal Division) was left with the task of reviewing whether the arrest of the defendant had been lawful when he was told by the police officer that he was to be 'arrested for breach of the peace'. It seems that the police officers had followed the defendant and others for some distance away from the party during which time the party leavers began to get more and more angry at the way they were being treated. Finally, as stated by the police, a policeman was about to arrest the appellant, when the appellant struck him in the face and a melee resulted. The defendant's story was that he was walking away from the scene peacefully when PC Lewis came from nowhere and said 'you are going to get it'.[11]

Lord Justice Watkins also mentioned that the defendant's version was supported by two other people, one of whom witnessed the event from nearby and did not seem to be one of those involved. The court specifically sets aside the question of whether an arrest 'for breach of the peace' could also have been good as an arrest under section 5 of the old Public Order Act. The case, therefore, remains important for the current law, since the demise of that section. The court attempts to deal with the wider concept in this way,

> a comprehensive definition of the term 'breach of the peace' has very rarely been formulated so far as we have been able, with considerable help from counsel, to discover from cases which go back as far as the 18th century. The older cases are of considerable interest but they are not a sure guide to what the term is understood to mean today, since keeping the peace in this country in the latter half of the 20th century presents formidable problems which bear on the evolving process of the development of this branch of the common law. Nevertheless, even in these days when affrays, riotous behaviour and other disturbances happen all too frequently, we cannot accept that there can be a breach of the peace unless there has been an act done or threatened to be done which either actively harms a person, or in his presence his property or is likely to cause such harm, or which puts someone in fear of such harm being done. There is nothing more likely to arouse resentment and anger in

---

[10] *R.* v. *Howell* [1981] 3 All ER 383.
[11] According to L. J. Watkins; ibid., 386.

him, and a desire to take instant revenge, than attacks or threatened attacks on a person's body or property.[12]

The court goes on to say that the description of a situation as being a 'disturbance' cannot constitute a breach of the peace.

> We are emboldened to say that there is a breach of the peace whenever harm is actually done or is likely to be done to a person or in his presence to his property or a person is in fear of being so harmed through an assault, an affray, a riot, an unlawful assembly or other disturbance. It is for this breach of the peace when done in his presence or the reasonable apprehension of it taking place that a constable, or any one else, may arrest an offender without warrant.

The court therefore held that there was a power of arrest for a police officer and for an ordinary citizen where

(1) a breach of the peace is committed in the presence of the person making the arrest; or
(2) the arrestor reasonably believes that such a breach will be committed in the immediate future by the person arrested although he has not yet committed any breach, or
(3) where a breach has been committed and it is reasonably believed that a renewal of it is threatened.[13]

Where a police officer exercises a power of arrest under (2) or (3) above it must 'be established that it is not only an honest, albeit mistaken, belief but a belief that is found on reasonable grounds'.[14]

In the case of *Wershof*[15] the plaintiff was a young solicitor of some 12 days standing who had been arrested by a police officer for wilfully obstructing him in the execution of his duty, contrary to section 51 (3) of the Police Act 1964, which as seen above contains no such power of arrest. The circumstances were as follows. The plaintiff's family business was that of a jeweller. One Saturday afternoon the plaintiff was telephoned by his younger brother, then in charge of the family shop, to come and deal with a dispute with a police officer over a ring which the officer alleged was stolen property. The plaintiff arrived at the shop and introduced himself as a solicitor. The plaintiff explained that he would not give up the ring unless the policeman gave a receipt for it

[12] Ibid., 388–9.
[13] Ibid., 338.
[14] Ibid.
[15] *Wershof* [1978] All ER 540.

and on a number of occasions asked for a receipt, which the police officer refused to give.

As a result the police officer arrested the plaintiff by taking 'a very firm and temporary, at any rate, painful grip of the plaintiff's arm and marched him out of the shop in front of his brother, two of their employees, Mrs Talbot and probably two customers'.[16] On the facts of the case it was held that the police officer had not been acting in the execution of his duty since his refusal to give a receipt for the ring was unreasonable and that the plaintiff was not being wilfully obstructive since he was making quite clear that he would hand over the ring if a receipt was given.

Since section 51 (3) of the Police Act 1964 did not constitute an arrestable offence, it was contended on behalf of the police that a power of arrest still existed under those circumstances where a breach of the peace was likely to occur. The court found that no breach of the peace was likely to have occurred in those particular circumstances and held that the common law power of a police officer to arrest without warrant a person who wilfully obstructed him in the execution of his duty only existed, if

(1) the nature of the obstruction was such that the offender actually caused or was likely to cause a breach of the peace or was calculated to prevent the lawful arrest or detention of another person; or

(2) at the relevant time the police officer was acting in the execution of his duty and honestly believed on reasonable grounds that the offender was wilfully obstructing him and that the obstruction was likely to cause a breach of the peace.[17]

It is interesting that this is an extreme case involving a solicitor acting reasonably, and one wonders whether the findings of fact and holding of law would have been the same in relation to a demonstrator or protester alleging similar reasonableness of behaviour in the circumstances of a public demonstration. Even in this most extreme of cases, Mr Justice May's advice to the plaintiff was that whether or not the police were correct in law the plaintiff should not have insisted on his right, but

> Nothing would indeed have been simpler than to give the ring to Sergeant Brand and immediately drive to the appropriate police station and, as a solicitor, make a formal complaint to the station officer or the station inspector.[18]

This is interesting because it does exhibit the judicial attitude to

16 Ibid., 546.
17 Ibid., 540.
18 Ibid., 546.

authority and the rule of law. Authority, whether it is right or wrong, should always be obeyed and the issue taken to law later. Such an approach does not seem to accord with personal intuition or reality at the time of such an event, as opposed to the position of the armchair critic subsequently. Neither is it clear that the system of complaint as advised in this case, or even using the judicial system in other ways, would necessarily gain the same effect as a reliance at the time on the specific rights which the court felt existed. It does not seem much for the court to recognize a 'right' which takes almost 3 years to prove in a case going up to the Divisional Court, at the same time as one is told one should not have exercised it.

In the perhaps equally bizarre case of *Gelberg* v. *Miller*[19] the defendant parked his car, contrary to the parking regulations in Jermyn Street, London, outside a restaurant whilst he was having his lunch. Noticing two police officers observing the position of his car, he went out to talk to them and they asked him to move the vehicle. He replied that he would be 3 minutes finishing his food and paying the bill. When they asked him to remove the vehicle again, saying that otherwise they would have to remove it, he removed the rotar arm from under the bonnet, went back into the restaurant, finished his meal and paid within the time previously stated.

On returning to his car he did not give his licence and other details to the policemen immediately on their request and was arrested for obstructing a police officer in the exercise of his duty. The further details of this case will be dealt with in a later chapter as the major decision rested on a somewhat different point. However, for our present purpose it should be noted that it was contended on behalf of the police, and agreed by the court, that a power of arrest for that offence existed where a breach of the peace was likely to be occasioned.

Lawyers tend to ignore the specific background of cases because only the distilled general principles are relevant to the next case. However, it is important for our study to note the somewhat bizarre circumstances under which cases arise that then prescribe applicable law for the area of interest covered by this book. It is clear that within a protest or demonstration it will almost always be easier for the police to suggest, where some unfortunate individual does not do immediately what the police officer desires, that a breach of the peace would also have occurred if the officer had not immediately arrested that individual under section 51 (3). Where the law has seen fit not to give the ultimate power of immediate arrest to a police officer whose whims have not been obeyed, it seems a great shame that as a result of this line of cases in the practical

---

[19] *Gelberg* v. *Miller* [1961] 1 All ER 291.

reality of a demonstration or protest such powers return to the police officer without judicial question.

Preventive Nature

The use of the powers mentioned above should be seen clearly in their intended light as aimed at prevention. It is 'conduct *likely to cause* a breach of the peace' which is criminal, and it was that sort of test which was applied in the older laws. It is still that form of test which is applied in relation to powers of arrest. This means that one person's discretion on the scene is trusted to make decisions about what might happen, even where no offence or disturbance has yet occurred. This intrusive intervention of the law may, on the one hand, be seen as a useful power in the prevention of disorder, but can also lead to strong misuse and abuse where insufficient guidelines are given to police officers as to how to employ their vague and vast powers.

Especially difficult in these circumstances must be the problem of the 'hostile audience'. If a breach of the peace is likely to occur only as a result of a particularly hostile, but small, part of the audience, it must be an exceptionally difficult question to judge whether the police officer on the spot should silence the speaker or silence the audience.

Binding Over

Williams[20] heads his chapter on binding over with the title 'Preventive Justice' taking from Blackstone the description,

> This preventive justice consists in obliging those persons, whom there is probable ground to suspect of future misbehaviour, to stipulate with and to give full assurance to the public, that such offence as is apprehended shall not happen; by finding pledges or securities for keeping the peace, or for their good behaviour.

Two separate powers of binding over order were recognized in *R.* v. *Aubrey-Fletcher*,[21] one arising out of the Magistrates Courts Act 1952, section 91[22] and the wider power in the Justices of the Peace Act 1361. With respect to the section 91 order, there has to have been 'a complaint

[20] D. Williams, *Keeping the Peace: the Police and Public Order* (London, Hutchinson, 1967), p. 87.
[21] *R.* v. *Aubrey-Fletcher* [1969] 2 All ER 846.
[22] Now the Magistrates Courts Act 1980, s. 115.

adjudged to be true',[23] whereas an order under the older jurisdiction 'can be made at any time without a formal complaint, and in the course of other proceedings, though if the order is to keep the peace, some threat must be disclosed by the evidence adduced'.[24]

Much disquiet has been voiced regarding the powers available under the 1361 Act, the oldest listed in Stone's Justice Manual. Particular complaints raised in 1980 related to the fact that magistrates may 'bind over not only defendants but also witnesses, solicitors or even onlookers in the public gallery, on pain of imprisonment'.[25] *The Times* noted that two hunt saboteurs who had appeared as prosecution witnesses in a case against hunt followers at Rye, Sussex who were charged with actual bodily harm, were jailed for 6 months when they refused to agree to being bound over to keep the peace for a year in the sum of £50.00. In another case arising out of the disturbances in Southall in 1979 two black witnesses were bound over after appearing for the defence. Binding over orders were said to be most common in 'domestic arguments' which include neighbour disputes where the magistrates, rather than deciding who started a fight, tend to bind over both sides to keep the peace and be of good behaviour. Some 7263 cases of binding over were made in 1978. The Law Commission has also recently asked for major reforms in this area suggesting the alternatives of conditional discharge and a fine.[26]

Binding over orders have been used frequently in protest and demonstration cases either as an addition to a fine after a finding of guilt; or as a preventive measure in order to stop individuals or organizers attending a planned demonstration. Such orders were used during the miners' strike of 1984. Although, as Williams points out,[27] since 1956 the statutory right of appeal to the Crown Court has meant that magistrates may now be less inclined to do so unless they can state their reasons with some clarity and force. Interestingly, in the next year it was shown in *R. v. Sharp* and *R. v. Johnson*,[28] that it was possible for all judges, 'who are also Justices of the Peace for every county'[29] to exercise the power of binding over. This power was used in that case to bind over appellants both of whom had their convictions quashed, but who had been involved in a vicious fight.

The origin of the forms of behaviour to be covered seems to relate

[23] Supperstone, *Brownlie*, p. 314.
[24] Ibid.
[25] *The Times*, 1 Apr. 1980.
[26] The Law Commission Working Paper 103, Sept. 1987.
[27] Williams, *Keeping the Peace*, p. 87 and D. G. T. Williams, 'Protest and Public Order' [1970] CLJ 104–6.
[28] *R. v. Johnson* [1957] 1 QB 552.
[29] Ibid., 561.

clearly to 'a breach of the peace', but its usage has widened considerably since then. Although the original 1361 Act was supposedly passed to deal with 'marauding ex-soldiers of the mid-fourteenth century',[30] it seems probable that it existed even before that Act back to the ninth century. In modern times it has been used against people who persistently annoy with phone calls or disturbances outside houses or places of work, writing poison-pen letters and even writing 'Donkey Watt, the railway Jackass' on the pavement.[31]

Williams documents numerous uses of the binding over order against demonstrators and marchers such as the Salvation Army, the Suffragettes, the Communists, the Fascists between the wars, the hunger marchers and Nuclear Disarmament demonstrators.[32] As Williams points out, where the binding over power is used in order to prevent speakers or organisers going to demonstrations, 'in effect, the authorities are sometimes able to use the binding over procedure as a means of "trying" political offences without having to have the issue thrashed out before a judge and jury'. The result is not very different from the sort of proscription or ban which *Beatty* v. *Gilbanks* states clearly is not available to the Justices of the Peace.

In the leading case of *Lansbury* v. *Riley*[33] the future leader of the Labour Party was bound over in the sum of £1000 with two sureties of £500 for his incitement to protesters on behalf of women's suffrage to

> burn and destroy property and do anything they will, and for every leader that is taken away, let a dozen step forward in her place; let us teach this make believe Liberal Government that this is a holy war, and is a war for women's and men's rights the world over; and it is a war that shall not end until our end is accomplished, and that it is a war in which we will do our best to preserve human life, but it is a war that will have no regard for property of any kind whatever.[34]

Lansbury took the matter to the Divisional Court which decided against him, in particular stating that there was no need to show that any particular person has been threatened and that a 'general threat' was sufficient for a binding over order. Lansbury refused to be bound over, was committed to Pentonville prison for 3 months, went on hunger strike and was soon released under the 'Cat and Mouse Act'.[35]

In 1922 Wal Hannington was imprisoned when he refused to be

---

[30] Williams, *Keeping the Peace*, p. 89.
[31] Ibid., pp. 91–2.
[32] Ibid., p. 93.
[33] *Lansbury* v. *Riley* [1914] 3 KB 229.
[34] Williams, *Keeping the Peace*, p. 97.
[35] Ibid., p. 100.

bound over after his arrest for a speech in Coventry. He and Elias, two leaders of the National Unemployed Workers Movement, were imprisoned again in 1931, refusing to be bound over after a speech made in Hyde Park. In December 1932 as 'several contingents of hunger marchers were approaching London where a mass demonstration was planned', Mann and Llewellyn, two other leaders of the NUWM were arrested and subsequently bound over. On refusal to accept being bound over they were committed to Brixton prison, which resulted in stormy debates in the House of Commons. Once again, the main cause of dissatisfaction was 'the manner in which preventive justice had been so readily resorted to in this case, whereas it was not used against those who allegedly incited anti-semitic demonstrations in the East End and elsewhere'.[36]

In the 1960s Bertrand and Lady Russell both declined to be bound over and received a sentence of imprisonment of 7 days for inciting others to commit breaches of the peace and breaches of the law in relation to demonstrations of the Committee of One Hundred on Sunday 17 September 1961. The imprisonment of these two elderly protesters was just long enough to keep them away from the demonstration itself, on which occasion 1314 arrests were made.

In *R. v. Central Criminal Court, ex. p. Boulding*[37] the Court finally criticized this use of the power saying that 'a binding over order must not be in such terms as effectively to inhibit a convicted person from exercising his right to free speech within the law'. This may herald a change in judicial approach.

The power is so vague and so wide that it has been used almost at whim. It seems quite wrong that people may be 'punished' without ever having committed an offence. It would be clearly possible to limit the Magistrates' power so that binding over orders could not be given in such circumstances, as the Law Commission seems to suggest.[38]

We have already noted the problem of the hostile audience or the tension between the 'taking your audience as you find it' approach and the 'first in the field' approach. Williams notes that the cases, previously mentioned, of *Beatty* v. *Gilbanks* and *Wise* v. *Dunning* both involved the court's use of the binding over power in circumstances where it is not completely clear which side was 'at fault' except from a highly subjective point of view. Using the power in this manner against people such as Pastor Wise in 1909, or the Reverend Ian Paisley in 1966, may be justified as Williams seems to suggest,[39] but does not seem to solve

[36] Ibid., p. 100.
[37] *R. v. Central Criminal Court, ex p. Boulding* [1984] 1 QB 813.
[38] Law Commission Working Paper 103, Sept. 1987.
[39] Williams, *Keeping the Peace*, pp. 107–10.

any real problems. The activities of the individuals concerned do not stop, and the general outrage at vague and discretionary powers being used against some, and not others, only brings Magistrates Courts, the law and the police into disrepute.

Recent cases have decided that where somebody has agreed to be bound over and enter into recognisances to keep the peace or be of good behaviour, the nature of the proceedings where it was alleged that he had not continued to be of good behaviour were civil proceedings in which the civil standard of proof applied.[40] This means that Justices have the power to bind someone over without making specific findings on evidence regarding previous behaviour, and then to order the forfeit of recognisances (which can be in excess of the amounts used as penalties for similar offences) on the basis of merely a balance of probabilities. This only seems to enlarge the magistrates' power. However, where a person under the age of 17 refuses to enter into recognisances when bound over to keep the peace, such a person cannot be imprisoned for such refusal since the Powers of Criminal Courts Act 1973 prohibits all such imprisonment.[41] Thus, the power cannot be used as a means of getting around one of the major safeguards for dealing with juvenile offenders.

Conclusion

The concept of a breach of the peace, conduct likely to cause a breach of the peace and binding over to keep the peace is therefore a central concept in the English legal system, and used heavily in cases of protest and demonstration. However specific new statutory offences are, the existence of such vague, catch-all offences or powers means that the police and magistrates will always be able to turn to those offences and powers rather than be tied up in more specific, narrower definitions. With a major new set of public order offences now on the statute book, two of which have specifically rejected use of the 'breach of the peace' formula, it would be a good time to look again at how these powers and defences could be limited. One simple way would be to limit their use so that a specific offence has to be found to be committed before a binding over order can be made.

[40] *R.* v. *Marlag Justices ex. p. O'Sullivan* [1983] 3 All ER 578.
[41] *Veater* v. *Gee and Others* [1981] 2 All ER 304.

6

Obstruction

In this chapter we move away from offences which seem more clearly, by their nature, to be intended to deal with public disorder to look at the two offences which are, in fact, most commonly used against demonstrators: obstructing the highway and obstructing the police in the exercise of their duty. These two offences belong together, not only because of the regularity of their usage,[1] but also because of the discretion available to police officers on the spot in relation to what conduct constitutes their commission.

This chapter therefore looks at the offence of obstruction of a police officer in the exercise of his/her duty, together with the allied offence of assault on a police officer in the exercise of his/her duty. It will also look at the statutory and common law offences of obstructing the highway, so far as they affect demonstrators and protesters. All of these offences are triable only at the Magistrates Court level and, therefore, involve a set of decisions which are rarely subjected to the scrutiny of higher courts and juries.

Obstructing the Police in the Execution of their Duty

The major offence is provided by section 51 (3) of the Police Act 1964 which states,

> Any person who resists or wilfully obstructs a constable in the execution of his duty, or a person assisting a constable in the execution of his duty, shall be guilty of an offence and liable on summary conviction to imprisonment for a term not exceeding one month or to a fine not exceeding level 3 on the standard scale or to both.

This offence is found under the title of the main section 'Assaults on

---

[1] A total of 8973 people were found guilty of obstruction of the highway, other than by a vehicle, in 1985, and 9864 were found guilty of assault on or obstruction of a constable (Home Office figures).

constables'. The first offence mentioned under section 51 (1) relates to
an assault on a constable in the execution of his duty, to which we shall
return. There is, therefore, some force in the argument that the offence
of obstruction was intended initially to deal only with a physical
obstruction of the police officer rather than the metaphysical obstruction
which will now be described. It is interesting to note that under the
law in Scotland the equivalent offence is limited to a physical
interference.[2]

The wider meaning of the word 'obstruction' was imported into the
law in the classic case of *Duncan* v. *Jones*.[3] Unlike many of the other
cases which are decisive on the conduct of protest and demonstration,
Duncan v. *Jones* actually concerned a protest meeting. The meeting was
held on 30 July 1934 at about 1.00 p.m. in Nynehead Street, New
Cross, outside an unemployed training centre. The meeting was organized
to protest against the Incitement to Disaffection Bill (see chapters 2 and
4 above) and was to be addressed by Mrs Katherine Duncan who was
a well known member of the National Unemployed Workers' Movement.
According to police evidence, she had addressed a meeting outside the
same centre some 14 months earlier, which had been followed by a
disturbance inside the training centre.

The district's Chief Constable, together with one of his inspectors,
arrived at the meeting as a result of being alerted by the superintendent
of the training centre. The Chief Constable told Mrs Duncan that she
could not speak there, but that she could hold the meeting at an
alternative site some 175 yards away. Mrs Duncan's response was 'I'm
going to hold it', and as she stepped up on to the box to speak she was
arrested by the inspector and charged with obstructing him in the
execution of his duty. David Williams[4] notes these facts and the
somewhat unsympathetic reaction of the Deputy Chairman of Quarter
Sessions to her appeal against conviction.

> What is the object of this appeal? Is it to establish a practice of ladies
> standing on boxes in public streets and addressing meetings?

It is clear from Mrs Duncan's reception at Tower Bridge Magistrates
Court where she was convicted and fined 40 shillings, from her appeal
to Quarter Sessions, and from the final appeal to the Divisional Court
before Lord Chief Justice Hewart, that the nature of the case made no
difference to their reactions to this offence. Lord Hewart, denying that

---

[2] See *Curlett* v. *M'Kechnie* [1938] SCJ 176, and Supperstone, *Brownlie*, p. 115.
[3] *Duncan* v. *Jones* [1936] 1 KB 218.
[4] D. Williams, *Keeping the Peace: the Police and Public Order* (London, Hutchinson, 1967),
p. 120.

this was 'a grave case involving what is called the right of public meeting' was not prepared to see any fundamental liberties or constitutional issues at stake. Mr Justice Humphries said, in words which must have echoed down the years after him, it was 'a plain case raising no question of importance or novelty'. The approach of the Divisional Court is simply geared in to the particular facts of the case, and the overwhelming need of the police to prevent any possible breach of the peace without any question entering into their minds of any importance involved in a freedom of speech.

In many of the more modern cases where freedom of speech or protest is denied to the individuals concerned, the courts have at least been careful to maintain the myth or chimera of a freedom of speech existing, whilst denying it in those particular circumstances. In *Duncan* v. *Jones* where the issue was explicit, and was made explicit by the appeal sponsored by the National Council for Civil Liberties, there is an outright rejection of the concept.

Supperstone states the effect of *Duncan* v. *Jones*,

> The upshot of *Duncan* v. *Jones* is the creation of an ambulatory offence based on a 'reasonable' (but in practice often very sensitive) apprehension of a danger to the peace. It is a new version of an inchoate or collateral offence. Apart from this offence, in most of the reported instances, including *Duncan* v. *Jones* itself, no offence had been committed.[5]

In other words, *Duncan* v. *Jones* allows a policeman on the spot the power to tell an individual to do something. In the event that the police officer is disobeyed, the officer may arrest the person for obstructing that officer in the exercise of the officer's duty.

Some of the effects of this approach have been seen in above chapters.[6] We have already noted how the police have viewed this offence mistakenly as being an arrestable offence, so that a police officer may have mistakenly believed until the case of *Wershof*[7] that it was possible to arrest somebody for not carrying out police demand. The legal manual used by the police, *Moriarty's Police Law*,[8] fostered this error. The immediate effect of such intrusion by the police on demonstrations and protests can be easily imagined, as well as seen clearly in the case of Mrs Duncan herself. There have been numerous academic attacks on

---

[5] Supperstone, *Brownlie*, p. 114.
[6] See ch. 5.
[7] *Wershof* [1978] 3 All ER 540, and see ch. 5.
[8] *Moriarty's Police Law*, 24th edn (London, Butterworth, 1981).

the principle[9] and it has also been attacked in some of the succeeding cases, but without any real success.

Supperstone makes a distinction between the major strand of cases following *Duncan* v. *Jones* and another set of cases where the strict rule does not seem to have been applied. He suggests that *Duncan*

> contains two principles:
> (a) that a police command may create a legal duty accompanied by a criminal sanction where no rule of common law or statute created such a duty; and
> (b) that the command is issued in the execution of his duty if the police officer reasonably apprehends a breach of the peace.[10]

Supperstone argues that when the second element (b) is not present, in other words where the police officer does not apprehend a breach of the peace, the courts do not seem so ready to justify the police action. He suggests that this is what occurred in the case of *R.* v. *Waterfield and Lynn*[11] in which a police officer was found not to be acting in the execution of his duty when attempting to prevent the removal of a motor car on the highway. Even though the police officer had a reasonable belief that the car had been involved in a serious offence, he was not in the execution of his duty when he tried to prevent it being driven away by blocking its path. Thus, when the car was driven at him by the defendants they were not guilty of assaulting him.

This case appears to be stating that although police officers may easily intrude upon a person's freedom of speech, they may not interfere with a person's property. However, it seems to be an anomaly decided on its own peculiar facts. Had the police officer attempted to stop the car and its driver by the use of powers under the Road Traffic Acts, etc., the case may never have arisen in that way.

The second strand of Supperstone's interesting distinction deals with the *Rice* v. *Connolly* type of situation[12] which has been followed to some extent in the equally bizarre case of *Wilmott* v. *Atack*.[13] Supperstone agonizes over the effect of these two cases, in an attempt to break down the structure of the reasoning in *Duncan* v. *Jones*. However, an inspection of each of these cases reveals somewhat strange facts, and the difficulty of reconciling them with the prevalent trend in the law seems to result

---

[9] See, e.g., T. C. Daintith [1966] *Public Law*, 248–61, V. Ross [1977] Crim. LR 187, A. L. Goodhart [1936] 6 CLJ 22, S. A. De Smith, *Constitutional and Administrative Law*, 5th edn (Harmondsworth, Penguin, 1985), pp. 495–6
[10] Supperstone, *Brownlie*, p. 114.
[11] *R.* v. *Waterfield and Lynn* [1964] 1 QB 164.
[12] *Rice* v. *Connolly* [1966] 2 All ER 649.
[13] *Wilmott* v. *Atack* [1976] 3 All ER 794.

from the court's difficulties in handling these facts, rather than any real will to change the rule in *Duncan* v. *Jones*.

In *Rice* v. *Connolly* a man who was stopped late at night in an area where there had been some thefts (but without any other reason for the policeman to suspect him) was asked his name and address, and gave only his surname and the name of the road he lived in to the police officer. He refused to give any further information and refused to go to a police box where the information that he had given might be checked saying 'if you want me, you will have to arrest me'. On these facts the Divisional Court decided that he was not obstructing the police officer in the exercise of his duty since there was no formal legal duty to answer a constable's questions. However, according to the facts, he did answer the constable's questions, if in a half-hearted fashion. Sufficient information had, in fact, been given to the police constable for this man's identity and address to be checked. It seems to have been more the officiousness of the police officer and the calm refusal of the defendant which the Divisional Court was addressing in making its decision than any more serious all-encompassing rule of law.

Wilmott v. *Atack* is bizarre in a rather different way. The facts seem to have arisen out of some sort of dispute between an off-duty police officer called Zieminski and a man called Howe, as a result of which Howe had taken Zieminski's warrant card.[14] Zieminski, determined to obtain the return of his warrant card, managed to stop a police car shortly before midnight on a Saturday night, and asked the police to pursue Howe who he thought had been consuming alcohol.[15] Howe, with the police car in pursuit, drove to a country club in Biggin Hill in Kent which was owned by a Mr Wilmott. The police constable driving the car, with the memorable name of Alan Atack, attempted to arrest Howe on the car park of the club, to the consternation of Wilmott. Wilmott seems to have interfered between the police officers (a number of others joined in the struggle) and Howe. His intention, according to the court's finding was to intervene 'in the belief that he could resolve the situation better than the police', and he was 'telling Howe not to be stupid and to get into the car'. On these facts Mr Justice Croom-Johnson, with whom Lord Chief Justice Widgery and Justice May agreed, found Wilmott not guilty. The case held that on a charge of obstructing a police officer the prosecution had to prove not only that the defendant had deliberately done an act which had resulted in the

[14] See *Wilmott* v. *Atack* [1976] 3 All ER 795. There are a number of cases which seem to involve off-duty police officers in this area of the law. See, e.g. *Ohlson* v. *Hylton* [1975] 1 WLR 724; *Albert* v. *Lavin* [1982] AC 546.
[15] Ibid., 795. It is an interesting point of conjecture exactly what occurred between Zieminski and Howe, in what sort of place and circumstances in order to give rise to those facts.

obstruction, but also that the act had been done 'with the intention of obstructing the officer in the sense of making it more difficult for him to carry out his duty'.

The *Wilmott* v. *Atack* circumstances are unlikely to give rise to a large number of cases and, even if they do, they would not necessarily be particularly important for freedom of speech or protest. *Wilmott* v. *Atack* appears to allow some lassitude to an officious bystander who gets in the way of the police whilst trying to be helpful, but not much more. In *Hills* v. *Ellis*[16] a man at a football match was arrested for obstructing a police officer because he was trying to tell the policeman that he was arresting the wrong man and 'the innocent party in the fight' to which the police officer's arrest related. The Middlesex Magistrates had found the appellant guilty of obstruction at the Tottenham Hotspur Football Ground, but had made an order discharging him absolutely, because they did not feel that his actions were worthy of any punishment. The Divisional Court distinguished *Wilmott*, by showing that Wilmott had intended to encourage the intended arrest, whereas Hills' interference was intended to persuade the policeman against the intended arrest.

Although one could wish every support to Supperstone's line of argument in undermining the effect of *Duncan* v. *Jones*, these cases do not seem to stand up to robust criticism on their general, as opposed to their factually specific, implication. Succeeding cases with not too dissimilar facts successively seem to distinguish and cut away the principles, if any, laid out in *Rice* and *Wilmott*.[17]

One particular use of the obstruction offence in relation to industrial picketing may well have an effect on non-industrial picketing used as a protest, similar to the circumstances in *Hubbard* v. *Pitt*.[18] In the 1961 case of *Piddington* v. *Bates*[19] a police officer in attendance at a small picket outside a factory decided that two pickets were enough for a picket on the back gate. The defendant disagreed and stated his intention to augment those numbers to above the permitted two. He 'pushed gently' past the police officer and was 'gently arrested', and charged with obstructing a constable in the execution of his duty. The Divisional Court held, dismissing the appeal, that on the police evidence there was a possibility of a breach of the peace and the police were entitled to take such steps as seemed proper to prevent a breach of the peace occurring.

In *Tynan* v. *Balmer*[20] some forty pickets were organized in a moving

[16] *Hills* v. *Ellis* [1983] 1 All ER 667.
[17] See, e.g. *Donnelly* v. *Jackman* [1970] 1 All ER 987.
[18] *Hubbard* v. *Pitt* [1975] 3 All ER 794, and see above, p. 64 ff.
[19] *Paddington* v. *Bates* [1961] 1 WLR 162.
[20] *Tynan* v. *Balmer* [1967] 1 QB 91.

circle at the main entrance to a factory where an official strike was taking place. A police constable asked the defendant, who was organizing the picket, to stop them from circling and entering into the public highway. The defendant refused to do so, and was arrested and charged with wilfully obstructing the police officer. Despite the express dispensation for industrial picketing in the Trade Disputes Act 1906 section 2 (now to be found in section 15 of the Trade Union and Labour Relations Act 1974) the Divisional Court found no difficulty in confirming the defendant's conviction. Mr Justice Widgery said that there had clearly been an unreasonable use of the highway and that the police officer on the spot had been within his rights. As Lord Wedderburn noted in relation to industrial picketing, 'the only indisputable lawful pickets... are those who attend in small numbers near the chosen place and keep out of everyone's way'.[21] If this is the situation for industrial picketing where a specific exclusion is granted, the decision of a police officer will a fortiori include even wider powers in cases involving other forms of protest activity.

Assaulting Police Officers in the Exercise of their Duty

As noted above the 'obstruction' offence comes under the heading of 'Assaults on Constables' at the beginning of section 51 of the Police Act 1964. Section 51 (1) reads,

> any person who assaults a constable in the execution of his duty, or a person assisting a constable in the execution of his duty, shall be guilty of an offence and liable on summary conviction to imprisonment for a term not exceeding six months or to a fine not exceeding level 5 on the standard scale or to both.

An assault on a constable under section 51 (1) *is* an arrestable offence. One way in which a police officer may avoid the problem of an obstruction not being an arrestable offence is that the police officer may place him/herself in such a manner in relation to a prospective defendant that a technical assault of the police officer will be inevitable and the police officer may thereupon legally arrest an individual for behaviour which amounted really only to an obstruction.[22]

Since this offence is punishable by a term of imprisonment exceeding

---

[21] Lord Wedderburn, *The Worker and the Law* (2nd edn), p. 325. See Supperstone, *Brownlie*, p. 68.

[22] These, it seems, are the circumstances referred to in *Piddington* v. *Bates* [1961] 1 WLR 162, although in that case the defendant was charged with obstructing a constable in the execution of his duty and *arrested* for that offence.

3 months, one might have thought that a person charged with the offence could claim to be tried by a jury, rather than in the Magistrates Court. However, in *Toohey* v. *The Woolwich Justices*[23] the House of Lords in a short (3 page) judgment held that an assault on a police officer came under the exception of the general term of 'assault' in section 25 (1) of the Magistrates Courts Act 1952 and, therefore, a defendant could not elect for jury trial. This means that a defendant's actions will always be judged by magistrates who have a closer connection with police officers and the policing of the area than a more independent jury. Magistrates are therefore more likely to believe a story told by the police than by defendants.

Some of the assault cases also seem to show liberal elements in line with the cases distinguished from *Duncan* v. *Jones* (see above). However, they mostly appear to concern the property element, and the view that the Englishman's home is his castle. Thus, in *Davis* v. *Lisle*[24] a police officer was found to become a trespasser and, therefore, not in the execution of his duty when he was assaulted by a garage owner. The officer had come to the garage in order to make enquiries about a possible obstruction on the highway, and was asked to leave by the appellant. Once he was told to leave he was not in the execution of his duty and, therefore, when he was assaulted the appellant had a right to do so. This was not, however, the situation in *Robson* v. *Hallett*[25] a case about a somewhat argumentative and pugnacious family in Gateshead. In that particular case in which the appellant, amongst other things, 'kicked Sergeant McCaffrey in the privates',[26] it was held that police officers do have an implied licence to walk through an unlocked gate and up to the door of a house, and to remain there until such licence is revoked and, thereafter, for such time as it would take to leave the premises. The police officers present were therefore acting in the exercise of their duty at the point in time when they were assaulted.[27]

Two cases seemed to show a willingness in the courts to constrain any exercise of police power to detain citizens without actually arresting them. In *Ludlow* v. *Burgess*[28] a plain clothes police constable was kicked on the shin whilst boarding a bus by one of three youths. The police constable decided to detain the youth 'for further conversation and enquiries', but did not have his warrant card with him to prove he was

[23] *Toohey* v. *The Woolwich Justices* [1966] 2 All ER 429.
[24] *Davis* v. *Lisle* [1936] 2 All ER 213.
[25] *Robson* v. *Hallett* [1967] 2 All ER 407.
[26] Ibid., 409.
[27] Item (g) of the contentions by counsel for the respondents at 410 reads 'when the appellant Dennis Robson kicked Sergeant McCaffrey in the privates, the sergeant was "trying to sort the position out".'
[28] *Ludlow* v. *Burgess* [1971] Crim. LR 238.

a police officer. The Divisional Court held that detaining someone against their will without arresting them was unlawful and, therefore, could not have been done in the execution of the constable's duty. When the youths assaulted the constable in order to get him away from their friend they were not guilty of a section 51 (1) offence.

Pedro v. *Diss*[29] concerned a policeman questioning a black man outside his brother's house. The man felt that he was being harassed by the police and did not answer questions, but replied as the case shows, in a rude manner. The policeman searched him and tried to take him 'around the corner to the house'. Finally, the man assaulted the police officer and was arrested. In this case, the policeman tried to found his detention of the appellant in reliance on section 66 of the Metropolitan Police Act 1839 which seemed to suggest that a power of 'detention' existed. The Lord Chief Justice, Lord Lane, said that if a Metropolitan Police Officer was relying on section 66, the rule in *Christie* v. *Leachinsky*[30] still applied and the detainee must be told that he was being detained, and on what grounds such detention was being made.

On the basis of these two cases it therefore seems that where the police have clearly acted officiously, so as to take themselves out of a reasonable approach in dealing with the public and using their (de facto) powers on the street, the courts may see their actions as not being in the execution of their duty in relation to a charge under section 51 (1). It does not, however, seem quite so clear that the courts are prepared to narrow down a police officer's exercise of duty in relation to the more minor offence of 'obstruction', as we have seen above.

The Police Federation Conference in Blackpool in May 1987 complained strongly against the growth of assaults on police officers,[31] and asked for mandatory prison sentences for those convicted. The Crown Prosecution Service was accused of not prosecuting for assaults on the police where there were no clear injuries and plea bargaining such charges for guilty pleas on more minor charges.[32] In October 1987, a policeman brought a successful private prosecution against a man who had assaulted him after the Crown Prosecution Service dropped the case.[33] It seems that the CPS may be exerting a strong influence in these cases and this may prove particularly important in relation to demonstrations.

[29] *Pedro v. Diss* [1981] 2 All ER 59.
[30] *Christie* v. *Leachinsky* [1947] 1 All ER 567.
[31] *The Times*, 21 May 1987.
[32] *The Times*, 20 May 1987.
[33] *The Times*, 18 Oct. 1987.

Obstruction of the Highway

In chapter 3 the importance and status of the public highway for demonstrations and protest was considered. In this section we will consider the specific charges of obstruction of the highway which so often occur in demonstration and protest cases. The bulk of the reported cases do not concern protesters. Some cases involve industrial unrest and a number of cases relate to stalls parked on a highway, used for the sale of food or other goods.

Williams[34] quotes numerous cases which did not reach appellate court level involving public speakers and protesters from Salvationists in 1886, through Suffragettes in 1905 and on to the Nuclear Disarmament supporters in the 1960s. He specifically quotes a 1939 case where five men sat down outside the Savoy Hotel with posters saying 'Hungry Leisure is no Pleasure'. There were also prosecutions for obstruction after road safety demonstrations in Putney Vale in 1961 and Camden in 1966. A very large number of the campaigners for Nuclear Disarmament in the early 1960s who demonstrated by sitting down in front of public buildings or in public squares were also arrested for obstruction of the highway.

Some of the most important cases did, however, actually concern demonstrators. In *Homer* v. *Cadman*[35] the defendant was convicted under section 72 of the Highways Act 1835 for obstruction of the Bull Ring at Sedgley (a highway) even though the whole area of the highway was not obstructed, and people and traffic could still pass and repass.

Two more recent cases in 1963 exhibit the workings of both the statutory and common law obstruction offences. In 1963 the case of Pat Arrowsmith, the veteran peace campaigner, came before the Divisional Court on a charge under section 121 of the Highways Act 1959,

> If a person without lawful authority or excuse in any way wilfully obstructs the free passage along the highway he shall be guilty of an offence and shall be liable in respect thereof to a fine...[36]

Pat Arrowsmith had been addressing a meeting in Nelson Street, Bootle, on 7 May 1962, at a place which had commonly been used for open air meetings and was the local equivalent of 'Hyde Park Corner' or 'Speakers Corner' in London. At one point during her speech the crowd blocked the entire road, but she asked them to move with the result that vehicles

---

[34] Williams, *Keeping the Peace*, pp. 205–16.
[35] *Homer* v. *Cadman* (1886) 16 Cox CC 51.
[36] Now s. 137 (1) of the Highways Act 1980.

could then pass. Miss Arrowsmith argued before the Divisional Court that any obstruction of the highway by her could not have been 'wilfully' since she had a genuine belief that she had 'lawful authority or excuse', even though that authority or excuse did not, in fact, exist. In other words, she attempted to use the word 'wilfully' as a means of attaching *mens rea* to the 'without lawful authority or excuse' clause. The Divisional Court spent little time in rejecting these arguments[37] and it seems clear that it would be difficult on this basis to defend successfully any charge of highway obstruction under the Act.

In the same year the case of George Clark, another veteran Nuclear Disarmament campaigner, came before the courts in relation to a procession he led around the Piccadilly area during the visit of Greek royalty on 9 July 1963. He was charged with incitement to the common law offence of public nuisance by causing an obstruction in the highway resulting from a crowd of 500 – 2000 people following him in an attempt to circumvent police cordons around Whitehall. Clark had been sentenced to 18 months imprisonment at the County of London sessions. The Court of Criminal Appeal allowed the appeal because the jury had not been directed to consider whether the use of the highway was, in all circumstances, unreasonable.[38] Since the issue of reasonableness had not been put to the jury Clark was allowed to go free. His counsel's contention was that,

> the question was whether, granted that there was an obstruction, there was an unreasonable use of the highway, bearing in mind that this procession on the face of it, and unless it did amount to a public nuisance, was, under our law, perfectly lawful.[39]

The result of this case would seem to suggest that a procession is not, by its very nature, an unreasonable obstruction of the highway, but it should be noted that no direct statement to that effect appears in the case. It should also be noted that this case was brought under the common law of nuisance rather than under the Highways Act. Nevertheless, it is an important decision and it should be noted that a moving procession which actually does proceed from one place to another, and does not simply go round in a circle, may well be a reasonable use of the highway.[40] Thus, a meeting on the highway may,

[37] *Arrowsmith* v. *Jenkins* [1963] 2 QB 561.
[38] *Clark* [1964] 2 QB 315.
[39] See Williams, *Keeping the Peace*, p. 216.
[40] See *Tynan* v. *Balmer* [1967] 1 QB 91, in which some forty pickets walked around in a circle in a service road which was part of the highway near the main entrance to a factory. Even though industrial picketing was allowed under s. 2 of the Trade Disputes Act 1906, obstruction of the highway was taking place and, therefore, the picket was stopped.

by its nature be an unreasonable user; but a procession will not *prima facie* be unreasonable.

Some of the non-demonstration cases have helped this form of argument in relation to cases under the Highways Act. *Nagy* v. *Weston*[41] stated that on a charge under section 121 (1) of the Highways Act 1959 it was necessary to prove that the use of the highway was unreasonable even if there was an obstruction. This was a question of fact

> depending on all the circumstances, including the length of time the obstruction continues, the place where it occurs, the purpose for which it occurs, and whether it does in fact cause an actual obstruction as opposed to a potential obstruction.[42]

This ruling was adopted recently in relation to demonstrations in a case involving an Animal Rights protest outside a fur shop. The line of nuisance cases starting with *Lowdens* v. *Keaveney*,[43] was linked into *Nagy* v. *Weston* for the first time. In *Hirst and Agu* v. *Chief Constable of West Yorkshire*[44] protesters were convicted of obstruction of the highway, contrary to section 137 Highways Act 1980 at the Magistrates Court, and this was confirmed on appeal to the Crown Court. The Divisional Court, however, quashed the conviction because the Crown Court had not considered the reasonableness of the appellants' conduct. 'Lawful excuse' would include activities otherwise lawful in themselves which were reasonable in all the circumstances. Mr Justice Otton said that reasonableness would allow a proper balance and 'freedom of protest on issues of public concern would be given the recognition it deserves'.

Master of the Rolls, Lord Denning's statements in *Hubbard* v. *Pitt* (in dissent and obiter) to this effect were given an airing and a three-question approach was adopted. The Court was to ask whether (i) there was an obstruction, (ii) whether it was wilful or deliberate, and (iii) whether it was without lawful authority or excuse. If a demonstration itself was reasonable any obstruction would have a lawful excuse.

Hirst seems to be an interesting departure both from an absolutist view of the section and the tradition of not advocating free speech in cases deciding in favour of such freedom. It is interesting to see that a subsequent case dealing with a fruit and vegetable stall on the highway, *Pugh* v. *Pigden and Powley*[45] has expressly followed Lord Justice Glidewell's adoption of *Nagy* in *Hirst*. Although *Pugh* is not a

---

[41] *Nagy* v. *Weston* [1965] 1 All ER 78.
[42] Ibid., 80.
[43] *Lowdens* v. *Keaveney* [1903] 2 IR 83.
[44] *Hirst and Agu* v. *Chief Constable of West Yorkshire* 85, Crim. App. Rep. 143, [1987] Crim. LR 336.
[45] *Pugh* v. *Pigden and Powley* (1987) 151 JP 664 and transcript.

demonstration case such support will still be useful for demonstrators. Some caution is still in order. So many cases had previously assumed that a standing demonstration on a highway was not, in fact, a lawful use of the highway, that the courts are likely to be a little wary in adopting the new approach too quickly. It should also be remembered that another line of cases says that it is extremely difficult to establish 'a lawful excuse'. Where a stall keeper had sought permission from police and local authority officials for a stall and been assessed for, and paid, rates on the stall in the highway he could still be guilty of obstruction under the Act.[46] This line of cases seems to have been contradicted in *Pugh*. These cases were not considered in *Hirst* and it will be interesting to see how these new developments progress.

In summary, therefore, most of the cases seem to show little difficulty in proving obstruction of the highway. There are some hiccups where trial courts do not seem to consider whether there was, in fact, an obstruction or whether such obstruction was unreasonable. Demonstrators may be able to find themselves under this form of defence if they have been involved in a procession, and even a standing demonstration, but probably not a meeting. It is a fairly narrow gateway since this defence hands back to the magistrates the decision of fact based upon 'all the circumstances' as set out in *Nagy* v. *Weston*. The magistrates may be keener to find an obstruction than Mr Justice Otton is to preserve freedom of speech.

Conclusion

Both offences of obstructing the police in the exercise of their duty and of obstructing the highway have been shown to be broad offences potentially covering a wide area of human activity, much of it unremarkable. By leaving a large amount of discretion to the police to decide whether to prosecute in any one particular case, these offences leave the police open to the charge of favouring one group as opposed to another.

Once again, the law has been left intentionally vague so that discretion can be used at police and court level. *Hirst* is an important step towards stating more clearly how far a police officer can haul demonstrators off the street whether or not they are blocking anyone's way. However, the

---

[46] *Cambridgeshire County Council* v. *Rust* [1972] 3 All ER 231; see also *London Borough of Redbridge* v. *Jaques* [1971] 1 All ER 262.

section 51 offence still leaves the constable with total discretion to create offences out of unobjectionable behaviour. The law remaining as it is, is clearly of benefit to the police, but the situation does not add to the clarity of the law or the general respect for it.

7

Preventing Violence and Extremism: Weapons and Uniforms

In previous chapters we have looked at a number of offences relating to behaviour on demonstrations, some of which have included offences of violence. Those offences such as riot and affray, which have included the use or threat of violence, are set within the context of speech or action tending to result in violence. In this chapter we look at offences dealing with behaviour on the other side of the line.

Where protesters or organized demonstrators dress in paramilitary uniforms, or involve themselves in illegal training and drilling or possessing offensive weapons, a different kind of protest exists with a prior intention of organization for (at least) the appearance of violence. This chapter will look at offences relating to these forms of behaviour against the background of some of the different groups who have been offenders against these crimes aimed at political extremism. Whilst looking at the law in this chapter no judgment is expressly made on the morality of the use of violence which was discussed in chapter 1.

Possession of an Offensive Weapon

There is now one major statutory offence of possession of an offensive weapon.[1] The Prevention of Crime Act 1963 section 1 contains this main provision amended slightly by the Public Order Act 1986 Schedule 2, and the Police and Criminal Evidence Act 1984 section 26 (1) (in relation to arrestability). A total of 5567 people were found guilty of possessing an offensive weapon in 1985.[2]

The main thrust of the offence is to prevent violence occurring as a

[1] Since the repealing of s. 4 of the Public Order Act 1936 and of the relevant part of s. 4 of the Vagrancy Act 1824 by the Public Order Act, 1986, Schedule 3.
[2] Home Office figures.

result of the possession or carrying of an offensive weapon in a public place. However, many of the prosecutions result from circumstances in which the weapon has already been used for violent purposes, which use is added to the evidence to prove the crime. Adding such charges of possession to existing assault charges has been frowned on by the courts

> in such a case the additional count does nothing except add to the complexity of the case and the possibility of confusion of the jury. This has in fact occurred.[3]

However, a prosecutor uncertain of a guilty verdict on an assault charge might well include the 'possession' charge in order to be sure of obtaining at least one guilty verdict, or in order to give some leeway for plea bargaining by the defendant who might feel that it was better to plead guilty to the lesser 'possession' charge if the assault charge were to be dropped by the prosecutor.

Section 1 of the Prevention of Crime Act 1953 (as amended) reads as follows,

> Any person who without lawful authority or reasonable excuse, the proof whereof shall lie on him, has with him in any public place any offensive weapon shall be guilty of an offence and shall be liable
>
> (a) on summary conviction, to imprisonment for a term not exceeding three months or a fine not exceeding the statutory maximum or both;
> (b) on conviction on indictment, to imprisonment for a term not exceeding two years or a fine, or both.

An offensive weapon is defined in section 1 (4) as,

> any article made or adapted for use for causing injury to the person, or intended by the person having it with him for such use by him or by some other person.[4]

The Act seems to create three different categories of offensive weapon:

(1) Any article made for use for causing injury to the person (including, e.g. clubs, coshes and flick knives).[5]
(2) Any article adapted for use for causing injury to the person (including,

---

[3] *Ohlson* v. *Hylton* [1975] 2 All ER 491 at 494, and see A. J. Ashworth, 'Liability for Carrying Offensive Weapons' [1976] Crim. LR 725.
[4] The last five words were introduced by Schedule 2 of the Public Order Act 1986.
[5] See *R.* v. *Hutchinson* [1784] 1 Leach 339, Police Truncheon – *Houghton* v. *Chief Constable of Greater Manchester, The Times*, 24 July 1986 and *R.* v. *Simpson* [1983] 3 All 789.

e.g. bottles with their tops broken, bicycle chains with edges sharpened, a sock filled with sand, and specially sharpened knives).[6]
(3) Any article intended by the person having it with him for such use by him or by some other person (including, e.g. a car jack, ordinary knives, drawing pins, and a tin of red paint).[7]

The system of proof in such cases is a little complex and worthy of some study. With respect to all three categories the prosecution have to prove that a defendant had the article with him in a public place, and in the case of category 3 also that the defendant had the intention to use the article for causing injury to the person. Articles falling under categories 1 or 2 are often referred to as articles which are 'offensive *per se*' and judicial notice may be taken of such fact in a direction to the jury. The main difficulties in the case law arise out of the third category, and often in cases where the prosecution attempt to prove the offence as a result of a subsequent use of the article for a violent purpose.

Where violence occurs on demonstrations and protests police often charge demonstrators with possession offences. Cases include a defendant alleged to have scattered drawing pins and upholstery pins on the Rugby Football pitch during a match involving visiting Springboks in 1976[8] and a defendant who threw a tin of red paint at the Prime Minister as a protest against the result of the 1970 election.[9] Although it is not known whether such practices have continued, the inquiry into the activities of Inspector Challenor in 1967 showed that there were occasions where police had 'planted' offensive weapons, such as pieces of brick in the pockets of demonstrators after their arrest, so that they could be charged with an offensive weapons offence.[10] The 'Agit Prop' publication, *Bust Book. The People versus Regina – about Law* published in the early 1970s contained the following advice for demonstrators under the heading 'Dressed for the Occasion',

7. Always check what you have in your pockets, bag etc., bearing in mind that if you have a penknife, nail file, marbles or even too many coppers they could use 'possession of offensive weapons' as their excuse

---

[6] See Supperstone, *Brownlie*, p. 149 and [1966] Crim LR 49.
[7] See *R.* v. *Dayle* [1974] 1 WLR 181, *Woodward* v. *Koessler* [1958] 3 All ER 557 and Supperstone, *Brownlie*, p. 150. Recent examples include a padlock and chain *R.* v. *Morgan*, *The Times*, 21 May 1987, machete knife and catapult used for killing grey squirrels (not offensive) *Southwell* v. *Chadwick*, *The Times*, 8 Jan. 1987 and a knotted chain *R.* v. *Lewis* [1986] Crim. App. Rev. 314.
[8] See *The Times*, 9 Jan. 1970 and Supperstone, *Brownlie*, p. 161.
[9] *Wright, The Times*, 23 June 1970 and see Supperstone, *Brownlie*, p. 150.
[10] The Challenor Inquiry, Cmnd 2735 and see ch. 8.

for charging you... Trousers with pockets sewn up can make planting a bit more difficult.

Placards or banners on sticks can end up being used for violent purposes on demonstrations, either by the person carrying the placard or banner, or by somebody else. One example is the wooden flag poles carried by the National Front at Red Lion Square on 15 June 1974,[11] which had sharp aluminium tops, and might easily have been used for violent purposes. Such articles in the possession of demonstrators would probably be considered under category 3 above (unless some attempt had been made specifically to sharpen the end with a view to causing injury). The question then arises whether if, in the heat of the moment, demonstrators use a category 3 article, they can be said to have had the article with them for the purpose of causing injury under category 3 above.

Doubt has been caused by contradictory statements in *R.* v. *Jura*[12] and the case of *Woodward* v. *Koessler*[13] as to whether it was possible to have formed 'the intention' 'by the person having it with him' to use such an article for causing injury to the person, instantaneously with the adoption of such an article for such use.

Woodward v. *Koessler* involved a sheath knife, of the sort used by boy scouts, intended to be used to force an exit door into a cinema by a youngster who was then confronted with the cinema commissionaire. The boy threatened him with the knife and was found to have been guilty of possession of an offensive weapon. In *Jura* a man shooting an air rifle at a funfair became annoyed, and turned round with the air rifle and fired it at his girlfriend. He was convicted of assault and also with possession of an offensive weapon. The Divisional Court held that no offence had been committed under the Prevention of Crime Act 1963 since it was the *use* of the rifle and not its *possession* which had been unlawful.

The dilemma caused by these conflicting cases seems to have been resolved by *Ohlson* and *Hylton*[14] which favoured the *Jura* approach. In *Ohlson* v. *Hylton* an altercation occurred at the door of a crowded underground train at Blackfriars Station in London during the afternoon rush hour in January 1974. As a result, the defendant, a carpenter returning home with his tools, reached for a hammer from his brief case and hit another passenger on the head with it. Lord Chief Justice Widgery in the Divisional Court held that there was no offence under

[11] See ch. 1.
[12] *R.* v. *Jura* [1954] 1 All ER 696.
[13] *Woodward* v. *Koessler* [1958] 3 All ER 557.
[14] *Ohlson* v. *Hylton* [1975] 2 All ER 490.

section 1 of the Prevention of Crime Act, 'where an accused seized a weapon for instant use on his victim'.[15] It would seem, therefore, that a placard bearer would not be guilty of possession of an offensive weapon under these circumstances. However, anybody walking around with stones, pieces of concrete or other items on a demonstration with no obvious lawful authority or reasonable excuse which could be proved, may well be charged and convicted.

It seems that it would not be possible for a demonstrator to plead possession of an offensive weapon for the purposes of self-defence. A large number of cases show that offensive weapons may not be carried, even by security guards[16] or taxi drivers at risk from violent passengers.[17] If there is a real threat it must be an imminent one and going to a demonstration with articles intended for self-defence simply because rival demonstrators may be expected to cause trouble is most unlikely to be accepted as a defence to the charge.[18]

Another possibility is that a demonstrator might form an intention to use an object such as a banner pole carried by somebody else, for causing injury on a demonstration if the occasion arose. This would set up the rather strange situation in which A is holding a banner on a demonstration and, unbeknown to A, B five rows back has formed the intention, if necessary, to use that banner for causing injury. If it can be proved that such intention was there (perhaps as a result of a police *agent provocateur* overhearing a comment), the offence would seem to have been committed.[19]

The Home Secretary, Douglas Hurd, reacting to representations by the Police Federation[20] announced at the Conservative Conference in October 1987 at Blackpool the Government's intentions to tighten the law in relation to the carrying of knives. The carrying of any knife would be made illegal and the burden of proof of showing a proper reason for carrying a knife would be on the defendant.

At a meeting of the Metropolitan Police federated ranks in September, Mr Hurd had amplified his plans of giving the police power to stop and search people on suspicion that they are carrying a knife or a blade. Such changes were to find their way into the Criminal Justice Bill.[21] It remains to be seen how such changes would affect demonstrators.

---

[15] Ibid., 491.
[16] See *R. v. Spanner, Poulter and Ward* [1973] Crim LR 704.
[17] *Grieve v. McCloud* [1967] Crim LR 424.
[18] See *Bradley v. Moss* [1974] Crim LR 430.
[19] As a result of the addition of the last five words to s. 1 (4) by Schedule 2 of the Public Order Act 1986 even A may be guilty if he formed an intention for someone else to use the banner. And see *R. v. Edmonds* [1963] 2 QB 142 for joint control and Supperstone, *Brownlie*, p. 153 for possession by an innocent agent.
[20] See *The Times* 12 Sept. 1987.
[21] See *The Times*, 21 Sept. 1987; but see letter from the 'Metropolitan Police "Knives"

Firearms and Explosives

Firearms and explosives are beyond the scope of this book which aims to deal with the general picture of protest rather than instances involving terrorism where severe violence and injury are caused or intended. However, one item which deserves a mention is *R. v. Bouch*[22] which decides that a petrol bomb, used frequently in the civil disorders in 1981, is an 'explosive substance' under the Explosive Substances Act 1883. A person can therefore be charged with making an explosive substance contrary to section 3 (1) (b) of the Explosive Substances Act 1883 with intent to endanger life or cause serious injury to property if they are involved in making petrol bombs.

Wearing Uniforms in Connection with Political Objects

The prohibition on wearing uniforms in connection with political objects contrary to section 1 of the Public Order Act 1936 (which is unaffected by the new Public Order Act) seems rather strange outside of the historical context in which the 1936 Act was passed, being the rise of the Fascist parties in England and their use of militaristic uniforms in order to signify and publicize their membership of those organizations.

Joseph Baker's book *The Law of Political Uniforms Public Meetings and Private Armies*[23] which was published 2 years after the Act notes some of the early cases including one relating to conduct on 2 January 1937 in Leeds, the day after the Act came into force. In *Wood*[24] the defendant was selling a political newspaper, whilst wearing a black peaked cap with a flash of lightning in a circle and the fasces (a hatchet bound up with a bundle of rods) which were the emblems of the British Union of Fascists. He also wore a black shirt, black tie and black overcoat. He was fined 40 shillings.

Four weeks later the prospective Fascist parliamentary candidate for East Hull was charged with wearing a dark navy blue woollen pullover tucked into black trousers, 'a black belt with metal buckles on which was the fascist badge, and a red brassard on the left arm'. *Charnley and Others*[25] were bound over to be of good behaviour for 6 months and

---

Campaign Co-ordinator' suggesting no additional powers are intended – *The Times*, 14 Nov. 1987.
[22] *R. v. Bouch* [1982] 3 All ER 918.
[23] J. Baker, *The Law of Political Uniforms, Public Meetings and Private Armies* (London, Gollancz, 1938), pp. 1ff.
[24] *Wood* (1937) 101 JP 90.
[25] *Charnley and Others* (1937) 81 Sol. J. 108.

ordered to pay prosecution costs. Similar cases occurred against *Irvine*, in Birmingham and the 'green shirt' cases of *Wright* in Lambeth, and *Taylor* in Luton.[26] In both *Wright* and *Taylor* the defendants appeared to be wearing the same sort of clothes, but in *Wright* the charge was proved whereas in *Taylor* the bench dismissed the case.

Section 1 of the Public Order Act 1936 provides:

Prohibition of uniforms in connection with political objects.
(i) Subject as hereinafter provided, any person who in any public place, or at any public meeting wears uniform signifying his association with any political organisation or with the promotion of any political object shall be guilty of an offence:
Provided that, if the chief officer of police is satisfied that the wearing of any such uniform as aforesaid on any ceremonial, anniversary, or other special occasion will not be likely to involve risk of any public disorder, he may, with the consent of a Secretary of State by order, permit the wearing of such uniform on that occasion either absolutely or subject to such conditions as may be specified in the order.

The consent of the Attorney General is required for a prosecution under section 1, which should have the effect of preventing an uneven prosecution policy.

The only major prosecutions since the 1930s which are documented involve *Percival and Others*,[27] twelve participants in a Ku-Klux Klan cross-burning rite in 1965, and *O'Moran* and *Whelan*[28] a prosecution of IRA supporters in 1975. In the Ku-Klux Clan case, seven people were charged under section 1 and received sentences ranging from fines of £20 to 3 months' imprisonment at Rugby Magistrates Court. The *O'Moran* case went to the Divisional Court on the question of how much of a uniform was necessary, and how to prove that a uniform signified the wearer's association with a political organization or promotion of a political object. *O'Moran* arose out of events involving the funeral march of Michael Gaughan, an IRA prisoner who died in the Isle of Wight. A military style march went in front of the coffin around Cricklewood and Kilburn, and into the church of the Sacred Heart in Quex Road, Kilburn in London. *O'Moran* called out commands to the 'party' or 'colour party'. Each of the defendants wore a black or very dark blue beret, dark glasses, black roll-necked pullovers and other very dark clothing. They were warned that they would be reported for wearing a political uniform, but continued to wear it. They appeared the next day in similar clothing and led the coffin to a meeting before

[26] *Taylor* (1937) 81 Sol. J. 509.
[27] *Percival and Others, The Times*, 8 Oct. 1965.
[28] *O'Moran and Whelan* [1975] QB 864.

a crowd of some 5000 – 6000 people. Sergeant Garnham of the Ceremonial Division at Cannon Row police station gave evidence about the wearing of dark glasses and dark clothing with black berets signifying connection with Irish political organisations. Under cross-examination 'he accepted that on the day previously a black beret and dark clothing had been the predominant dress at a demonstration by Greek Cypriots and that black berets were habitually worn by French onion sellers'.[29]

The case of *Whelan*, heard at the same time by the Divisional Court involved a group of 300 people gathered at Speakers Corner intending to march to Downing Street with a petition and then on to the Embankment. Black berets were distributed from a box and a number of people placed them on their heads. A chief inspector warned the marchers that the wearing of political uniforms was a criminal offence and told them 'that included the black berets and sunglasses and asked the marchers to remove their berets'. One of the leaders, according to the case stated, said words to this effect:

> Supporters of the Political Hostages Campaign, we have been warned by the fascist police that anyone wearing the black beret will be arrested before he leaves the park. You know what to do. You know what the beret means to the Provisionals.[30]

The defendants continued to wear black berets, and some of them also had a flag or a banner and dark glasses. One James Henry DeVere was discharged by the magistrate because 'although he was satisfied that DeVere was wearing a black beret at the march and distributing IRA badges, he accepted DeVere's evidence that he wore a black beret as his usual headdress and had not adopted it for this occasion in order to signify his association with the Provisional Sinn Fein'.[31]

Lord Chief Justice Widgery, in the first case to go on appeal under the section, said that 'wearing' implied an 'article of wearing apparel' and, therefore, would not include a badge by itself. However, a 'beret, dark glasses, the pullovers and the other dark clothing, were clearly worn and therefore satisfy the first requirement of the section'.

Where people were marching together and in association even one common article 'such as a beret' 'can be regarded as uniform without any proof that it has been previously used as such'.[32] The deliberate adoption of an identical article of attire shows that it is intended to be a uniform showing association between the people. Although he suggested

[29] Ibid., 475.
[30] Ibid., 477.
[31] Ibid., 479.
[32] Ibid., 480.

that this would be subject to the *de minimis* rule, he felt that was not important in this case where many of the defendants wore more than just a beret. Lord Widgery said it was also possible to prove that an article constituted uniform by showing that it 'was commonly used, or had been frequently used' by members of a particular organization. It was not necessary to prove previous use of the article if on the day in question it was used by people 'adopting a similar style of dress in order to show their mutual association one with the other'.[33]

The next question was how to prove that the uniform signified the association of the wearer with a political organization. Lord Chief Justice Widgery said that the prosecution could show that the article 'has been used in the past as the uniform of a recognised association' and 'is associated with a particular organization'. However, he felt it was not necessary for a particular organization to be specified provided it could be 'capable of identification in some manner'. Alternatively, it was possible to show the significance of the uniform and its association with a political organization simply 'from the events to be seen on the occasion when the alleged uniform was worn'. Assembling together and wearing a piece of uniform to indicate association one with the other, and with other activity of a political character would be enough for the purposes of that section. In the particular circumstances of the case issuing banners carrying political slogans and black berets to persons taking part in a demonstration with political object, or being involved in a colour party at a militaristic IRA funeral involving highly political speeches 'was ample evidence that the black berets were being worn to signify the wearers' association with a political organisation or with a promotion of a political object'.[34]

Under the Prevention of Terrorism (Temporary Provisions) Act 1984 section 2 it is also prohibited to wear any item of dress or wear, carry or display any article, in a public place, in such a way or in such circumstances as to arouse reasonable apprehension of membership or support of the IRA and the Irish National Liberation Army.[35]

In summary, the wearing of any apparel signifying association with other people and some political object would be sufficient to fall foul of section 1 of the 1936 Act. Offences under that section are punishable on summary conviction by a maximum of 3 months' imprisonment or a fine not exceeding level 4, or both.

[33] Ibid., 481. Twins wearing the same clothes would of course be wearing a 'uniform' under this definition, but not for political purposes.
[34] Ibid., 474.
[35] See Prevention of Terrorism (Temporary Provisions) Act 1984 Schedule 1.

Prohibition of Quasi-Military Organizations

Carrying on its philosophy of controlling the (then) new fascist organizations, section 2 of the 1936 Public Order Act aimed at preventing the organizing, training or equipping the members of an association for using or displaying physical force in promoting a political object. Section 2 is wordy and difficult to read. Joseph Baker[36] makes much of a distinction between paragraphs (i) (a) and (i) (b) of section 2. The section reads as follows:

(i) If the members or adherents of any association of persons, whether incorporated or not, are –
(a) organised or trained or equipped for the purpose of enabling them to be employed in usurping the functions of the police or of the armed forces of the Crown; or
(b) organised and trained or organised and equipped either for the purpose of enabling them to be employed for the use or display of physical force in promoting any political object, or in such manner as to arouse reasonable apprehension that they are organised and either trained or equipped for that purpose; then any person who takes part in control or management of the association, or in so organising or training as aforesaid any members or adherents thereof, shall be guilty of an offence under this section:

There is a proviso allowing a defence for anyone so charged to prove that they neither consented to nor connived at the organization, training or equipping of members or adherents of the association. The consent of the Attorney General is needed for a prosecution. Special rules are contained in section 2 (4) allowing the prosecution to use material in evidence (to show the purpose or character of the association and to prove the manner in which its members are organized, trained and equipped,) which would otherwise be inadmissible. According to Baker, 'for example, it will not be necessary for the prosecution to show that, say, the drilling of members was done in the presence of the accused, or that orders were given in his presence'.[37]

Section 2 (1) (a) seems to be aimed at any militaristic organization which might 'usurp' the functions of the police or the armed forces. Section 2 (1) (b) is a little bit clearer in its aim of reference to the promotion of a political object, an object that must have been clear to the legislators at the time, but does not wear well with age. It should

[36] Baker, *The Law of Political Uniforms*, pp. 37–41.
[37] Ibid., 40.

be noted that it is not the members or adherents of the association who commit the offence, but only a person who takes part in the control or management of the association, or in organizing or training. Offences under this section are liable to a maximum penalty on indictment of 2 years imprisonment and/or a fine, and on summary conviction to 6 months imprisonment and/or a fine not exceeding the statutory maximum.

Only two major cases are known, one involving a Fascist movement in 1963 and the other involving the Free Wales Army in 1969. In the Free Wales Army case in 1969 three of the nine defendants were convicted of taking part in organizing and training a quasi-military organization, two of whom were sentenced to 15 months imprisonment and a third to 9 months imprisonment.[38]

R. v. Jordan and Tyndall[39] was also a prosecution under section 2 (1) (b) relating to the activities of a neo-Nazi movement known as Spearhead. The evidence which was well publicized by photographs in a popular Sunday newspaper of the time, was that in August 1961 eighteen members of Spearhead had been wearing items of uniform and practising foot drill. In April and May of 1962 members 'were seen carrying out attack and defence exercises at a tower building. They were wearing items of uniform and exchanged Nazi salutes; on the second occasion they made the salutes to a Nazi flag'. In August of 1962 they held a camp at which speeches were made about the Aryan race and the Horst Wessel song was sung. Documents were found at the area headquarters of the movement containing references to the German National Socialist Storm Troopers, and phrases such as 'Task Force', 'Front Line Fighters' and 'Fighting Efficiency'. Tins of sodium chloride were found which would have been enough to make 100 mills bombs and on one tin the words 'weed killer' had been struck out and substituted with the words 'Jew Killer'.

The question left to the jury was whether the manner in which the members of Spearhead were organized was such as to arouse reasonable apprehension that they were organized to be employed for the use or display of physical force in promoting a political object. The Court of Criminal Appeal held that it was not necessary to show evidence of specific trainings for particular attacks, general training was enough for the second part of section 2 (1) (b). Jordan (the same Colin Jordan as in *Jordan* v. *Burgoyne*)'s sentence of 9 months and Tindall's sentence of 6 months imprisonment were upheld, 'the only doubt the court had felt was whether the sentences were adequate'.[40]

[38] *The Times*, 2 July 1969. *R.* v. *Callinan* is also reported in *The Times* on 20 Jan. 1973; see Supperstone, *Brownlie*, pp. 185, 186.
[39] *R.* v. *Jordan and Tyndall* [1963] Crim. LR 124.
[40] Ibid., 126.

It is interesting to note that the information on the National Front 'defence party' adduced in the Red Lion Square Inquiry may be close to behaviours which could be charged under section 2 (1) (b). The section 2 (1) (b) is quite wide and it could contain this form of behaviour if perhaps the members of a 'defence party' were in uniform giving rise to an impression of their being 'organized and trained or organized and equipped'.

Police Reaction to the Fascists and other Extremist Organizations

No statutory provisions could have been more precisely aimed at a specific mischief than sections 1 and 2 of the Public Order Act 1936, aimed at the Fascists. However, this seems to have been in direct contrast to the manner in which the police were favouring the Fascists at the time of the passing of the Act. Kidd, Bowes, Thompson and others all show strong evidence of the manner in which police discretion was organized. Bowes continues such evidence into the 1960s, way beyond the passage of the Act.[41]

The police reaction to the Fascists as compared to their reactions to the hunger marchers in the 1930s is legion. It is so well documented that it does not seem necessary to mention too many details here. The example most often mentioned is the 10,000 police who were provided in 1936 'through the Jewish quarters of the East End of London, ... to help 2,500 Fascists to march'.[42] This is contrasted with the 'Trenchard Ban' forbidding the holding of 'any public meeting in the vicinity of a labour exchange'[43] where many of the 1930s unemployed held their demonstrations.

According to Pritt and Bowes the pro-Fascist police attitude continued well beyond the war. Pritt specifically mentions the police practice of 'taking names' at public meetings.[44] Section 6 of the 1936 Public Order Act had made it possible for the chairman of a meeting to use a police constable to obtain the name and address of any person who according to the chairman of the meeting 'acts in a disorderly manner for the purpose of preventing the transaction of the business for which the

[41] See R. Kidd, *British Liberty in Danger*, ch. 5 (London, Lawrence & Wishart, 1940), ch. 5, 'The Police'; *The Autobiography of D. N. Pritt, Part II, Brass Hats and Bureaucrats* (London, Lawrence & Wishart, 1966), ch. 4, 'Government Favouring Fascists'; and S. Bowes, *The Police and Civil Liberties* (London, Lawrence & Wishart, 1966), ch. 3, 'The Police and the Fascists'.
[42] Pritt, *Brass Hats and Bureaucrats*, p. 74.
[43] Ibid., p. 74.
[44] Ibid., pp. 58–64.

meeting was called together, or incites others so to act'.[45] This power was being misused by chairmen of Fascist meetings to obtain the names and addresses of any hecklers, and as a result numbers of people were subsequently attacked by the Fascists in or around their homes, after their names had been taken at meetings. These events, monitored by Pritt and made known by him to the Home Secretary, occurred in 1947.

Thus the Act, which was supposedly intended to deal with the horrors of Fascist marches and meetings, was being used by the police directly to favour them. Pritt notes how, towards the end of 1946 and through 1947, there were Fascist meetings week after week in Ridley Road, Hackney, a largely Jewish area, 'at which they both preached and practiced violent brutalities against Jews and Communists'. Although the Second World War had recently been fought against Fascism, it was always outsiders to the meetings who were prosecuted while the Fascists were allowed to continue using language clearly calculated to cause a breach of the peace.[46]

The result of allowing the Fascists to continue in this controversial manner was clear. In April, only eight policemen were needed at the meetings. By July of 1947 fifty constables were needed and on 7 September this grew to some three hundred. Numerous reports exist of police violence and bad language to Jewish protesters. One infamous case concerns the comment of an inspector, asked by a reporter how they had allowed some thugs to beat up a Jewish man, who was then charged by the police 'with creating a disturbance'. His answer was, 'if a few more of the bleeders got that treatment, we'd be freer of Jews along here'.[47] It was the police officers on the spot, with views such as these who were (and are) given the power of discretion.

Continuing into the late 1940s the banning powers of section 3 of the Public Order Act (passed with the intention of dealing with Fascist marches) was used cleverly by the Fascists to obtain a ban on May Day marches for some years running. According to Pritt, the Fascists would attempt to stage a provocative march for that day. The result was that the Metropolitan Police Commissioner would have to ask the Home Secretary for a ban on marches. May Day workers' processions, which had become traditional, were thereby also stopped. Bowes[48] sets out a table of occurrences between 1960 and 1962 in which Mosleyite and other Fascist supporters had no police action taken against them, compared with numerous arrests and prosecutions against anti-Fascist

---

[45] Section 6, Public Order Act 1936.
[46] Pritt, *Brass Hats and Bureaucrats*, p. 67.
[47] Ibid., p. 71.
[48] Bowes, *The Police and Civil Liberties*, pp. 68–9.

demonstrators on the same occasions, often for relatively mild comments and actions compared with those of the Fascists (table 7.1).

Although tables such as 7.1 are clearly selective in approach, the legal background of discretion and the degree of historical corroboration gives some pause to consider whether more control needs to be taken over police action. Since the police officer is the person on the spot the Crown Prosecution Service will not make much difference to this particular aspect of discretion. The police decision is exercised on the spur of the moment and it would be difficult for the Prosecution Service to contradict a *prima facie* case.

It seems clear that neo-Fascist extremist groups such as the National Front, the National Front Support Group and the British National Party are still among the most likely to commit the forms of violence and offences dealt with earlier in this chapter.

In December 1985, the European Parliament reported on its enquiry into the Rise of Fascism and Racism in Europe.[50] The Report charted the beginnings of the extreme right in Britain from 1902, with the formation of the British Brothers League at the time of large scale immigration from Eastern Europe, on through the 1930s and Sir Oswald Mosley's British Union of Fascists. The enquiry followed the growth of

Table 7.1

1962	Offence	Consequence
August 14	Spitting to show disgust at a Nazi salute.	£1 fine for 'insulting behaviour'.
August 14	Directing Nazi salute at a crowd outside Bow Street Court.	No police action against the culprits who had arrived at court by taxi.
August 21	Booing as Colin Jordan arrived at Bow Street Court.	Arrest for 'insulting behaviour'.
August 21	Directing a Nazi salute outside Bow Street Court against a crowd of 200, many of whom responded by hissing and booing.	No police action against the offender, Colin Jordan, who had just been sent for trial at the Old Bailey.[49]

[49] Ibid., p. 70.
[50] Draughtsman: Mr Dimitrios Evrignis. See also the resolution of the European Parliament adopted 16 Jan. 1986 as a result of the findings of the Committee of Inquiry.

the Mosleyite Union Movement, the National Labour Party of John Bean and Andrew Fountaine, the White Defence League, the Racial Preservation Society, the British National Party, the Greater Britain Movement (under John Tyndall), the National Socialist Movement becoming the British Movement, and the emergence of the National Front in 1967.[51] The report also remarks on the 'entryism' of extreme right wing groups such as Tory Action, Wise, The Swinton Circle and David Irving's Focus Policy Group.

International links were shown to exist between certain Arab embassies, Palastinian groups and right wing extremist groups, as well as international collusion between the National Front, the British Democratic Party and Column 88 with other neo-Nazi groups in Germany, Belgium and Italy. In view of this situation it is surprising to see such collusion as occurred in October 1977 between James Anderton the Chief Constable of Greater Manchester and the National Front National Activities organizer Martin Webster.[52] Anderton fooled counter demonstrators to the National Front demonstration by 'conniving' at the organization of a march in an unannounced area with Martin Webster heavily guarded by a police presence.

National Front officials have been charged in recent years, and sentenced for possession of offensive weapons and using threatening behaviour during rallies in Bury St Edmunds, Oldham and Stockport.[53] In November 1986, Philip Andrews, a member of the National Front National Directorate, was sentenced to 6 months imprisonment for causing actual bodily harm to a police officer after the National Front St Georges Day pageant in April 1986. John Tyndall and John Morse, both leaders of the British National Party were sentenced to 6 months imprisonment for offences under the Race Relations Act in 1986.

In November 1986, Tony East, the Youth Organizer of the British National Party, was sentenced to 3 years imprisonment for conspiracy to cause explosions. A home-made bomb exploded in his car close to the Workers Revolutionary Party headquarters in South London.[54] In 1986, Joe Pearce, the Deputy Chairman of the National Front, was sentenced to serve 12 months in prison for Race Relations Act offences and Martin Wingfield, the National Front chairman, was sent to prison after refusing to pay a fine on conviction for Race Relations Act offences.[55] Ian Stuart, a member of the National Front National Directorate and lead singer in the National Front Band 'Screwdriver'

---

[51] See pp. 48–51.
[52] See *The Times*, 8 Oct. 1977 and 12 Oct. 1977.
[53] Ajex Action Briefing March 1987.
[54] Ibid.
[55] Ajex Action Briefing, June 1986.

was also convicted of causing actual bodily harm to a number of black people he had assaulted.

Conclusion

This chapter has looked at the mid-range of offences dealing with violence and extremism on demonstrations. It has not concerned itself with either terrorism at one end of the spectrum, or insulting words or behaviour tending to cause some violence, on the other. We have looked at behaviour specific to protesters intending to cause violence or adopting a paramilitary approach to their demonstration and protest activity.

Apart from the possession of an offensive weapon offence, the other offences have rarely been charged and are little used. Offensive weapons may well undergo a major change in characterization of the offence if the government proposals go ahead. At present the major use of the offence is not against protesters, but against others carrying a weapon in a public place.

8

Control of the Police and Police Control of Demonstrations

In this chapter the focus moves away from the law as used by the police and prosecutors against demonstrators, to the law as it may be used by demonstrators against the police. We begin by considering complaints against the police, civil and criminal legal actions against the police, political control of the police at local government and central government level, criticism of police methodology and official inquiries into police action, all in the context of demonstrations.

The chapter then goes on to consider the problem of demonstrations from the police point of view. Often the police seem the major enemy of the demonstrators, whereas the real object of the demonstrators' enmity is usually some building or group of people which the police find themselves defending. As noted above, demonstrations therefore become a ritualistic game between the demonstrators and the police. Many of the problems of respect for the police force in recent years have resulted from the disparate functions they perform. For example, there are the needs of community policing with a low profile for normal police activity, and 'hard' policing of riots and major demonstrations where crowd control can get out of hand. The text therefore considers whether a 'Third Force' is advisable in the United Kingdom, to go in-between the police and the army for dealing with demonstrations. Rubber bullets and the use of other riot equipment will also be considered as will police training methods since Lord Scarman's report on the Brixton disturbances. The chapter will therefore conclude with a description of the policing of a demonstration from planning, through control and on to prosecution and review.

In this way, the two sides of the equation of controlling the police and police control will be considered and weighed.

Individual Remedies

Riot Damages

The Riot (Damages) Act 1886, which was passed after 'a spectacular outburst of rioting in the area of Trafalgar Square on 8 February 1886'.[1] enables a person who has suffered damage or loss 'by any persons riotously and tumultuously assembled together',[2] to apply for compensation from the local police authority of the district, to be 'paid out of the police rate'.[3] Where the police authority refuses or fails to fix compensation for any such claim a civil action can be bought against the police authority under the Act to recover such compensation. Cases under this act including *Field*[4] and *Munday*[5] have been mentioned in chapter 4.[6] The definition of 'riotously' in the Riot (Damages) Act is to be construed according to the definition of 'riot' in section 1 of the Public Order Act 1986.[7] This means that the number of persons involved now increases to twelve or more, as opposed to the three or more persons that would have been sufficient for the common law definition of riot.[8] It has to be proved that persons were not only 'riotously' but also 'tumultuously' assembled together. This has been taken to mean that there must be such commotion that the police ought to have taken some action in order to prevent the damage.[9]

Although it may be more difficult to prove riot since the Public Order Act 1986, it will still be an effective method for obtaining compensation where twelve or more people are involved in disorder affecting houses, shops or buildings, or any property inside them. Many insurance policies specifically exclude damage resulting from riot or civil disturbance, and it is therefore useful for there to be another form of compensation available. Compensation may also be obtained from those actually causing the damage either through a compensation order made in the Magistrates Court or through civil action. However, it may not be possible to determine the specific people involved and the police authority will therefore be a more certain defendant.

[1] D. Williams, *Keeping the Peace: The Police and Public Order* (London, Hutchinson, 1967), p. 11.
[2] Section 2 (1), Riot (Damages) Act 1886.
[3] Ibid.
[4] *Field* [1907] 2 KB 853.
[5] *Munday* [1949] 1 All ER 337.
[6] See p. 88–9.
[7] See s. 10 (1) Public Order Act 1986.
[8] See *Field*, at 853.
[9] See *J. W. Dwier Ltd.* v. *Metropolitan Police District Receiver* [1967] 2 QB 970.

The existence of this right of compensation will also, to some extent, have an effect on the police reaction to disorder, and in that sense may exert some control over a police decision whether or not to take action against those involved in a riot. In the disorders on the Broadwater Farm estate in 1985, and in disorders in the St Pauls area of Bristol in the early 1980s, the police seemed to make active decisions to withdraw from the area, either because their very presence was helping to inflame the disorder or simply to regroup for a more effective dispersal operation.[10] The Riot (Damages) Act means that the police have to think carefully before making such a decision whatever the strategic needs of the moment.

Complaints Against the Police

The Police Complaints Authority with supposedly greater powers to supervise the investigation and handling of complaints than the old Police Complaints Board, was established on 29 April 1985. Some 17,000 complaints were made in 1984 under the old system,[11] the larger proportion resulting from incivility, assault, irregularities in procedure, neglect of duty, and oppressive conduct. The chances of complaints being upheld vary between the different types of complaint[12] and also vary between types of complainant.

Although this is clearly the simplest form of action against the police and does not necessarily need the assistance of a lawyer to formulate the complaint, it also appears to be one of the least successful. Less than 10 per cent of complaints lodged in 1984 were upheld and less than 1 per cent resulted in a disciplinary hearing that went against the police officer.[13] According to the Home Office's own study 'The Police Complaints Procedure – A Survey of Complainants Views',[14] 60 per cent of respondents expressed overall dissatisfaction with the system and a further 20 per cent had mixed feelings about it.

There are also numerous disincentives for making complaints. The Police National Computer includes a special code for people who have made 'false complaints against the police'. This would include 90 per cent of those who complain. This means that if a person has a search made against them in the computer subsequently, the police would have

[10] See J. Benyon and J. Solomos, 'British Urban Unrest in the 1980s' in *The Roots of Urban Unrest*, eds Benyon and Solomos, (Oxford, Pergamon, 1987), pp. 7–10, 15–21 etc.
[11] Annual Report of Police Complaints Board 1984, Appendix C Tables II and VI (HMSO, 1985).
[12] John Harrison, *Police Misconduct: Legal Remedies* (Legal Action Group, 1987).
[13] Harrison, *Police Misconduct*, p. 9.
[14] Home Office Research Study No. 93 (HMSO) September 1987 (relating to old scheme).

reason not to treat them kindly.[15] Horrifying stories have appeared in the press regarding harassment by police officers over a 6-year period of a black man in Liverpool, who was subsequently awarded £4000 in damages as a result.[16] There have also been reports of major harassment of some Manchester students who complained about police misconduct in 1986, which harassment had caused one student to flee the country.[17]

Lord Scarman's Report on the Brixton disturbances advocated more independent control of police complaints, which resulted in the new Police Complaints Authority.[18] As quoted by Harrison[19] even the old Police Complaints Board thought that there would not be much change as a result of the new system:

> The new Authority under the reformed system are unlikely to produce more thorough results or a different outcome, but the Authority should be in a position to provide a further measure of assurance.[20]

One of the changes seems to involve more of a possibility of reconciliation between complainant and police officer concerned. However, there is a great deal of scepticism about the independence of the police in conducting their own inquiries. The report of the Home Office Research Unit itself showed that complaints by white people were three times as likely to be substantiated as those of blacks, and complaints from Asian people were about twice as successful as those of black people.[21]

Since the police conduct inquiries into their own misconduct, albeit through senior police officers from another region, there is bound to be suspicion of the manner in which such inquiries are conducted. As the police see themselves in an adversarial role,[22] it is not surprising that bringing a complaint against a police officer often results in charges, or further criminal charges, being brought against the complainant by the

---

[15] Ibid., p. 10; see also C. Pounder, *Police Computers and the Metropolitan Police* (London, GLC, 1985), p. 11.

[16] *The Times*, 9 Jul. 1985.

[17] See *The Guardian*, 22 Jul. 1985, regarding the unofficial inquiry into the original police misconduct during and after a demonstration against Mr Leon Brittain, the Home Secretary, at Manchester University, and *The Times*, 14, 15 September 1987 on the subsequent plight of police victims of harassment after their complaints; and charges of perjury against the police involved in *The Times*, 27 Feb. 1987.

[18] 'The Brixton Disorders 10–12 April 1981': Report of the Inquiry by the Rt. Hon. the Lord Scarman OBE (London, HMSO, 1981) Cmnd. 8427.

[19] Harrison, *Police Misconduct*, p. 7.

[20] Report of the Police Complaints Board 1983 (HMSO, London, 1984).

[21] P. Stevens and C. Willis, *Ethnic Minorities and Complaints Against the Police* (London, Home Office Research and Planning Unit, 1981). See also L. Lustgarten, *The Governance of Police* (London, Sweet and Maxwell, 1986), pp. 153–8.

[22] Lustgarten, *Governance of Police*, pp. 1–9.

police. These have the effect of holding the complaint in abeyance until the criminal prosecution has been heard. It also means that the first hearing of the issues involved will be in front of magistrates, where the complainant is accused rather than the police, and in a venue where police testimony is more likely to be believed.

A straw poll of fifty-five criminal specialist barristers conducted in 1986 for the *New Law Journal* found that the barristers believed that police officers committed perjury on average in three out of every ten trials.[23] The ability of the police to cover up each other's errors was shown clearly in the 'Holloway Road Transit Case' in which a conspiracy of silence prevented the truth about a vicious assault on five youths by police officers from being known for 4 years.[24]

It will be seen, therefore, that there are serious difficulties in the way of obtaining a fair or just conclusion to a police complaint. This situation only encourages a major suspicion of the police and police activities among groups in society who feel they are more likely to be oppressed by the police. It does not help the police community role, nor does it assist in the atmosphere of policing on demonstrations. This particular element of the independence of the police force seems to be a quite unnecessary barrier to trust and obedience from the general population and has probably had the effect of hiding major corruption and bribery within the police as well as more minor misconduct.

Civil Actions Against the Police

It seems to be accepted practice not to make an official complaint against the police if there is a possibility of bringing a civil action[25] since the effect of making a complaint is to give away some of the evidence, names of witnesses and the surprise element involved in trial. The most likely civil actions against the police in relation to their conduct on demonstrations would be assault, false imprisonment and malicious prosecution.

A civil suit for assault against a police officer would need to show that the officer intentionally used some physical force on the demonstrator that was not justified by law. The police officer may be able to show that only reasonable and necessary force was used according to the circumstances. It may well be especially difficult for a plaintiff to show that police action was unreasonable if the assault occurred whilst the

[23] D. Wolchover, 'Police Perjury in London', NLJ, March 1986.
[24] See R. East, 'Police Brutality: Lessons of the Holloway Road Assault', NLJ, 30 Oct. 1987 and B. Hilliard, 'Holloway Road: Unfinished Business', NLJ, 6 Nov. 1987.
[25] J. Harrison, 'Police Complaints: Pitfalls for the Unwary Litigant' [1985] 135 NLJ 1239.

police officer was involved in policing a demonstration. However, where assaults occur subsequent to the arrest of demonstrators, considerable damages can be awarded. Three women involved in a feminist demonstration, who had been assaulted with truncheons after being arrested in Soho were awarded damages ranging from £400 to £3000 in 1983.[26]

Where a demonstrator is confined by the police without any lawful excuse, a civil suit for false imprisonment against the police authority may secure damages for false imprisonment, as obtained by the young solicitor in *Wershof*.[27] Even if an original arrest is lawful, the confinement itself may be unreasonable. Where a man suspected of being a Free Wales activist was held for 21 hours in a cell and given only one 10-minute interview during that period before he was released, a jury still awarded damages of £600 although his original arrest was considered lawful.[28] A similar amount was awarded to somebody arrested unlawfully and detained for over $2\frac{1}{2}$ hours because he was wearing a police uniform and carrying a truncheon after a fancy dress party.[29]

Where the arrest itself is unlawful from the beginning it is possible to sue for wrongful arrest and false imprisonment. The veteran campaigner Pat Arrowsmith received £200 for a wrongful arrest in 1976.[30]

It is also possible to sue in court for malicious prosecution. However, for this purpose it is necessary to show that there had been some damage as a result of a police prosecution which was (i) not successful, (ii) lacked reasonable and probable cause, and (iii) in which the police acted maliciously. It is unlikely that the last element can be proved unless it can be shown that the police have concocted evidence or in some other way attempted to cover up their own wrong doing.[31] Perhaps the most memorable account of police concoction of evidence relating to demonstrations comes out of the Challenor Affair in which parts of bricks were 'planted' on demonstrators after their arrest.[32]

Suing the police takes a good deal of time, effort and finance. Legal Aid is available for such cases, provided the plaintiff is within the capital

---

[26] *Ballard, Stewart-Park and Findlay* v. *Commissioner of Police for the Metropolis* [1983] 133 NLJ 1133. Private prosecutions for assault by police officers have also had some measure of success; see Supperstone, *Brownlie*, p. 332 fn. 9 and R. Clayton and H. Tomlinson, 'Assessing Damages in Civil Actions Against the Police', LSG 25 Nov. 1987.

[27] *Wershof* [1978] 3 All ER 540.

[28] *Lawrence* v. *Chief Constable of Dyfed–Powys Police* [1983] CEL 973.

[29] *Houghton* v. *Chief Constable of Greater Manchester*, *The Times*, 24 July 1986.

[30] *The Times*, 12 Nov. 1976.

[31] See, e.g., *White and Another* v. *Metropolitan Police Commissioner*, *The Times*, 14 Apr. 1972 and *Brown* v. *Hawkes* [1891] 2 QB 798 at 722; *Sam* v. *Cluney* [1956] Crim. LR 271.

[32] See Supperstone, *Brownlie*, p. 333 and M. Grigg, *The Challenor Case* (Penguin, Harmondsworth, 1965).

and income limits and the case is considered strong by the Legal Aid scheme. Even if legal aid is available, knowing how to proceed and finding a suitable solicitor can be difficult.[33] Witnesses and other evidence have to be secured, and it may be difficult in relation to a demonstration to find witnesses who may have come from far away. Even if such witnesses can be identified, they may not wish to be involved.[34] They may specifically be wary of police retaliation against them.

However, the burden of proof is lower in the civil court, being on the balance of probabilities, than in a criminal court where guilt has to be proved beyond reasonable doubt. Although civil proceedings may be difficult, the damages obtainable can be high. A sum of £51,000 was awarded to one couple who were very badly treated by the police.[35]

In cases of false imprisonment and malicious prosecution the plaintiff has a right to have the case decided by a jury, both in the High Court and in the County Court, unless the character of the evidence cannot be conveniently dealt with by a jury. The judge has the discretion to order a jury trial in assault cases as well. A judge may be more likely to accept the police version of events than a jury. However, Harrison[36] points out that the largest ever award was made by a judge sitting alone.

A civil suit can be an effective remedy against the police, provided that evidence and legal assistance is available. On an individual basis this is probably the most effective remedy against police misconduct on demonstrations.

Criminal Injuries Compensation Board

Where it has been proved that a demonstrator is the victim of a crime of violence carried out by a police officer, a claim can be made for personal injury to the Criminal Injuries Compensation Board. However, the level of compensation is lower than in the courts and the procedures do not favour a complainant in the same way. This may still be a useful method of individual remedy where a complainant does not want to have to carry the conduct of a case themselves. Once the application form has been filled out, the process is carried through by the Criminal Injuries Compensation Board.[37]

[33] See Harrison, *Police Misconduct*, pp. 91ff and R. Clayton and H. Tomlinson, *Assessing Damages in Civil Actions Against the Police* (London, Sweet & Maxwell, 1987), *passim*.
[34] See A. Sherr, *Client Interviewing for Lawyers: An Analysis and Guide* (London, Sweet & Maxwell, 1986), pp. 115–17.
[35] *White* v. *Metropolitan Police Commissioner*, *The Times*, 24 Apr. 1982. And see *The Times*, 21 July 1988.
[36] Harrison, *Police Misconduct*, p. 95.
[37] Ibid., pp. 105–13.

Inquest

In 1974 Kevin Gately died during an anti-National Front demonstration in Red Lion Square. In 1980 Blair Peach died as a result of an attack during a demonstration. Where allegations are made that a death has resulted from an injury inflicted by a police officer in the purported execution of his duty then the Coroner must sit with a jury.[38] Although coroners' inquests have rather limited objectives they have been used in recent years by the families and friends of those who have died in controversial circumstances allegedly at the hands of the police.[39]

Inquests have not been found to be particularly effective in establishing the cause of death. The Kevin Gately inquest specifically left the question of direct cause to the Inquiry by Lord Scarman into the events at Red Lion Square. Lord Scarman's Inquiry felt that the circumstances of Kevin Gately's death should rather be decided by an inquest, or as a result of criminal charges against particular officers. In the event no such decisions or charges were made. In the Blair Peach case the High Court refused to allow disclosure of witness statements taken by the police to the family[40] although the situation may now be different.[41] Although legal advice is available under the Green Form scheme for preparatory work regarding an inquest, there is no legal aid available for family representation. The family of Blair Peach were said to have faced legal bills of around £14,000.

Inquests are 'inquisitorial' rather than adversarial and certain people or organizations may not be recognized as 'a properly interested person' to appear before the coroner. They therefore have a limited use in questioning police conduct on demonstrations, but it may sometimes be the only public forum available.

The European Commission on Human Rights

England has ratified the European Convention on Human Rights, thus enabling individuals to complain to the European Commission of Human Rights regarding a violation of the convention by the state signatory. Police misconduct on a demonstration could, in theory constitute a violation of Article 11 of the Convention,

---

[38] The Administration of Justice Act 1982, amending the Coroners (Amendment) Act 1926 s. 13. See also T. Ward, 'Death and Disorder', *Inquest*, London, 1987.

[39] Harrison, *Police Misconduct*, p. 120 and Scraton and Gordon, *Causes for Concern* (London, Pelican, 1984), p. 62.

[40] *R.* v. *Hammersmith Coroner ex p Peach* [1980] 2 All ER 7, p. 10.

[41] *Peach* v. *Commissioner of Police for the Metropolis* [1986] 2 All ER 129. See now agreed compensation of £75,005 and costs of £50,000 paid to Peach's brothers, *Legal Action*, August 1988, p. 4 by the MPC.

1. Everyone has the right to freedom of peaceful assembly and to freedom of association with others...
2. No restrictions shall be placed on the exercise of these rights other than such as are prescribed by law and are necessary in a democratic society in the interests of national security or public safety for the prevention of disorder or crime, for the protection of health or morals or for the protection of rights and freedoms of others. This Article shall not prevent the imposition of lawful restriction of the exercise of these rights by members of the armed forces, of the police or of the adminstration of the State.

A complainant must show that the case is admissible before the Commission, with all domestic remedies exhausted; and the application must be made within 6 months of the date of the final national decision.[42]

If the Commission, on investigation of the facts, cannot negotiate a 'friendly settlement' with the government subject of the complaint, the case may be referred to the European Court of Human Rights which may award compensation to an aggrieved individual. Admissible cases can take several years to be dealt with by the Commission and longer if the case goes before the Court. Legal Aid is not available, but can be granted by the Commission and a worthy case might be supported by such organizations as the National Council for Civil Liberties.[43]

The second part of Article 11 seems to make available almost every possible defence in relation to a breach of the first part of the Article. It may therefore be exceptionally difficult to prove a case under this head. In *CARAF* v. *UK*[44] a complaint was taken against the unfair use of section 3 of the Public Order Act 1936 for banning of a demonstration, but was not allowed by the Commission since Article 11 (2) provided an easy 'let-out' for the Government.

This is essentially a remedy for individuals against individual abuse of power, but it involves an excessively lengthy procedure and is not easily accessible for most complainants. It is therefore likely to be used only for major test cases regarding high profile issues. Although no successful cases have yet been taken regarding demonstrations, there have been significant successes against the British Government on a number of other issues. This might, therefore, prove a fruitful avenue in the future. The general effect of accession to the Convention and attempts to enact it within English law will be considered in chapter 9.

---

[42] See Article 26. For more general information see F. G. Jacobs, *The European Convention on Human Rights* (Oxford, Clarendon, 1975) and *European Convention on Human Rights: Collected Texts* (annual; Brussels, Council of Europe).
[43] See Harrison, *Police Misconduct*, p. 130 and Supperstone, *Brownlie*, p. 333.
[44] Application 8440/78 21 DR of European Commission of Human Rights 138 and see p. 77 above.

Administrative Law

Attempts have been made to use the judicial review power of the High Court in order to compel chief officers of police to carry out specific public duties[45] and unsuccessful attempts have been made to use this form of power to demand that a chief constable remove demonstrators who are protesting at the site of a proposed nuclear power station.[46]

Attempts have also been made to use the High Court's power to quash decisions of police commissioners, such as those taken in banning demonstrations under section 3 of the Public Order Act 1936.[47] The Court has, however, consistently refused to substitute its judgment for that of the police. The recent *Holgate-Mohammed* case,[48] which involved allegations of false arrest, and seemed to import the *Wednesbury* principles[49] into reviewing police discretion, will probably not effectively give more power to the Divisional Court.[50]

Therefore, although such cases gain a certain amount of public attention and are heard at a high level of the judiciary, this method has not yet been found to be successful in querying or changing police action.

Collective Remedies

High profile cases of individual complaint or action against the police, such as those listed above, could also bring about a more general change in police practice and behaviour. The remedies listed in this part though are directly aimed at investigating and correcting more general police behaviour.

Requiring a Report

Under section 12 (2) of the Police Act 1964 a local police authority may require its chief officer of police to submit a written report on any policing matters that they may specify. As far as is known this power

---

[45] See, e.g. *R.* v. *Metropolitan Police Commissioner ex p. Blackburn* (No. 3) [1973] 1 All ER 324.
[46] *R.* v. *Chief Constable of Devon and Cornwall ex p. CEGB* [1981] 3 All ER 826.
[47] See *Kent* v. *Metropolitan Police Commissioner, The Times* 13 May 1931, and transcript.
[48] *Holgate-Mohammed* [1984] AC 437.
[49] *Associated Provincial Picture Houses Limited* v. *Wednesbury Corporation* [1948] 1 KB 223.
[50] See Lustgarten, *Governance of Police*, p. 71, who seems at first to be arguing that *Holgate-Mohammed* is a liberalizing influence, and then that it is not.

is not used frequently, but reports are not published and it is therefore difficult to judge.[51]

Under section 30 (1) and (3) of the Police Act 1964 the Home Secretary may require any chief constable or the Police Commissioner of the City of London to submit a report on specified matters connected with policing of their area. The Home Secretary may also require reports from any police authority including the Metropolitan Police Commissioner under section 1 of the Metropolitan Police Act 1829. As noted by Harrison[52] one of these was published in 1974[53]

Where a police authority or the Home Secretary are convinced by public outcry that the policing of a demonstration has been conducted badly by the police, a report could be ordered from the chief officer of police in order to ascertain what went wrong. This could be a step prior to taking other action, or may be considered in itself to be a rap on the knuckles for the chief officer of police.

Inquiry

Under section 32 of the Police Act 1964 the Home Secretary may order a local inquiry into any matter connected with the policing of any area. The two inquiries by Lord Scarman into 'The Red Lion Square Disorders of 15 June 1974'[54] and 'The Brixton Disorders'[55] were both conducted under this power.

Prior to the 1964 Act, inquiries were held into a wider range of issues including misconduct by individual police officers such as that of Challenor.[56] However, calls for inquiries into the deaths of Blair Peach, Jimmy Kelly and Liddle Towers or the serious public disorders in Lewisham in 1977, Southall in 1979 and Bristol in 1980 have all been refused. Jefferson and Grimshaw suggest that an inquiry can now be expected only when disorder amounts to an operational defeat for the police.[57] Witnesses may be summonsed to the inquiry and evidence may be administered on oath. Section 32 (5) allows the cost of legal representation to be met from police funds if the Home Secretary agrees, and this was done in the Brixton inquiry.[58]

[51] See Harrison, *Police Misconduct*, p. 123.
[52] Ibid., p. 123.
[53] Report to the Home Secretary from the Commissioner of the Metropolis (HMSO, 1974 HC 351).
[54] Cmnd. 5919 (HMSO, London, 1974).
[55] Cmnd. 8427 (HMSO, London, 1981).
[56] Report of Inquiry into Det. Sgt. Challoner, Cmnd. 2735 (HMSO, London, 1965).
[57] Muller, 'Controlling the Constable', quoted in Harrison, Police Misconduct, pp. 127–32 at 122.
[58] The Scarman Report, Appendix A paras. 15–17.

Judging from Red Lion Square and Brixton such inquiries will deliver a fair amount of whitewash to cover police action regarding the precipitating events of the inquiry. However, reading in between the lines of the reports, where they make suggestions for the future, seems to reveal any police mishandling and misconduct.[59] Such an inquiry is therefore worthwhile, but difficult to obtain. The ritual blood letting effects of the Brixton inquiry may mean that it will be a long time before similar inquiries will be ordered by the Home Secretary.

Lord Scarman's suggestions for the future at Brixton have certainly been noticed, seemingly more by the police than by the government. However, urban unrest remains and the real lessons of the inquiry did not seem to have been learned by the time of the disorders on the Broadwater Farm Estate in 1985.[60]

Control of Chief Police Officers

Lustgarten portrays the different genesis of the 'head constables' in the boroughs and the chief constables in the Counties, as well as the special position of the Metropolitan Police Commissioner, throughout the nineteenth century.[61] Although originally local watch committees, police committees or the justices seemed to have more power, by the 1930s the chief constables seem to have become relatively free of local control. Centralisation of information, advice and pay structure within the Home Office led to a greater homogeneity among police forces. The Police Act 1964, and the cases of *Ridge* v. *Baldwin*[62] and Captain Popkess and The Nottingham Watch Committee[63] only served to confirm the independence and power of the chief constable. This independence seems to cover all 'operational matters' and it is even difficult for a police authority to question eccentric behaviour of a chief constable, as shown by the recent controversy surrounding James Anderton in Manchester. Anderton used his position to make comments, seemingly motivated more by his own religious persuasion than policing needs, regarding the background to the spread of the AIDS virus, in favour of castration of sex offenders and his willingness to flout police authority wishes.[64] Even though complaints were taken to the Home Office, it

---

[59] See A. Sherr, 'The Scarman Report on "The Brixton Disorders 10–12 April 1981" – a Retrospective Review' [1985] 7 *Urban Law and Policy*, 227–41.
[60] Benyon and Solomos, 'British Urban Unrest in the 1980s' in *The Roots of Urban Unrest*, op. cit.
[61] Lustgarten, *Governance of Police*, pp. 33–43.
[62] *Ridge* v. *Baldwin* [1964] AC 40.
[63] See, e.g., Lustgarten, *Governance of Police*, p. 49, or T. Critchley, *A History of the Police in England and Wales* (Constable, London, 1978), pp. 270ff.
[64] See *The Times*, e.g. 15, 23, 24, 28 and 31 Jan., 21 Feb, 18 Sept. and 17 Dec. 1987.

was not clear that the right of criticism of the employing local authority police committee was in any way established.

If it is not possible to criticize a chief constable regarding such issues, it is clearly *a fortiori* far less possible to call a chief constable to question in relation to operational decisions such as those involved in policing a demonstration.

We have already noted that it is not possible to question a chief constable's decision relating to a ban or the imposing of other conditions on a demonstration.[65] Although unofficial inquiries have been used considerably in recent years, and Harrison notes nine unofficial inquiries between 1977 and 1986 some of which were actually set up by the local authority police committee,[66] such inquiries may only be effective in an informal way. A chief officer of police may also be asked for reports, as seen above, but it will still be difficult to effect direct and purposeful changes through these means.

Control, if it exists at all in relation to chief police officers, is therefore of a very vague and informal nature. It will depend upon the individual chief officer, how much any criticism is taken to heart and acted upon. The policing of large demonstrations will often be an issue considered by the chief officer of police and at that general level within the police force. Leaving such officials such enormous power, with little control is a significant element in the British system which seems to rely so much on the personnel involved for their correct discretion and behaviour, without outside check or interference.[67]

The View from the Thin Blue Line

Sir Robert Mark in 'Policing a Britain Under Threat'[68] stated,

> My first task is to say something about the reality of what is loosely called Law and Order, and in doing so I suspect I may shatter a few long cherished illusions. Most of you will have formed a general impression that effective law and order depends on an efficient and honest police force serving an effective justice system ... This is not true. There never has been a reliable evaluation of the effectiveness of the police and the justice system and only in recent years have the curious begun to suspect

[65] See ch. 3.

[66] See Harrison, *Police Misconduct*, pp. 123–4.

[67] On alternative means of controlling the police and the unnecessary accent on 'independence' see Lustgarten, *Governance of Police* pp. 160–82 and D. Kretzmer, 'Demonstrations and the Law' (1984) 19 Israel LR p. 47.

[68] Sir Robert Mark, 'Policing a Britain under Threat', in R. Clutterbuck, ed., *The Future of Political Violence: De-stabilization, Disorder and Terrorism* (RUSI Defence Studies series) (London, Macmillan, 1986), pp. 159ff.

that whilst the police and the courts have an important part to play, their importance lessens in relation to some crimes which are now so commonplace that they are now accepted as part of the pattern of our daily lives....

A similar situation is to be found in relation to offences against public order, arising from political demonstrations, strikes, football and other hooliganism, and racial tensions. The most the police can do is to contain them, sometimes with great difficulty.

Following Sir Robert Mark's line, the government too have been keen to redefine and refocus the public perception of problems relating to crime. The public is seen as a number of 'D.I.Y. crime fighters'[69] by Douglas Hurd the Home Secretary and John Patten the Minister of State at the Home Office. Crime is to be seen as something householders must take personal precautions against, rather than viewed as a problem of society which needs direct attention. The result of this attempt at a new focus is to remove the police from criticism and to prevent them from becoming the 'meat in the sandwich'.

However, by taking more part in political decision making, by becoming more public and open to the media, police officers have made it difficult for the public to ignore their central role and function in making decisions which affect public order.

The fulcrum upon which any balance between police control of demonstrations and control of the police must sit is the question of the cost of policing demonstration. This has increasingly become a major issue in the Annual Reports of Metropolitan Police Commissioners[70] and other chief officers of police.

Assistant Commissioner John Dellow[71] in his essay 'Political Violence and the Response' charts how the police adapted their style of reaction to 'demonstrations and riots in London' since 1970.

The police strategy became one of allowing both sides to demonstrate but separately. The judge's words about escape routes and converging marches in The Red Lion Square inquiry were burned into the souls of police Commanders. We learned that to preserve the basic but unwritten rights to demonstrate and yet preserve order by separation was a delicate exercise and extremely expensive in manpower and other resources. You will remember the phalanxes of police officers used to contain and protect marchers and the strong cordons of foot and mounted officers used to seal off assembly and dispersal areas and the route between. More manpower was needed to sweep the routes of opposition and contain it

[69] See *The Times*, 26 Oct. 1987.
[70] E.g. 1983, 1984, 1985, 1986, 1987.
[71] Dellow was in command of the siege of the Iranian Embassy in Princes Gate, London, in 1980.

at places where it could demonstrate but without risk of confrontation and consequent violence. This did not always prevent violence towards police. In general, however, the tactics proved successful and demonstrations did take place in the most sensitive areas without disorder but at the cost of deploying thousands of police officers per demonstration and the temporary curtailment of liberty for many law abiding local residents and business people.[72]

The issue of cost, which must be determined by local and central government funding authorities, once again attempts to place policy and political issues regarding 'the right to demonstrate' back in the laps of the politicians rather than in the hands of the police. However, this must of necessity go in a circle. Such decisions of policy can be made only with police expertise involved. Decisions may well depend on which demonstrations or protests the police consider to be less likely to cause them more difficulty.[73] Should a right or liberty of demonstration simply be dependent upon police strategy, police effectiveness or cost? Whatever the answer, there must come a time when ratepayers (or their poll tax equivalent) and taxpayers themselves decide that too much of their money is being spent on maintaining the right to demonstrate. This is an issue which is yet to be faced.[74]

If the British police are still to maintain the crowd control strategy articulated by Sir Robert Mark as being 'to win by appearing to lose' they need to maintain public sympathy.[75] Sir Robert Mark apparently claimed that the Metropolitan Police had trained a horse to collapse, pretending to be dead, at a word of command. This was apparently guaranteed to win the support of the animal loving British public.[76] However, it has simply not been possible to maintain this 'soft' policing approach in the face of major urban unrest, which may itself be the product of complaints against police racialism and the redefinition of crime.[77]

[72] J. Dellow, 'Political Violence and the Response' in Clutterbuck, ed., *The Future of Political Violence*, pp. 167ff.
[73] See also the reasoning in *Harris* v. *Sheffield United F.C.* [1987] 2 All ER 839, where a bill for £51,699 was delivered to a football club for policing matches. Is this a possible future step against organizers of demonstrations?
[74] In terms of the Metropolitan Police, independent financial audit will soon be carried out by the Inspectorate of Constabulary which already reports to the Home Secretary about all other police forces. This will strengthen central government's financial control and may force the issues discussed here into a more political arena. See *The Times*, 21 Nov. 1987.
[75] See Robert Reiner, *The Politics of the Police* (Brighton, Wheatsheaf, 1985), p. 54.
[76] Ibid.
[77] See Stuart Hall et al., *Policing the Crisis – Mugging, the State and Law and Order* (London, Macmillan, 1978) for an account of who the police managed to label and produce a particular crime which would feed the needs of the media and fit in with popular mythology. See also M. Kettle and L. Hodges, *Uprising* (London, Pan, 1982), esp. ch. 3, 'Black People and the Police'.

We are left, therefore, with some mixed images of the police position. They see themselves as the meat in the sandwich between the protesters and the object of their protest. However, they are more active than this passive role would suggest. Their adoption of media assistance and the manipulation of it has left them as major actors on the scene, at the same time as they are involved in a circular movement of protested independence, pretending to hand back the real decisions to their political 'masters'.

In truth, these decisions should not be the decisions of the police. Our police have become so 'independent' that they decide for themselves not only how they should do their 'job', but also what that job entails. Reiner[78] suggests that the conflicting political mythologies are both wrong because, as the empirical evidence shows, 'police work is more complex, contradictory, indeed confused, than either model allows'.[79] Reiner's survey of the empirical studies shows that much of police work is not too different from that of social workers, and sums up the view of one American patrolman,

> Every time you begin to do some real police work you get stuck with this stuff. I guess 90% of all police work is bullshit.[80]

One description is that most police work is 'neither social service nor law enforcement, but order maintenance – the settlement of conflicts by means other than formal law enforcement'.[81] What seems important here is not to note how the job has evolved historically or how it exists empirically, but who decides what the job will be now, and why it will be thus. The police should not arrogate to themselves the power of deciding that part of their role is the maintenance of freedom of speech. They should not do so because the decision in itself is undemocratic and makes it less likely that any such freedom would be maintained by them. Comparisons exist in both the United States[82] and Israel[83] where more legal control of the police is possible.

The issue of police control or 'governance' is not singular, but another example of the English determination to rely on selecting the 'right' people for the right jobs, and socializing them into particular forms of behaviour afterwards. A more open and homogenous society, with more equal opportunities has made such a system more difficult to operate.

[78] Reiner, *Politics of the Police*, p. 111.
[79] Ibid.
[80] A. J. Reiss, Jr, *The Police and the Public* (New Haven, Yale University Press, 1971), p. 42.
[81] Reiner, *Politics of the Police*, p. 114.
[82] Lustgarten, *Governance of the Police*, pp. 6–7.
[83] Kretzmer, 'Demonstrations and the Law.'

'The Big Boot' on the Other Foot – Inquiring into and Controlling Police Strategy

It is not easy to discover police planning systems and strategies for dealing with demonstrations and protests. Police operational memoranda are not published and will be seen by them as part of their confidential documents in the adversarial 'battle' of the streets. *The Times* reported on 23 November, 1987 the existence of a new manual for policing public order allegedly drawn up by the Association of Chief Police Officers. It was said to include details of 'highly aggressive tactics bordering on the operations of the famed French riot police. The public cannot read it.'

Four Codes of Practice under the Police and Criminal Evidence Act 1974 have so far been published, dealing with powers of stop and search, searching of premises and seizure of property, detention treatment and questioning, and identification parades, etc. It is a disciplinary offence to fail to comply with any requirement of these Codes, although such an offence will not, by itself, make a police officer liable to criminal or civil proceedings.[84] However, no code of practice has yet been published in relation to police conduct on demonstrations or dealing with demonstrators and protesters.

Some information has become public knowledge as a result of inquiries such as Red Lion Square and Brixton. Police rules about the use of truncheons, both by mounted and unmounted police officers, became known, for example, as a result of inquiries at Red Lion Square and the inquest into the death of Blair Peach. One unremarked record of police systems which came out in the Brixton inquiry, concerns the chain of command operating in Brixton during the disorders there in April 1981. The two charts of the police chain of command at Brixton (Figures 8.1 and 8.2) show the chain of command and time of involvement on Friday 10 April 1981, which was the first day of the disorders, and Saturday 11 April 1981. Although this 'chain of command' deals with a situation described as a 'riot' rather than demonstration or protest, it seems clear that the same chain of command and decision making would still have been applicable to a less violent protest. In any event, a demonstration may be seen as an incipient riot, especially a demonstration generated by some precipitating immediate cause rather than one planned with full information in advance.

It is interesting to note that there is little difference between the chain of command shown for Friday 10 April and for Saturday 11 April as stated in Lord Scarman's Report. Friday 10 April was the beginning of

---

[84] See Police and Criminal Evidence Act s. 67 (10) and Harrison, *Police Misconduct*, p. 136.

172

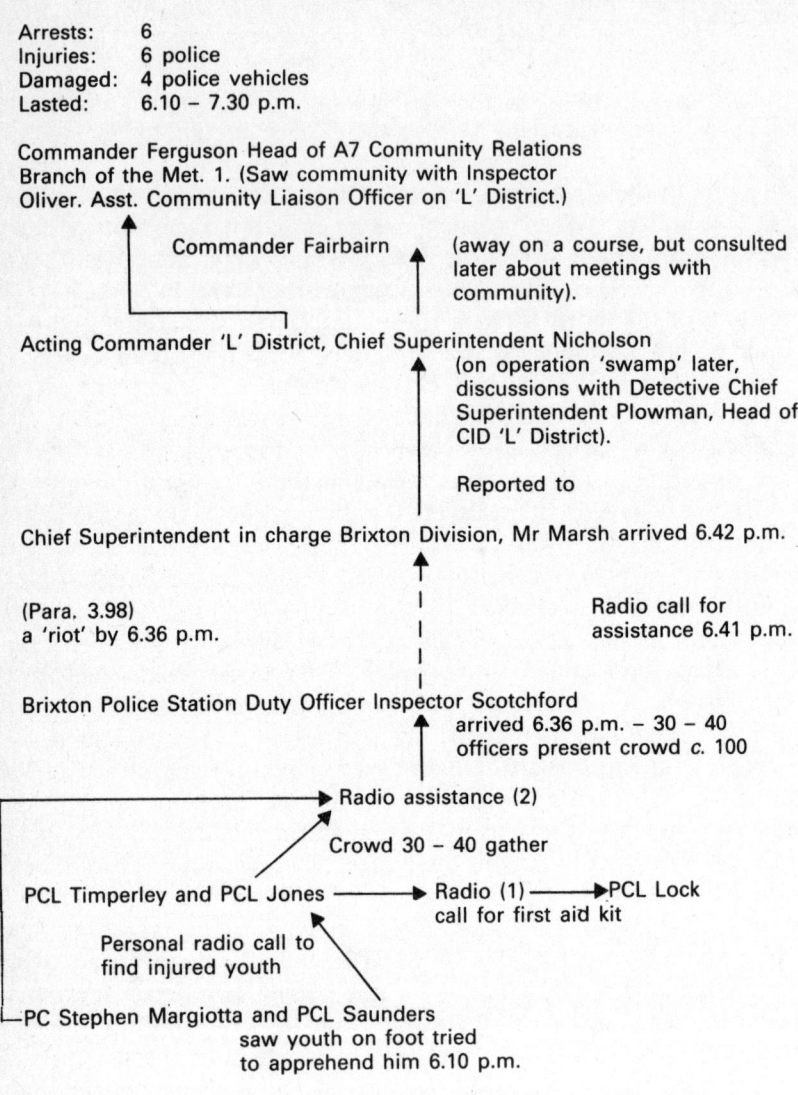

Arrests: 6
Injuries: 6 police
Damaged: 4 police vehicles
Lasted: 6.10 – 7.30 p.m.

Commander Ferguson Head of A7 Community Relations
Branch of the Met. 1. (Saw community with Inspector
Oliver. Asst. Community Liaison Officer on 'L' District.)

Commander Fairbairn   (away on a course, but consulted
later about meetings with
community).

Acting Commander 'L' District, Chief Superintendent Nicholson
(on operation 'swamp' later,
discussions with Detective Chief
Superintendent Plowman, Head of
CID 'L' District).

Reported to

Chief Superintendent in charge Brixton Division, Mr Marsh arrived 6.42 p.m.

(Para. 3.98)   Radio call for
a 'riot' by 6.36 p.m.   assistance 6.41 p.m.

Brixton Police Station Duty Officer Inspector Scotchford
arrived 6.36 p.m. – 30 – 40
officers present crowd c. 100

Radio assistance (2)

Crowd 30 – 40 gather

PCL Timperley and PCL Jones ──→ Radio (1) ──→PCL Lock
call for first aid kit

Personal radio call to
find injured youth

PC Stephen Margiotta and PCL Saunders
saw youth on foot tried
to apprehend him 6.10 p.m.

Source: Reconstructed from Brixton Report paras. 3.4 – 3.27 and 3.98

Figure 8.1 Police chain of command at Brixton on Friday 10 April 1981.

Arrests: 82
Injuries: 279 police, 45 public
Damaged: 56 police vehicles, 61 private vehicles, 145 premises (28 by fire)

Lasted 4.40 – 11 p.m.

Attempts at mediation (1) (Para. 3.36) 5.00 p.m. Iron bars in bags; (2) (Para. 3.37) 5.10 p.m. Tony Morgan. (3) (Para. 3.47) 6.00 p.m. white American woman. (4) (Para. 3.57) 7.00 p.m. 4 VIPs (local).

                    Deputy Asst. Commissioner Walker No. 4. Area of
                        ▲ Met. ('L' District is part of
                        | this) arrived 6.30 p.m.
    Commander Adams arrived |
    3.30 p.m. (Fairbairn's |
    predecessor) |
                                  |
Commander 'L' District, Commander Fairbairn, arrived 6.15 p.m.
                                  |
(Para. 3.99)   ▲
A 'Riot' by 5.15 p.m. |
'Windsor Castle' burning |
started c. 6.30 p.m. |
Looting began 6.00 p.m. |
                                  |
            Acting Commander 'L' District Chief Superintendent Nicholson
                        ▲ (3) Call to 5.27
                        | (2) Further assistance and 1
                        | ambulance and fire brigade
                        | (1) Urgent assistance from all
                        | over the Met.
                        |
Chief Superintendent Boyling and Chief Inspector Benn arrived 5.10 p.m.
                        ▲   50 – 60   police
                        | Radioed to 200   crowd
                        |
                        |
Brixton Police Station Duty Officer Inspector Scotchford
                        |
                        ▲ 4.52 p.m.
                        | Radio call of 'stabbing'
                        |
Plainclothes 'Swamp' officers PC Cameron (aged 20) and PC Thornton (aged 24)

            Start of S & M incident 4.40 p.m.

Source: Reconstructed from Brixton Report paras. 3.28 – 3.80 and 3.99.

Figure 8.2 Police chain of command on Saturday 11 April 1981 at Brixton.

the disorders. Although operation 'Swamp '81' was already under way, no immediate expectation of a grand protest, building to a riot existed on the Friday. Reports go from the police officers on the scene, Margiotta and Saunders to the Brixton police station duty officer, Inspector Scotchford, and from him to Chief Superintendent Marsh in charge of Brixton Division. They both appear on the scene with amazing speed at 6.36 p.m. and 6.42 p.m., respectively. Marsh reports to Chief Superintendent Nicholson, who was the acting Commander 'L' District. He reports to Commander Fairbairn who was away on a course at that time, and Commander Ferguson, who was the Head of A7 Community Relations Branch of the Metropolitan Police.

On the next day when the number of arrests and injuries and the damage to vehicles and premises was much greater, the chain of command was remarkably similar. The police officers on the scene, Cameron and Thornton, radioed to Duty Inspector Scotchford at Brixton police station. He radioed to Chief Superintendent Boyling and Chief Inspector Benn. They made an 'urgent assistance' call to officers from all over the Metropolitan Police, and then reported to Acting Commander Chief Superintendent Nicholson. He, in turn, reported to Commander Fairbairn, who this time reported to the Deputy Assistant Commissioner Walker of No. 4 area of the Metropolitan Police (of which 'L' District was a part).

No major differences appear, even though by the second day the police must surely have expected trouble. This seems to suggest that the chain of command is fairly fixed in this manner. Tracing through the time of arrival of each upper link in the chain of command, it seems that the more senior police officer arrives on the scene, makes an assessment of the problem and then very soon afterwards calls either for further assistance or to the next upper link in the chain of command. The response rate seems quite fast, if the times recorded are accurate. The first senior officer on the scene appears to be able to call for immediate 'further assistance'. This was done by Scotchford on the Friday 5 minutes after arriving on the scene. Major demands for 'urgent assistance from all over the Met' may need to await the arrival of more senior officers, such as Chief Superintendent Boyling and Chief Inspector Benn on the Saturday.[85] It is not clear whether it is possible for even the most junior officers on the scene to make an assessment such that immediate general assistance from all over the Metropolitan force could be brought to bear. Although one might have thought that different systems or more specialist officers might be employed in differing

[85] See 'The Brixton Disorders, 10–12 April 1981': Report of the Inquiry by the Rt. Hon. The Lord Scarman, OBE, Cmnd. 8427 (HMSO, Nov. 1981), pp. 17–41.

circumstances, especially when some foresight of major difficulties exist, the system of command seems to stay very much the same.

Based on the availability of this form of information, a researcher may piece together small nuggets of information which have become public as the result of inquiries, but not in an ordered or comprehensive manner. Another approach is to carry out a 'laboratory' type exercise to see how policing needs might be met in a real demonstration.

Such an exercise is carried out by the author annually with a group of students learning about demonstrations and the law. The law students are split into groups of two or three, and are advised that they are to carry out the role and functions of a committee of police officers faced with the likelihood of a particular form of demonstration at a particular place and time. Each 'police officer committee' is given the instructions and map shown in figure 8.3.

'Police Officer Committees' are asked to plan in detail the policing of the demonstration including detailing the control of traffic in the immediate and surrounding areas, number of police needed, method of deployment of police, initial plan for controlling demonstration and fall-back plans in the event of disorder.

Although it sounds more like a parlour game than a laboratory experiment it is fascinating to watch the committees plan and it is interesting to see what decisions they make. Students who are normally suspicious and even cynical about the police, find themselves deeply involved in behaving like police officers. Those who have been on a number of demonstrations themselves seem to be much better at the policing exercise than others. Police Inspectors who have attended the exercise confirm that the atmosphere and method of decision making, and even some of the better decisions made, is not unlike a police planning meeting.

The adversary nature of the process becomes obvious immediately they begin the task. The uncertainty of the crowd and crowd reaction, together with the associated temptations to 'over police' is an important factor. Some 'committees' come up with police numbers that would require almost the entire West Midlands Police force.

The 'Committees' are then asked also to consider what their main priorities are in planning the policing of the demonstration. Where real police officers have been invited and have given a note of their priorities in such circumstances, they have tended to differ from the student committees in only one way. The real police officers (who have all been of the rank of Inspector or above) have included as a priority 'attempting to ensure the freedom of speech of the protesters' or words to that effect. Interestingly, however, their suggested mode of policing the demonstration does not differ markedly from many of the student

Event: HRH Princess Anne the Princess Royal is opening the new headquarters of the British Foxhunting Society and is being accompanied by her husband Captain Mark Phillips.

Venue: The building is situated at the junction of Fletchamstead Highway and Sir Henry Parkes Road (marked Fire Station on map). The opening ceremony will be conducted inside the building.

Arrival and departure: Arrival will be at 2.00 p.m. by Rail at Canley Halt and from there the Royal party will travel by direct route by road to the venue. Departure will be at 3.00 p.m. by the same means.

Estimated attendance: The Anti-Hunt Society intend vigorously to oppose the event, and intend to get into the meeting and prevent it from taking place. Preliminary information indicates that there will be between 750 and 1000 demonstrators from all over the country.

It is expected that other factions may be present, viz. Anti-Royalists and Anti-Armed Services to an estimated total of 250.

There will be an unknown quantity of ordinary members of the public who will be merely interested in the Royal family and who will be present throughout the route.

Manpower: The Force has an establishment of 4000 and 650 of these are stationed at Coventry. Normal daily duties throughout the Force have still to be covered and to facilitate coverage of the demonstration all leave has been cancelled. There are four Territorial support Groups of 75 men who are based in Birmingham, but who would be available if required. The Mounted Branch are based in Birmingham, but are similarly available. There is a dog section at Coventry. Transport of all descriptions is available as required.

Pre-event negotiation: Due to the fact that the demonstrators are from all over the country there have been no communications with any Organizers.

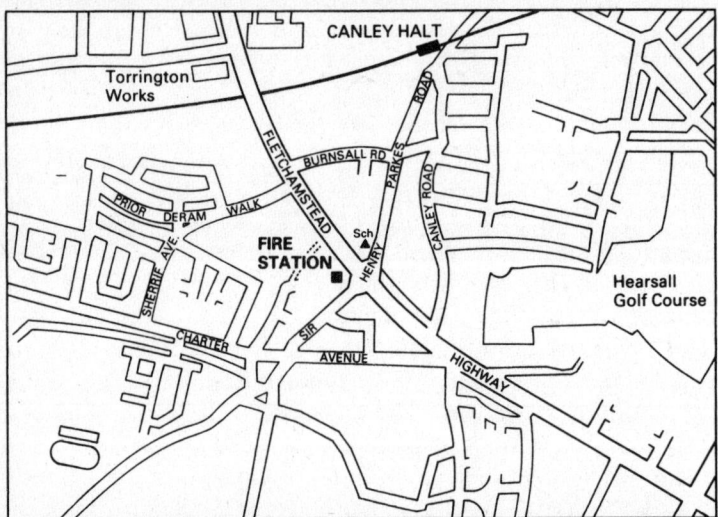

Figure 8.3 Planning the Policing of a Public Demonstration: Exercise

'committees', whose priorities do not include that stated aim. It may be, therefore, that police officers are taught to pay lip service to that particular ideal, even though it may make little difference to their mode of operation in dealing with demonstrators.

Some of the students who have been involved in this exercise are quite surprised at their reactions whilst in the role of police officers, and gain considerable insight into the problems police face on demonstrations. There is no doubt that policing demonstrations is a difficult task both for the senior police officers planning and for the individual police officers on the street. A poorly thought out scheme of control, or a bad manoeuvre on the day can cause disorder, violence and even loss of life. Poor police communication between different groups of police officers at Red Lion Square, for example, caused two lines of police to be advancing towards each other with a packed crowd in between them each in an effort to move the crowd in the opposite direction.[86] We have already noted in chapter 2 how different policing arrangements for the Vietnam demonstration in September 1978 changed the whole character of the demonstration, compared with the demonstration in March of that year.

It is important, therefore, to note that policing demonstrations is a difficult job. This knowledge must reflect also on the need for control of the police. The more difficult the job is, the more likely the failure to carry out the job properly. The more the likelihood of failure, the greater the necessity for a sensible method of advising and controlling police behaviour in relation to such a central social liberty as the right of protest.

Image, Training and Equipment – a 'Third Force?'

The problem of the split image between the 'hard' policing needs of a violent demonstration and the 'soft' policing needs of general community work could be overcome by setting up a specialist branch of the police, or some force in between the police and the army, to deal with mass demonstration and crowd control, and situations worsening from that level into violence. The need to have special riot equipment including CS gas, plastic bullets, shields, etc., and to have appropriate officers ready who are trained in their use also makes the idea of a third force sound reasonable.

Unlike the CRS in France or the Kidotai in Japan, England has never

[86] The Red Lion Square Disorders 15th June 1974: Report of Inquiry by the Rt. Hon. The Lord Justice Scarman OBE, Cmnd. 5919 (HMSO, Feb. 1975), pp. 14–15.

had a separate force to deal with public disorder. According to Stewart Tendler[87] London now has some ninety-six constables, twelve sergeants, five inspectors, one chief inspector and an overall commanding superintendent involved in Territorial Support Groups aimed at handling major public disorder as well as specialized areas of crime. These new TSGs sound not too dissimilar from the previous 'Special Patrol Groups' which had received a poor press during the previous decade. Changes, however, are clearly occurring in terms of the specialist police firearms units, and instead of police officers in each area being trained to use guns there will be far fewer officers of this type in the future. The fatal errors involved in the shootings of the 5 year old John Shorthouse and Cherry Groce have caused the police to think again about the use of such equipment.

However, the question of whether special riot equipment will be available to a particular police area is not a matter for the decision of the Police Authority. In *R. v. Secretary of State for the Home Department, ex parte Northumbria Police Authority*[88] it was stated that the Home Secretary has express statutory power to supply plastic batton rounds and CS gas equipment, etc., from central stores without charge and without the consent of a local police authority under section 41 of the Police Act 1964, as well as under the general power of Royal Prerogative. Once again the local police authority is shown to have very little control over its police force, but here the central power of the Home Office over the theoretically 'independent' local areas is strengthened considerably. The National Reporting Centre deals with 'mutual aid' between the police forces and the Association of Chief Police Officers. The effective centralization of the police force in organizations 'with no statutory existence, who took decisions with major implications for policing in both receiving and sending areas independent of any democratic authority (during the miners' strike), central or local, is constitutionally unprecedented and cannot be justified in a democratic polity'.[89] The question of local or central police control is wider than this book, but it should be noted, particularly in relation to public order weaponry, how much central and how little local power exists.

In respect of riot equipment, the police were testing military armoured personnel carriers known as 'Pigs' which would 'deliver police teams with CS gas or plastic bullets' in a riot, in February 1987.[90] The incoming Metropolitan Police Commissioner, Mr Peter Imbert, within a few months of taking up his new position, told the Howard League

[87] S. Tendler, *The Times*, 17 Feb. 1987.
[88] *The Times LR*, 14. Jan., 19 Nov. 1987.
[89] Lustgarten, *Governance of Police*, p. 109.
[90] See *The Times*, 13 Feb. 1987.

for Penal Reform that the police needed more equipment to deal with disorder,

> The necessity for such equipment and training, which must be reluctantly acknowledged, should not be confused with any general desire to possess and use it.[91]

Horses remain 'a tried and tested strategy'. Even though their use in public order situations seems more reminiscent of the nineteenth century battlefield, with both horse and riders wearing body protectors and body armour.[92]

The problems of equipment and training go beyond the possibilities of using a third force or even the TSGs. Lord Scarman commented in Brixton about the poor training of, especially young, police officers. Although attempts have been made to lengthen their training, by May 1987 Sir Lawrence Byford, retiring as Chief Inspector of Constabulary was still saying

> I feel sorry for the difficulties faced by young policemen. They are in the front line in less than three years. I wonder if we really do enough for them. It's almost like waving them off when we were in the Second World War.[93]

A special recovery home has been set up for Metropolitan Police victims of stress and physical violence in Hove on the Sussex coast.[94] Fifteen officers have been retrained by Warwickshire to provide a confidential counselling service for their own staff.[95] The Metropolitan Police have even courted Saatchi and Saatchi (the Conservative party publicists) to change their image not only for the public, but also to encourage recruits.[96]

Specially trained squads and special equipment do not appear to be the real answer for dealing with demonstrations (as opposed to violent riots). Indeed, it may well be that the use of specially trained and easily identified forces with special equipment could, in itself, provoke the disorder they intend to avoid or control. There is much to be said for local police officers knowing the terrain, being recognizable to the local people, and having a community-based approach to their work. Special groups are distant people whose training is more likely to be to control others than to control themselves, and they will have no ongoing

[91] *The Times*, 10 Sept. 1987.
[92] *The Times*, 19 Jan. 1987.
[93] *The Times*, 14 May 1987.
[94] *The Times*, 4 July 1987.
[95] *The Evening Standard*, 10 Dec. 1987.
[96] *The Times*, 3 June 1987.

responsibility in a community for the effect of their actions. Once again, a careful balance needs to be maintained even in terms of training and equipment.

Conclusion

In this chapter we have considered the demonstrators' response to police misbehaviour or misconduct on demonstrations by looking at the methods of complaint and civil or criminal redress against the police or more political methods of calling inquiries. At the same time, we have considered some of the problems faced by the police in relation to demonstrations.

As Roger Birch, Chief Constable of Sussex and the new President of the Association of Chief Police Officers said in October of 1987,

> The reassuring and much loved Mr Plod has gone forever and we are approaching a crossroads in the philosophy of policing.[97]

Whether or not police are as open to suggestions as he states, it certainly does seem that they are not pretending to know too many answers. If they find themselves caught in between the two sides physically on the streets, they also find themselves caught between the two main political parties, and between being independent and responsible all at the same time. The police need more guidance both on a central and local basis. They have not been prepared to accept local guidance and central guidance has been minimal. Statutory structures, such as those suggested by Lustgarten[98] are essential for regulating properly the role of the police. Legal controls and complaints procedures should be real and not illusory, and debate between the police and the public on such questions should be open and not affected by party politics or crime figures.[99]

[97] R. Birch, 'What kind of policeman do you want?', *The Times*, 12 Oct. 1987.
[98] Lustgarten, *Governance of Police*, pp. 177–82.
[99] See the 'false' crime figures allegations in Kent in *The Times*, 4 Feb. 1987.

9

Constitutionalism and Society

In setting out the major issues relating to the law of protest and demonstration one cannot escape from the vision preferred by some writers of a particular panacea for the difficult problems in this area. This chapter concludes the main part of the book by carefully examining this claim and raising some questions about the environment for a Bill of Rights or a constitutional type guarantee of freedom of protest.

A debate at the Bar Conference in September 1987 on the question of whether the European Convention on Human Rights should be enacted as part of the law of the United Kingdom, seems to set out the issues well, as between two points of view both in favour of a right of freedom of speech.

> The *Spycatcher* case demonstrates how the United Kingdom law has failed to provide for the basic right of freedom of speech, Mr Anthony Lester, Q.C., told lawyers at the conference.
>
> In arguing a case like that one, lawyers were unable to point to any concrete right to freedom of expression, other than the residual right which existed in that it was not specifically denied by any law.
>
> Mr Lester, who represented the *Sunday Times* in the recent proceedings, said that the freedom of speech was one of many such fundamental rights not enshrined in UK law. He urged a charter of human rights based on the European Convention.
>
> However, Mr Tony Blair, Labour M.P. and Barrister, said in his view the *Spycatcher* case had demonstrated the case against a Bill of Rights as advocated by Mr Lester. 'It had shown the "inherent conservatism of the judiciary' and it was "bizarre" to argue that a Bill of Rights which would hand over civil liberties to the judges, was now needed', he said.[1]

Anthony Lester pointed out that there were no domestic remedies for

---

[1] *The Times*, 28 Sept. 1987, reporting the Bar Conference on the previous day. *Spycatcher* was the title of a book by Peter Wright, an ex-MI5 employee, which purported to give details of the classified work of the secret services and which had therefore been banned from publication in the UK, even though it was being published in many places abroad. Anthony Lester had been the first to raise the subject in a considered way in *Democracy and Individual Rights* (Fabian Trust No. 390, 1968). See generally, summarizing the debate, M. Zander, *A Bill of Rights*, 2nd edn (Barry Rose, 1979) and J. Jaconelli, *Enacting a Bill of Rights* (Oxford University Press, 1980).

executive violation of fundamental rights and freedoms, causing more complaints against the UK government *per capita* to the European Commission and Court of Human Rights in Strasbourg, than from any other country. From his point of view, the United Kingdom was 'almost alone among democratic countries' in that it did not have an enforceable Bill of Rights or the equivalent and only 'complacency, conservatism and insularity' prevented reform.

Tony Blair, on the other hand, saw the *Spycatcher* case as a question of the conflict of rights between national security and freedom of speech. Even if there were some form of Bill of Rights the choice would be the same and it would still have to be made by the judges 'guided by their own use of civil liberties and human rights'.[2] He considered that such decisions ought to be made by politicians who could be controlled by the public, as opposed to the judiciary who were totally independent and made their decisions by 'making a personal and often political judgement based on individual politics'.

The Great Debate – Some Background

The 'great debate' concerns exactly this issue: whether or not the problems faced in England regarding human rights and civil liberties would be answered by a constitution, or constitutional approach.

Every schoolchild knows that the United States of America has a constitution and that Great Britain does not. However, this simple distinction hides a great deal. We must have a constitution of sorts, since there must be some conceptual or formal structure which defines our legal and political institutions, and the inter-relationship between them and our citizenry. In that sense every polity has a constitution. It is next suggested that the difference is that we have no 'written' constitution. Some would argue that the British Constitution can be read as the summary of all the statutes, caselaw, statutory instruments and legal conventions which are to be found in the books. It may therefore be 'written' but not finite.[3]

One does not need to go as far as this in order to find a written constitution; since some 'fundamental laws' exist including the Act of Union of 1707 between England and Scotland and the Articles of Union 'the treaty' upon which the Act was based.[4] These would be fundamental

---

[2] *The Times*, 28 Sept. 1987.
[3] See John Kenny, 'The Advantages of a Written Constitution Incorporating a Bill of Rights' [1979] 30 NILQ 189; Colin Munro, 'What is a Constitution?' [1983] Pub. L. 563.
[4] See, e.g. J. D. B. Mitchell, 'What Happened to the Constitution on 1st January 1973?' [1986] Cambrian L. Rev. 69. Although C. G. Fritz disagrees – 'An Entrenched Bill of Rights

laws in the sense that some of them are unalterable by parliament. Professor deSmith has suggested that such Acts 'provide a rudimentary framework of a written constitution' so that it can reasonably be argued that the Acts of Union with Scotland and Ireland were constituent acts in the sense that they established a new United Kingdom parliament. This background remains as sophistry, except to patriotic Scots who object to the current Queen Elizabeth being referred to as Elizabeth *the Second* when the first Elizabeth reigned before the Treaty of Union of 1707.[5]

The great debate, however, concerns a smaller element in what 'constitutionalism' may mean: the adoption of a set of fundamental rules which would delineate 'civil' or 'human' rights. English reaction to such a set of rules has historically been negative. It was not long after the American Declaration of Independence of 4 July 1776 when a somewhat crusty Jeremy Bentham fired off a salvo against such ideas as the natural and unalienable rights of men by characterizing such doctrine as so much 'bawling upon paper' and 'nonsense upon stilts'. Such chauvinism, utilitarian in background or otherwise, has continued in England to hold the higher ground from which scorn is poured on legal guarantees of human rights such as those adopted in the French Declaration of the Rights of Man and Citizen of 1791, and in the American Bill of Rights. In 1963, for example, Sir Ivor Jennings was stating that

> in Britain we have no Bill of Rights; we merely have liberty according to law, and we think – truly I believe – that we do the job better than any country which has a Bill of Rights or a Declaration of Rights of Man'.[6]

It should be noted that in this particular football match it is very much England versus The Rest of the World. Constitutionalism has won the day. The only states which do not boast of the classical 'written' and finite constitution are England, New Zealand and Israel. Even Israel has a growing set of laws judicially formed by the Israeli Supreme Court which define the human rights of the individual vis-à-vis the state including freedom of expression, religion and movement.[7] The Israeli Supreme Court in its consideration of such basic laws looks directly to

---

for the United Kingdom: The Constitutional Dilemma' [1981] Anglo-Am. L. Rev. 105 – P. L. Fitzgerald does not – 'An English Bill of Rights? Some Observations from Her Majesty's Former Colonies in America' [1982] 70 Geo. LJ 1229. See also Lawrence Goldstein's 'Paradox of Sovereignty' in 'Four Alleged Paradoxes of Legal Reasoning' [1979] CLJ 377.

[5] This was the contention in the famous case of *MacCormick* v. *The Lord Advocate* [1953] JC 396, but the issue was decided against the petitioners. See Neil MacCormick (whose father was the leading petitioner), 'Does the United Kingdom have a Constitution? Reflections on *MacCormick* v. *Lord Advocate*' [1978] 29 NILQ 1.

[6] Sir I. Jennings, *An Approach to Self Government* (Cambridge University Press, 1956), p. 20.

[7] See D. Kretzmer, 'Demonstrations and the Law' [1984] 19 Israel LR 47.

the American Supreme Court for its discussions of constitutional rights issues in similar contexts.

Constitutional rights have arrived through the back door to every country which has become a signatory to the Universal Declaration of Human Rights proclaimed by the General Assembly of the United Nations in 1948 as a reaction to the atrocities committed during the Second World War. They have also come through the back door by way of the European Convention for the Protection of Human Rights and Fundamental Freedoms signed in 1950 by the governments which were then members of the Council of Europe including the United Kingdom.

Anthony Lester has recently written up the cabinet and state papers of the British Government covering the period of drafting and signing the European Convention.[8] A similar chauvinism to that of Bentham 200 years before is clear from the cabinet papers, without, however, quite the same flair or logic. Those in the cabinet who were against signing the Convention felt that it was good for everyone else, but not for Great Britain. It was essential that foreigners and their governments, who could not be relied on to do the decent thing should be bound by such rules. However, it was not necessary for the British who can rely on the decency of their own people. Lord Jowitt the Lord Chancellor informed the cabinet,

> That we were not prepared to encourage our European friends to jeopardise our whole system of law, which we have laboriously built up over the centuries, in favour of some half-baked scheme to be administered by some unknown court.[9]

He also noted that the draftsman of the convention, 'does not seem to me to be highly skilled either in Constitutional Law, Comparative Law or in drafting'. It was regarded as an 'unqualified misfortune' for the administration of the law when for political reasons the government realized it would have to accept the convention. The Lord Chancellor described it as

> so vague and woolly that it may mean almost anything. Our unhappy legal experts – two distinguished home office officials – who would probably have expressed their complete inability to draft a bill (for example to prevent the docking and nicking of horses) – have had to take their share in drawing up a code compared to which the Code Napoleon – or indeed the Ten Commandments – are comparatively insignificant....

[8] Anthony Lester, 'Fundamental Rights: the UK Isolated? [1984] Public Law 46. These have only recently, under the 30-year rule, been released and made available to the public.
[9] Lester, 'Fundamental Rights', pp. 51–2.

It completely passes the wit of man to guess what results would be arrived at by a tribunal composed of elected persons who need not even be lawyers, drawn from various European states possessing completely different systems of law, and whose deliberations take place behind closed doors.... Any student of our legal institutions.... must recoil from this document with a feeling of horror ... I have appointed the Evershed Committee to advise me upon the desirability of cutting down the double appeal (both to the Court of Appeal and House of Lords). I cannot view with equanimity a still further appeal to a secret court, composed of persons with no legal training, possessing the unfettered right to expound the meaning of seventeen articles which may mean anything, or – as I hope – nothing.[10]

The political reasons for accepting the Convention were clearly that the British Government could not say to every other government that it was necessary for everyone else to have such a Convention which affected them, without the British Government also being included and bound by the Convention as a signatory.

The cabinet papers then go on to show that, for the British Government, the signing of the Convention was considered an end in itself. It was quite another question whether the United Kingdom should accept the right of an individual to petition directly to the European Court about a breach of the Convention; or whether the UK would recognize the jurisdiction of the European Court of Human Rights; or whether there should be any legislation to alter existing domestic law; and whether specifically to incorporate the rights and freedoms of the Convention into UK law.

In short, the right of individual petition was accepted by the new Labour Government at the end of 1965 without (as far as can be ascertained) much discussion at all. This right of individual petition began to cause 'problems' within a year and since then some 80 cases have been declared admissible by the Commission of Human Rights. In 1982 alone some 800 files were opened by the Commission against the UK and by September 1983, of the 34 cases in which the European Court had found a breach of the Convention, *seven* of these were against the UK.

In a very strong sense, therefore, human rights or civil liberties issues have already been incorporated by the back door into British jurisprudence. Even though we may not have a constitutional system or a set of such human rights incorporated within our own laws, there is a possibility of applying above the heads of our judiciary to the structures set up by the European Convention.

[10] Ibid., pp. 52–3.

Signing the Convention in 1950 and agreeing individual petition in 1965 might have been small steps for the rest of mankind, but were giant leaps for the British legal system. This is not, however, the end of the constitutional story. As Lester points out,[11] another chapter begins if one looks at the context of a new constitution for most of those countries who have one. Apart from a small number of cases, including the recent Canadian instance,[12] adopting a constitution has been the formal part of a political revolution. A complete change in political power and government has been formalized into the wording of a constitution, the adoption of which has signalled the advent of the new regime.

This has certainly been true for the countries which were part of the British Empire. As each of the Commonwealth countries adopted an Independence Constitution it looked to the Mother Country for guidance, or such guidance was forced upon it as a price of independence. Not having too many other constitutional models, the wording and framework the Mother Country suggested for civil liberties came straight out of the European Convention. It was, after all, to hand and, as stated above, was considered to be good for everyone else. Beginning with Nigeria in 1958, the constitution of the great majority of the newly independent Commonwealth countries have incorporated almost the entire European Convention as their model for the codes for fundamental rights contained in them. The independence constitutions of Cyprus and Malta are also largely based on the Nigerian model, but have certain differences. Similar provisions have been made in some remaining British dependent territories such as Bermuda, Gibraltar, and the Gilbert and Ellice Islands. The British Parliament has therefore exported wholesale the fundamental rights and freedoms of the Convention to the New Commonwealth, as Lester explains, 'on a scale without parallel in the rest of the world'.[13] The country that most clearly rejects constitutional rights for itself once again seems to be strongly in favour of it for everybody else.

It has not been possible to create such waves without some of them finding their way back to lap against the shores of our precious isle set in a silver sea. Many of these Commonwealth Countries still have appeals to the Judicial Committee of the Privy Council. The Judicial Committee is staffed by the judges who normally sit as the Judicial Committee of the House of Lords, sometimes joined by a judge or two from the commonwealth country itself. The Judges in the highest court in our

[11] Ibid., pp. 55ff.
[12] See P. A. Bender, 'The Canadian Charter' [1983] 28 McGill LJ 811 and R. S. Kay, 'The Creation of Constitutions in Canada and the US' [1984] 7 Can.–US LJ 111.
[13] Lester, 'Fundamental Rights', p. 56.

land, therefore, habitually sit and review the constitutionality of legislation and administrative action against standards which are directly derived from the European Convention. Many of the commonwealth countries utilizing this form of constitution, in the absence of any history of fundamental rights in their own country, increasingly refer to United States caselaw when interpreting their own codes. The Privy Council is therefore often constrained to look at cases coming to them in this guise in the light of the decisions of the US Supreme Court.[14] Constitutionalism in this sense has, therefore, not so much been knocking at our back door, but it has been sitting in the chambers of the highest court in the land.

These issues have gone almost unnoticed in the great debate. However, the existence of this available system and judicial resistance to it are important in understanding where the real distinctions between the constitutional rights and non-constitutional models lie.

The Real Distinctions

A different approach to how a constitution/human rights system and our own system operate may be shown graphically in a manner which takes us a little further than the 'every school child knows' statement with which we began. On one side of the diagram is a straight horizontal line and on the other side is a circle. The line demonstrates the constitutional system in which there is a 'floor of rights'. At some point to be decided by the judiciary and certain other officials, it is possible to stand on this floor of rights and say 'this I can do, it is my right'.

On the other side of the diagram, in the circle, is the goldfish bowl of human behaviour in the 'non-constitutional' system. Inside the goldfish bowl exist all sorts of sponge-like and amoebal creatures called laws, including crimes and civil obligations. One may swim around in this behavioural sphere wherever it is possible to do so without coming up against these areas of 'no right'.

There are problems with both systems. In the goldfish bowl the edges of the crimes are not always clear and they have the tendency of expanding (and sometimes, but rarely, contracting) at the whim of prosecutors, magistrates and judges. The effect is that, especially in the area of civil liberties, it is not possible to tell exactly where one can swim; although some areas are clearer than others. Over on the floor of rights, although it is clear that, at some point, you will hit that floor it

---

[14] But see an American's reaction to this: William Van Alstyne, 'Interpreting *THIS* Constitution: The Unhelpful Contributions of Special Theories of Judicial Review' [1983] U. Florida LR 209, where he discourses on the problems of an 'aged' constitution.

may take a long time to get to the Supreme Court which decides exactly where that floor is. This may be too late for an individual whose human rights have been ignored or who has suffered in contravention of the constitution at the hands of the local police force or local institutions.

There are many other approaches to portraying and understanding the difference between the two systems. The graphical approach above attempts to conceptualize from a theoretical standpoint what the difference might be. Another approach would be a 'comparative law' view involving the comparison of a case in each jurisdiction covering similar behaviour, and the outcome of each case and the manner in which they are decided. In order to understand this, one first has to appreciate how the other system works.

The Constitutional Way: The USA, A Case in Point

In 1791 the First Amendment to the Constitution of the United States was adopted, declaring that,

> Congress shall make no law... abridging the freedom of speech,... or the
> right of the people peaceably to assemble, and to petition the government
> for a redress of grievances.[15]

The Fourteenth Amendment applied the force of the First Amendment to all of the individual States.[16]

The First Amendment appears to have been framed and adopted as a reaction to the eighteenth century prosecutions in England for seditious libel directed against political discussion. The First Amendment was intended to show 'the essential difference' between the new America and the old Britain.[17] In America it was to be the people and not the government who were absolute sovereign.[18]

In the 'market place of ideas' truth would finally win, as Mill has suggested.[19] Some of the cases, including one which will be dealt with

---

[15] For an excellent review of the way in which the First Amendment was passed and the general background to it, see N. Dorsen, P. Bender and B. Neubourne, *Emerson, Haber and Dorsen's Political and Civil Rights in the United States*, 4th edn (Little, Brown, Boston, 1976).

[16] Adopted in 1868, part of it reads 'no State shall make or enforce any law which shall abridge the privileges or immunities or citizens of the United States; nor shall any State deprive any person of life, liberty or property, without due process of law; nor deny to any person within its jurisdiction the equal protection of the law.'

[17] Maddison, *Report on the Virginia Revolution, 1799.*

[18] Z. Chafee, *Free Speech in the United States* (Cambridge, Mass., Harvard University Press, 1941), p. 18.

[19] J. S. Mill, *On Liberty* (1859).

in this chapter, seem to take this belief literally. There is, however, plenty of observation among the academic texts to the contrary[20]

The 'market place of ideas' has indeed become a market place controlled by the economic and political interests which control the media.[21] The early American faith in the literal text of the First Amendment does not match with the real world of ideas, and has been quite strongly cut back in many of the Supreme Court cases. Emerson, Haber and Dorsen also chart how immigration, the slavery controversy leading to the Civil War, the work of radicals in the early 1900s, the impact of the First and Second World Wars and McCarthyism all caused heavy state incursions into the freedom of expression doctrine.

The Supreme Court have used three basic methods in order to exclude cases from an absolute right of free speech.[22] Some expression has been termed 'non-speech' including, for example, 'the lewd and obscene, the profane, the libelous and the insulting or "fighting" words – those which by their very utterance inflict injury or tend to incite an immediate breach of the peace'.[23] Obscene publications are also not protected on this basis[24] nor is 'commercial speech' of some sorts. There are some doubts about whether 'speech-plus', speech with action, and 'symbolic speech', such as the displaying of a red flag,[25] are protected.

The next set of procedural techniques resolve First Amendment issues by deciding whether rigorous standards of acceptable procedure were used by the government in attempting to suppress the speech. These include the ban on prior restraints; the 'void for vagueness' doctrine used where a state law does not express its meaning with sufficient clarity, e.g. where a vague proscription may have 'a chilling effect' on speech; and 'over-breadth' where state statutes sweep too broadly or outlaw protected and unprotected conduct or allow for discriminatory enforcement. Also included under this heading are principles of equal access to and due process of the law.

Where the Supreme Court cannot avoid a decision on a substantive First Amendment issue through one of the two previous methods it is forced to adjudicate directly using 'the bad tendency' test, the 'clear and present danger test', the 'incitement test' and differing forms of *ad*

---

[20] See, e.g. A. M. Bickel, *The Morality of Consent* (New Haven, Yale University Press, 1975), pp. 76–8; L. W. Tribe, *American Constitutional Law* (Mineola, Foundation Press, NY, 1978), p. 577 and others referred to in Supperstone, *Brownlie*, p. 84.
[21] An observation by Malcolm Muggeridge in his autobiography exposes another possible reasoning: 'People, after all, believe lies, not because they are plausibly presented, but because they want to believe them.'
[22] See Dorsen, Bender and Neuborne, *Emerson, Haber and Dorsen*, pp. 37–45.
[23] *Chaplinsky* v. *New Hampshire* (1942) 315 US 568.
[24] *Roth* v. *United States* [1957] 354 US 476.
[25] *Stromberg* v. *California* [1931] 283 US 359.

hoc balancing. Against these tests Justices Black and Douglas have expressed, in dissent, an 'absolute' view of freedom of speech protection which stated that once the court acknowledges that a government has imposed a restriction on freedom of speech no further room exists for weighing values.[26]

It is worth making a particular case study, in order to compare how the First Amendment may work in the United States with how similar cases operate in this country. For example, the question of the way each jurisdiction deals with the 'heckler's veto' can be studied in this manner. Comparative law is a somewhat risky business and it is not always clear whether one is comparing like with like, but it may be worthwhile attempting this approach with two direct cases one in each jurisdiction such as *Feiner* v. *New York* and *Jordan* v. *Burgoyne*.

These two cases both consider whether freedom of speech should only be given to those who speak with the agreement of their audience. Should freedom of speech be given only to those who speak with what would be the agreement of any 'reasonable' audience? Should the first person to reach the field have freedom of speech, but the second person, the hostile audience, not have freedom of speech there or at that time?

In *Feiner*[27] the accused was standing on a wooden box on the sidewalk in Syracuse addressing the crowd through a loud speaker system attached to a car. He was inviting listeners to attend a meeting whose venue had been changed at the last moment because the local authorities cancelled the permit to use a school building. In this context, according to the findings of the court, Feiner was making derogatory remarks concerning President Truman, the American Legion, the Mayor of Syracuse and other local political officials. The trial court found that as his speech went on he gave the impression that he was endeavouring to 'arouse the negro people against the whites, urging that they rise up in arms and fight for equal rights'.

Some of the onlookers, one of whom had been standing in the crowd quite far from the speaker, together with his wife and children, complained to a police officer that if the policeman did not stop the speaker, he would stop him. After being asked twice to stop, Feiner was arrested and went meekly. Feiner was charged with the offence of disorderly conduct, which included using 'offensive, disorderly, threatening, abusive, or insulting language, conduct, or behaviour', as well as congregating 'with others on a public street and refusing to move on when ordered by the police'.

The United States Supreme Court found that the police had properly

[26] Dorsen, Bender and Neuborne, *Emerson, Haber and Dorsen*, p. 45.
[27] *Feiner* v. *New York* (1951) 340 US 315.

exercised their discretionary power to prevent a breach of the peace, as had the trial court and two other courts on review. The opinion of Chief Justice Vinson says quite clearly 'Petitioner was thus neither arrested, nor convicted for the making or the content of his speech. Rather it was the *reaction which it actually engendered*'. Whilst the Court recognized Feiner's right to express even unpopular views, they found that he had gone beyond 'argument or persuasion and undertook incitement to riot'. It should be noted, in passing, that the facts, as given in the dissenting judgment of Justice Black, suggest a very different scenario.

Whether or not Feiner is still law (and there is some question about this) it is interesting to compare it with the English case of *Jordan* v. *Burgoyne*[28] Feiner took place in 1949, whereas *Jordan* v. *Burgoyne* took place in England in 1962. This was a public meeting in Trafalgar Square, at which two people, Colin Jordan and John Tyndall, addressed the public. It was found that there was a crowd of some 2000 people of which about 200 or 300 young people were positioned together immediately in front of the speaker's platform. This mixed group contained 'many Jews, supporters of the Campaign for Nuclear Disarmament, and Communists'.[29] Colin Jordan in his opening words said'

> As for the Red rabble here present with us in Trafalgar Square, it is not a very good afternoon at all. Some of them are looking far from wholesome, more than usual I mean. We shall of course excuse them if they have to resort to smelling salts or first aid. Meanwhile, let them howl, these multi-racial warriors of the Left. It is a sound that comes natural to them, it saves them from the strain of thinking for themselves.[30]

A little bit later, at about 5.15 p.m., when the crowd had grown to about 5000 people, Colin Jordan said,

> More and more people every day are opening their eyes and coming to say with us 'Hitler was right'. They are coming to say that our real enemies, the people we should have fought, were not Hitler and the National Socialists of Germany, but world Jewry and its associates in this country.[31]

At this point there was disorder, an outcry, and a general surge forward by the crowd towards the speaker's platform, although a large police cordon surrounded the platform. Jordan was arrested and charged with

[28] *Jordan* v. *Burgoyne* [1963] 2 QB 744, and sec pp. 81, 82, 92, 94 and 149 above.
[29] Ibid.
[30] Ibid., 749.
[31] Ibid., 745.

using insulting words whereby a breach of the peace was likely to be occasioned, contrary to Section 5 of the Public Order Act of 1936.[32]

The trial court found as a fact that a great many of the words used by the defendant were highly insulting, but were not likely to lead ordinary, reasonable persons attending the meeting in Trafalgar Square, to commit breaches of the peace by committing assaults and, accordingly, allowed the defendant's appeal against conviction. On further appeal by the prosecutor (Jordan appearing in person not represented by a barrister) to the Queens' Bench Divisional Court, Lord Chief Justice Parker disagreed with the previous Court, saying,

> I cannot, myself, having read the speech, imagine any reasonable citizen, certainly one who was a Jew, not being provoked beyond endurance, and not only a Jew but a coloured man, and quite a number of people in this country who were told that they were merely tools of the Jews, and that they had fought in the war on the wrong side, and matters of that sort.[33]

'A man is entitled to express his own views as strongly as he likes, to criticise his opponents, to say disagreeable things about his opponents and about their policies, and to do anything of that sort',[34] but the words spoken 'were words which were intended to be and were deliberately insulting to that body of persons restrained by the police, and on that alone it seems to me that there was a contravention of Section 5 of the Act of 1936'.[35]

So, in both of these cases one could say that the heckler's veto applied. As with Feiner it is difficult to reconcile Jordan with other cases, including, for example, *Beatty* v. *Gillbanks*,[36] where the heckler's veto of the skeleton army was not allowed to prevent the Salvation Army from conducting its usual business.

This form of comparative analysis, however, does not always lead to such certain conclusions. The accidents of litigation (i.e. that cases only occur to define the law in the peculiar ways in which cases find their way to appellate court level) result in no well defined areas in either jurisdiction. It is, therefore, extremely difficult to compare in a sufficiently broad manner; to make judgements across the board about the effects of constitutional rights protection.

What is more obvious and clearer is the manner or form in which the decisions are arrived at. It is very clear, for example, that the given reasons in judicial writings under the constitutional system appear to

[32] Repealed by the Public Order Act 1986.
[33] Ibid., 748.
[34] Ibid., 749.
[35] Ibid.
[36] See above pp. 79–82, 122–3.

address the exact question of principle of the civil liberties involved. The judicial writings in deciding public order cases under the non-constitutional system only consider the question of whether a crime or another law has been broken. It is rare to see even lip service paid in the English cases to the subject of the actual liberties or rights of the individual such as, for example, some of the wording mentioned above in *Jordan* v. *Burgoyne* or the recent comments by Mr Justice Otton in *Hirst* and *Agu*. Where it *is* mentioned a right is almost always expressed in hypothetical terms which do not apply to the case in question.

Although in theory this is a substantial, substantive difference between the two approaches it may not be quite as important as it appears. The fact that in one case judges express their opinions in a particular format which *appears* to address the relevant issues and in the other case they explain the reasons for their decisions in a completely different form, does not necessarily mean that the two sets of judges have actually reached their decisions in any very different manner. This view does not necessarily belittle the importance of providing judges with the ability to make decisions about civil liberties with at least the articulation of theories of civil liberty in mind. It says, however, that this factor may not be quite as important as many suggest.

The argument then also becomes somewhat circular. The UK system is problematic because it relies too heavily on the officials within the system: the police, the magistrates, the prosecutors and the judges. However, a system which relies more on rule and regulation, such as that in a written Bill of Rights, also needs judges at an even higher level to interpret those rules and regulations. If one is not happy with the views of the judiciary then the same problems apply.[37]

Another way of assessing the different systems is to look more closely at how they work not only in law but also in practice. This may help to break the circle in which theory seems to place us. The case study that we will look at in some detail is the 'Skokie–Nazi' litigation in the United States in 1977 and 1978.

The Village of Skokie and the National Socialist Party of America

The 'Skokie–Nazi' case involved a number of law suits and even more decisions. The litigation concerned the efforts of the Village of Skokie to obtain an injunction against the National Socialist Party of America

[37] See Mauro Cappelletti, 'The "Mighty Problem" of Judicial Review and the Contribution of Comparative Analysis' [1980] 53 So. Cal. LR 409, for a more European view. See also, for example, the furore over Reagan's appointment of a new Supreme Court judge, the Robert Bork episode – *The Times*, e.g. 6 Sept. 1987. For a review of Dworkin's 'inherent rights' theory, see Neil MacCormick, 'Jurisprudence and the Constitution' [1983] CLP 13.

('the NSPA') to prohibit them from marching in Skokie on May 1st 1977; the NSPA's action which challenged the village of Skokie's march related ordinances; the NSPA's law suits which challenged the City of Chicago's practices regarding rallies in Marquette Park; the Anti-Defamation League of B'nai Brith's law suit against the NSPA and other more minor efforts to frustrate Nazi freedom of expression. The present study will be confined to a discussion of the major court decisions through which most of the issues are portrayed.[38]

The case is interesting because it tested out the realities of free speech for people with unpopular views together with the realities of a nation's belief in freedom of speech under all circumstances for all people. The case concerned Frank Collin 'a racist and a fascist, a bigoted totalitarian, a self-avowed Nazi'.[39] Collin was head of the National Socialist Party of America which among other things called for the forcible deportation of Jews, Blacks, Latinos and other non-whites from the USA.

Collin and his organization were adept at obtaining publicity in the Chicago area where he was based. In particular, his marches in and around Marquette Park, where racial tension on the south-west side of Chicago was high, had caused violence including rock throwing between the NSPA on one side and blacks, and supporters of their right to live where they choose, on the other. These marches resulted in Collin's arrest and an insurance requirement for $250,000 prior to the issuing of a demonstration permit in one of the city parks.

At this point, Collin applied to the local branch of the American Civil Liberties Union (ACLU) for assistance.[40] The ACLU support for Collin and his Nazi group was to bring about an enormous rift in the ACLU itself, between those who were prepared to give help to anyone who wanted freedom of speech and those who were not prepared to fight for the freedom of speech of those who would not guarantee freedom of speech to everyone else. In particular, large scale funding of the ACLU by Jewish people and Jewish organizations was withdrawn as a result of this case.

Meanwhile, apparently, Collin was looking around for other places to march and wrote to a number of Chicago suburbs asking for permission to stage rallies in their parks. Among these was the Village of Skokie, Illinois, a small suburb on the north of Chicago more than 50 per cent

[38] *National Socialist Party of America et al.* v. Village of Skokie (1977) 97 S. Ct. 2205, 14 June 1977; *Village of Skokie* v. *National Socialist Party of America et al.* (1977) 366 NE 2d 347, 12 July 1977; *Village of Skokie* v. *National Socialist Party of America et al.* 373 NE 2d 21, 27 Jan. 1978.

[39] David Hamlin 'Swastikas and Survivors: inside the Skokie–Nazi free speech case'. *Civ. Lib. Rev.*, March/Apr. 1978, p. 8.

[40] Ibid., p. 12.

of whose residents were Jewish. 'While other communities largely ignored Collin's letter or simply replied no, Skokie took action'.[41]

It seems that the Village of Skokie, with some reason, thought that they had been singled out for this provocation. They therefore passed an ordinance legislating an insurance requirement for a rally in any park in the Skokie Park district with $350,000 in insurance cover prior to a rally permit being granted. The intended effect, as with the similar requirement for Marquette Park, was to make a rally in Skokie too expensive for Collin. Even if he could find insurance to cover his activities, with the record of violence arising out of his rallies, the cost would be more than he could raise.

The Village of Skokie replied to Collin informing him of the ordinance, which had the effect of waving 'a red flag at a charging bull'.[42] Collin knew already as a result of his experiences with the ACLU at Marquette Park that such an ordinance was unconstitutional. He therefore wrote back to the Village of Skokie announcing that he intended to picket the village hall on Sunday 1 May 1977 in protest at the City ordinance, at which time his followers would wear their uniforms.

Initial efforts in the Village were aimed at a calm reaction and a policy which would allow the demonstration, but ignore it. However, opposition soon grew to this reaction and, coupled with the threat of a massive counter-demonstration from left-wing groups and late night telephone calls to Jewish-surnamed residents, the Village decided to seek an injunction preventing Collin and the NSPA from parading through the streets of Skokie in uniform on 1 May.

Despite the backing of the ACLU for Collin, Judge Wosik issued an injunction against the march on 28 April 1977. On 29 April the Illinois Appellate Court denied Collin's appeal without giving reasons. Collin immediately announced his intention to march the next day, 30 April, a date not mentioned in the injunction against him. The Village of Skokie thereupon obtained an injunction banning Collin and the NSPA from parading in uniform in Skokie on 30 April and 'until further order of the court'.

The basis of the Village of Skokie's arguments all the way through these cases had been not that Collin was intending to do anything illegal, but that the effect of what he was going to do would cause others to carry out violent and illegal acts against him and his supporters. They were in effect using the 'heckler's veto' argument against Collin, or in English terms the argument of 'taking your audience as you find it'.[43]

[41] Ibid.
[42] Ibid.
[43] See p. 94 above.

A notice of the new injunction was served on Collin as he arrived just outside the Village of Skokie and the projected march was averted on Saturday 30 April. The US Supreme Court on 14 June 1977 ruled that an expedited hearing must occur on the merits of the injunction. Collin took advantage of this to announce his intention to march in Skokie on 4 July 1977. The Illinois State Supreme Court, reacting as slowly as it could to the US Supreme Court's ruling on expedition scheduled a hearing for 8 July.[44] The Illinois Appellate Court removed the ban on uniforms, but left standing the remainder of the original order modified as follows,

> (Defendants) be and hereby are enjoined and restrained from engaging in any of the following actions within the Village of Skokie until further order of the court: Intentionally displaying the swastika on or off their persons in the course of a demonstration, march, or parade.

The appellate court also suggested that the Village of Skokie might have made a case for a 'clear and present danger' by offering testimony regarding the previous actions of Collin and his followers from law enforcement officials. The entire matter was therefore remanded back to the lower court for further hearings on that particular issue. The court did, however, reverse the elements of the original injunction which purported to enjoin Collin and the NSPA from marching, walking or parading in the Village of Skokie whether or not dressed in their 'storm trooper' uniforms. The wearing of the storm trooper uniform 'was considered only the communication of ideas' and therefore protected speech. The court drew a distinction between wearing the uniform without the swastika and wearing the uniform with the swastika, which might constitute 'fighting words' and, therefore, not be part of protected speech. The last part of the injunction which had prevented the NSPA from 'distributing pamphlets or displaying any materials which incite or promote hatred against persons of Jewish faith or ancestry or hatred against persons of any faith or ancestry, race or religion' was also reversed on the basis that no need was shown for it in this particular case.

In summary, therefore, all that remained of the original injunction was the restraint against displaying the swastika. This then became the subject of appeal to the Supreme Court of Illinois which ruled on 27 January 1978. The Court ruled clearly that it was bound by previous United States Supreme Court cases to 'permit the demonstration as proposed, including display of the swastika'.[45]

[44] See *Village of Skokie* v. *National Socialist Party of America et al.* (1977) 366 NE 2d 347, 12 July 1977.
[45] *Village of Skokie* v. *National Socialist Party of America* (1977) 373 NE 2d 21.

Especially important was the case of *Cohen* v. *California*[46] during the Vietnam War in which the defendant had worn a jacket with the words 'Fuck the Draft' on it in a state courthouse. Ideas could not be prohibited merely because they were offensive to some of their hearers. Wearing some distinctive clothing was 'symbolic expression' which falls within the free speech clause of the First Amendment, as was also decided in *Tinker*, in which children at school wore black armbands to show their disagreement with the Vietnam war.[47] There was a specially heavy burden on the Village of Skokie to justify imposing a prior restraint on the Defendants' right to freedom of speech. This could not be met by applying the 'fighting words' doctrine which was designed 'to permit punishment of extremely hostile personal communication likely to cause immediate physical response'.[48] The court did not consider that the swastika fell within the definition of 'fighting words' and, therefore, that it could not be used to overcome the heavy presumption against the validity of a prior restraint.

Neither could the swastika be restrained on the basis that it would cause violent reaction from an 'hostile audience' by operating a 'hecklers veto'. The court quoted comments made by a New York Supreme Court in relation to a projected public demonstration by another American Nazi leader, George Lincoln Rockwell,

> So, the unpopularity of views, their shocking quality, their obnoxiousness, and even their alarming impact is not enough. Otherwise, the preacher of any strange doctrine could be stopped; the anti-racist himself could be suppressed, if he undertakes to speak in 'restricted' areas; and one who asks that public schools be open indiscriminately to all ethnic groups could be lawfully suppressed, if only he chose to speak where persuasion is needed most.[49]

Those who would be offended by the swastika should be forewarned and place themselves in a position where they would not need to view it. As a result of this appeal to the Illinois Supreme Court all elements of the original injunction were therefore now removed.

Finally, on 23 February 1978 the Illinois District Court ruled in detail on the constitutionality of the three village ordinances passed by Skokie on 2 May 1977. The first ordinance had required all applicants for parade or public assembly permits to obtain $300,000 in liability insurance and $50,000 in property damage insurance. The second ordinance had made criminal the dissemination of material inciting racial

[46] *Cohen* v. *California* [1971] 403 US 15.
[47] *Tinker* v. *Des Moines Independent Community School District* (1969) 393 US 503.
[48] *Village of Skokie* v. *National Socialist Party of America et al.* (1977) 373 NE 2d 21.
[49] *Rockwell* v. *Morris* 12 AD 2D 272, 282–1 [1961].

or religious hatred, with intent to incite such hatred. The third ordinance prohibited public demonstrations by members of political parties wearing military style uniforms.

District Judge Decker, in short, found that the insurance ordinance imposed a 'virtually insuperable obstacle' to the exercise of First Amendment rights 'which may be disposed of at the uncontrolled and standardless discretion of the village government'.[50] The inciting racial or religious hatred ordinances were also found to be unconstitutional on the basis that unpopular ideas were protected unless they were likely to incite 'imminent lawless action'. Neither could the racial slurs be classed as unprotected speech under the 'fighting words' test since for that they would have to be 'abusive and insulting rather than a communication of ideas'.[51] Though 'the line between protected and unprotected speech in matters relating to race and religion is an extraordinarily difficult one to draw',[52] an ordinance which punishes language which intentionally incites hatred is 'subjective and impossible to clearly define'[53] and the ordinance was therefore unconstitutionally overbroad, and could not be considered to be limited in its scope only to racial libel.

Finally, the Court found the ordinance providing that:

> No person shall engage in any march, walk or public demonstration as a member or on behalf of any political party while wearing a military-style uniform.... patently and flagrantly unconstitutional on its face.[54]

All of the ordinances passed by the Village of Skokie were therefore ruled as unconstitutional and the village was enjoined from enforcing any of the ordinances against Collin and the NSPA. The judge pointed out, as Mr Justice Harlan had in *Cohen* v. *California*, 'that the air may at times seem filled with verbal cacophony is ... not a sign of weakness but of strength'.[55]

Comparison The major differences between the law, as it is written, in the USA and England regarding the issues raised in the Skokie case study are clear. Section 1 of the English Public Order Act, 1936 prohibits the wearing of uniform signifying association 'with any political organization or with the promotion of any political object'.[56] Section 2 prohibits the organization and training or equipping of persons for 'the

[50] *Collin* v. *Smith* [1978] 447 F. Supp. 676.
[51] Ibid.
[52] Ibid., 17.
[53] Ibid., 19.
[54] Ibid., 32.
[55] Ibid., 34.
[56] See p. 144 above.

use or display of physical force in promoting any political object'.[57] These would both, if applied to the USA, have prohibited some of the NSPA's suggested activities. The use of words or behaviour intended to stir up racial hatred or likely to do so is an offence under section 18 of the Public Order Act 1986. The publishing or distributing of similar written material is an offence under section 19 of the Act. Section 11 of the Public Order Act 1986 provides that advance notice must be given of public processions to the police[58] and sections 12 and 13 allow the police to impose conditions on public processions or to ban them.[59] Conditions may also be imposed on public assemblies under section 14 of the 1986 Act.[60]

It would seem, therefore, that under English law all of the forms of behaviour which the Village of Skokie was attempting to prohibit, could be controlled and prohibited by law. It is not clear whether a local authority or even central government could impose an insurance precondition on the use of a public open space, since the issue has not been litigated, although contractually it may be possible to do so for use of a building.[61]

With all of this written prohibition operative and available on this side of the Atlantic, and the complete written freedoms demonstrated on the other side of the Atlantic, it is interesting to note what actually occurs in practice. Frank Collin and the National Socialist Party of America never did march in the Village of Skokie, Illinois. Regularly, members of the Sinn Fein, the political wing of the Irish Republican Army, march here wearing berets and dark glasses (held to be political uniforms),[62] and the National Front in their 'colour parties' have marched often on the streets of London and other English towns.

The constant restatement in the American cases of the ability of minority rights protesters to speak freely under the constitution in areas where their views are not respected was clearly shown to be impractical and impossible during the American Civil Rights campaigns of the 1960s. The physical violence to which campaigners were exposed and even the attempts through litigation to stop such marches made such absolute freedom of speech a fond, but derisory hope. The control of the market place of ideas by media serving their own interests, and not

---

[57] See p. 148 above.
[58] See p. 69 above.
[59] See p. 74 above.
[60] See p. 68 above.
[61] A local authority may not change its mind, even if its political complexion has changed, over whether a Nazi organization may use one of its halls for their annual conference – *Verrall* v. *Great Yarmouth Borough Council* [1980] 1 All ER 839.
[62] See, e.g. *O'Moran* and *Whelan*, p. 145 above.

necessarily those of fairness and justice also calls into question the reality of freedom of speech.

As between the two jurisdictions compared here, the position on the statute and casebooks can be quite different, and sometimes exactly opposite to, the reality of demonstration and protest on the streets. A constitution *in itself*, or any form of words legislating for human rights, is therefore clearly not a complete answer. This returns us to the question with which we began.

The Great Debate and the Human Rights Bill

The great debate (which touches not the heart or mind of the man or woman on the top of the Clapham Omnibus, but has raised some judicial eyebrows and has spawned some fifteen to twenty pieces in the Anglo-American literature over the last decade)[63] is the question of whether Great Britain should adopt a constitutional Bill of Rights such as that contained within the European convention.

Foremost among the protagonists for a Bill of Rights has been Lord Scarman, the Law Lord who has acted as a government trouble shooter in chairing Inquiries into problems in Northern Ireland, Red Lion Square in 1974 when a student was killed and the Brixton disorders 1981. In almost every case he has seen his function as being to deliver some whitewash regarding the police or government forces at the same time as making suggestions for the future which clearly show some transparency in the whitewash.[64] His twenty-sixth Hamlyn Lecture in 1974 in which he advocated a Bill of Rights for the UK began, in the academic world at least, renewed interest in a constitutional Bill of Rights.[65] Most of the argument in the literature is *for* change, seeking to push the UK into adopting some constitutional form. The minority view, once again held not necessarily by those one would think of as

[63] See the articles cited here and P. G. Schrag, 'By the People: the Political Dynamics of a Constitutional Country' [1984] 72 Ge. LJ 819–1108; R. A. Bust, 'Constitutional Law and the Teaching of the Parables', 93 Yale LJ 455–502 [1984]; J. H. Ely, 'Professor Dworkin's External/Personal Preference Distinction' [1983] Duke LJ 959–86; R. M. Cover, 'The S.C. 1982 Term-Foreword: Nomos & Narrative' [1983] 97 Harv. LR 68; M. K. Curtis and R. Berger, '9 Lived Cat – Incorp. of Bill of Rights' [1982] 43–4 Ohio St L. 3 89–124 1982, 1–19 1983; G. Marshall, 'UK Parl. and Brit. N. American Acts', Alberta LR 352–62; L. G. Scarman, 'Law, Lawyers and Government', 14 Bracton LJ 1–6; Conference on Comp. Con. Law [1986] 53 So. Calif. LR 401–785; P. Allot, 'Courts and Parliament' [1979] 38 Camb. LJ 79–117.
[64] See A. Sherr, 'The Scarman Report on "The Brixton Disorders 10–12 April 1981" – A Retrospective Review', *Urban Law and Policy* 7 (1985) 227–41.
[65] L. Scarman, *English Law – the New Dimension* (London, Stevens, 1974), pp. 18–21.

chauvinists (including Professor John Griffith of the LSE),[66] is against the idea.

The modern-day mother of democracy, who has in one way or another given birth to constitutions or foisted constitutions on a large part of the world, is therefore being forced to rethink her own form of existence.[67] Such rethinking, however sporadically repeated, does not look likely to achieve imminent success; and the most recent attempt to incorporate the European convention into British law was foiled in the House of Commons in February 1987.[68] Some have suggested that judicial review will finally be brought to Great Britain through the 'chunnel' or channel tunnel on the back of the European Economic Community caselaw. As Ken Karst explains, the American constitution was similarly brought to all the states through its commercial and economic importance initially.[69]

Society and Constitution

Whether or not our constitutionalization is imminent, there are other issues which also need to be explored relating to the effects of such a change. What differences, for example, are engendered generally in the culture of a society by the presence of a constitution and a constitutional system of rights as opposed to their absence? This does not mean the narrow differences relating to these civil liberties themselves, but the differences which may be affected by the constitutionalism, or rule orientation, or higher norm orientation, of that society. If perceivable differences exist between 'constitutional' countries and 'non-constitutional' countries, are they the cause or effect of constitutionalism? This is important to know because the answers may affect the decision whether the UK is a good subject for a constitution. If the UK is a good subject, what other effects may a constitution have on it, and what else will we need to change in order to accommodate the constitution? The USA is, for example, a society more based on legalism, conscious

[66] J. Griffith, 'The Political Constitution' [1979] 42 MLR 1.
[67] The author likened this, in the title of a paper given to the Law Faculty at UCLA, to the God figure who having originally created man in his own image, is being forced to reconsider remaking God himself in the image of God's own creation as it has evolved. ('Recreating God in the image of man.')
[68] See *The Times*, 7 Feb. 1987. For a discussion of some previous attempts, see John Kenny, 'The Advantages of a Written Constitution Incorporating a Bill of Rights' [1979] 30 NILQ 189; Glenn Abernathy, 'Should the UK Adopt a Bill of Rights?' [1983] Am. Jo. Comp. Law 431.
[69] K. Karst 'Judicial Review and the Channel Tunnel', [1980] 53 SO. Calif. LR, 401–785 and J. D. B. Mitchell, 'What Happened to the Constitution on 1st January 1973?' [1980] 11 Camb. LR 69–86.

of legalisms and quite heavily burdened with rules. There appear to be
far more rules and laws guarding and guiding every possible way of life
than there appear to be in England. Secondly, there appears to be very
little reliance on internal morality inculcated as part of the system
generally and as part of the educational system in particular. Obediance
to outside rules and recourse to externally imposed rules of morality
seems to be considered more important than relying on engendering or
installing internal codes of discretion of certainty of limits and knowledge
of what is right and wrong.

A simplistic example is the ABA Model Rules of Professional Conduct
the new code of ethics for the legal profession. For the fifty-two rules
in the new ABA code the English solicitor had until recently nine basic
rules dealing with the same subject areas. Such questions, which are
difficult to answer, have not received attention in the literature or in
public debate.[70] Clearly, the British system and the British mentality
would not change over-night with a Bill of Rights. But does having a
constitution lead to some of these effects or is it necessary for these
factors to be present for a constitution to work?

Another order of questions not yet addressed is whether the
'constitutional' approach encourages one style of 'lawyering' as opposed
to another. The particular pair of opposites of styles which it may be
worth studying are what might be called the *principled* approach or style,
as opposed to the *letter of the law* approach. The 'principled' lawyer
takes on every question of law head on and goes directly to attack the
issue at stake. The 'letter of the law but not the spirit' lawyer works
out what the law says and finds ways of avoiding it.   Would, or does,
the ability to discuss the issues of principle on civil liberty cases in the
constitutional system encourage much more of the *principled style* of
lawyer which does appear to be more straightforward, more direct and
more honest, but is also more argumentative, more time consuming and
more litigious, than the *avoiding style*?

Other social differences between the USA and the UK include a much
more rational, simplified approach to both life and change in the USA.
Does the simple statement of freedoms give rise to a simpler approach
to life and change? There seems to be a more mechanical approach to
emotional questions as well as a more mechanical approach to political,
social and economic change in the USA. England is so encrusted with
tradition that it is extremely difficult to change even the smallest item.
Such questions may not necessarily be directly related to a constitutional
system in which a basis of first principles can be adverted to. However,

---

[70] But see Michael Asimow's discussion of similar issues in 'Delegated Legislation: United
States and United Kingdom' [1983] 3 Ox. Jo. Leg. St. 253.

it is worth remembering how they were used in order to make grand social changes such as those that have occurred since the 1960s regarding racial issues in the USA. There does seem to be a common belief in the USA that change is easily possible and that the face validity or external validity of such change can be equated with social change itself. There are clear advantages in a system which promotes (necessary) change. There are also clear disadvantages in too simplistic a view of such issues.

Two other factors may well be equally important in noting such distinctions. In England, and perhaps in the whole of Europe, the much stronger class system has kept a surprising stronghold on normative values and behaviour. There are just certain things which certain people would not do. One question is whether, if England becomes a less homogenous society and the class system is no longer adhered to, a constitution would be more applicable. England is also a much smaller country. It could fit well within California and, therefore, it is much easier to instill and maintain normative control through values, than over such a wide expanse as in the USA.

A more rigorous examination along these lines would entail consideration of other countries as well. But in terms of common law jurisdictions the United States has the most mature constitution. Such issues also need to be properly examined before a considered decision can be made whether a constitution will answer the more fundamental problems involved in freedom of demonstration and protest. If we are to enact a Bill of Rights and attempt to make that change meaningful, we need to know what other concomitant circumstances are necessary and what effects will occur.

Conclusion

This chapter has reviewed the question of whether the main problems involved in dealing with protest and demonstration could be dealt with better under a system of constitutional rights or freedoms. It does not seem that there are any easy answers.

Comparing different systems takes us some of the distance, but provides no certainty. Many of the difficulties in handling a bill of rights, are difficulties which are in any event endemic in the problems of the law relating to demonstration and protest. Other issues relating to the culture of the society in which a bill of rights is to operate have not yet been fully explored. For many of the writers, the system they know is the system they prefer. For others, rather like Dryden,

For forms of government let fools contest,
What e'er is best administered is best

Absalom and Achitophel

It would be difficult to transplant something so clearly different from the rest of the legal structure, without a major fear of rejection of the transplant by the rest of the system.

The question of enacting such a Bill of Rights in relation to freedom of protest has an intrinsic value quite outside of the merits of the issue. But Article 11 of the European Convention portrays how weak such statements can be,

1. Everyone has the right to freedom of peaceful assembly and to freedom of association with others, including the right to form and to join trade unions for the protection of his interests.

2. No restrictions shall be placed on the exercise of these rights other than such as are prescribed by law and are necessary in a democratic society in the interests of national security or public safety, for the prevention of disorder or crime, for the protection of health or morals or for the protection of the rights and freedoms of others. This article shall not prevent the imposition of lawful restrictions on the exercise of these rights by members of the armed forces, of the police or of the administration of the State.

And the CARAF case only underlines this fact.[71]

The value of the debate has been to show how similar and how difficult the problems are of providing for real freedom of protest and demonstration under both forms of legal system. The comparisons have shown that it is not necessarily the legal form, but more the will of the government, prosecutors and police, that decides how much, or how little, freedom to protest exists.

[71] See ch. 8 above.

10

Epilogue

A recent, curious attempt at legislating for 'freedom of speech within the law' came into force on 1 September 1987 as a result of section 43 of the Education (2) Act 1986. In itself it shows how easy it can be to confuse rhetoric with reality.

Section 43 requires universities, polytechnics and colleges to 'take such steps as are reasonably practicable to ensure that freedom of speech within the law is secured for members, students and employees ... and for visiting speakers'. Such institutions are also required to issue a Code of Practice dealing with procedure for meetings organized on university premises (section 43 (3)) and to take such steps as are practicable to ensure observance of the code, including where necessary disciplining offenders.

As may be gathered from the public and parliamentary debates prior to the enactment of this section, the government was particularly worried about incidents in which government ministers had been heckled or prevented from speaking on university premises. Tettenborn suggests that the section is extremely vague, has few teeth, and is more likely to limit the range and number of speakers than it is to encourage any real freedom of speech.[1] It is curious that institutions of higher learning should be singled out by statute to ensure 'freedom of speech within the law', whereas no other public institutions are similarly charged. Since no specific sanctions are given to the section for enforcement it is not clear what would happen in the event that section 43 were to be ignored or broken. Conceivably an injunction would be available to prevent the denial of freedom of speech to a particular speaker or an order of mandamus might force an institution to carry out the section.[2] However, beyond these it is not clear that the section gives any more legal rights than are already available.

Since there is no definition of what may be meant by *'reasonably*

[1] A. M. Tettenborn, 'Universities: A Boost for Free Speech?' [1987] NLJ 30 Oct. 1021–3.
[2] Ibid., 1022.

practicable' in the circumstances or 'freedom of speech *within the law*'
it is not clear how important such let-outs will be. Altogether it seems
to be a somewhat feeble attempt at legislating for such freedom, in
fairly specific circumstances relating to government officials. Such
attempts cannot enhance the likelihood of a more general 'freedom of
speech' being adopted usefully by the legislature. However, it does show
that government is prepared to consider and foster such concepts where
it suits them whether or not the results will be meaningful in practice.

It is hoped that this book may have provided the reader with some
food for thought regarding demonstrations and protest, liberally spiced
with an approach that does not allow anything to be taken at its face
value, especially the law. The idea of a freedom of protest, the law of
protest and the realities of protest itself are all inextricably linked with
the rhetoric of politics. With section 43 of the Education (2) Act 1986
and even in relation to the more detailed and better thought out Public
Order Act 1986, it is never clear how much is an attempt to sway public
opinion or make a statement, without necessarily having effect in the
real world. However, that real world, and the rights of individuals to
voice their grievances undeterred by the powerful forces of, and within,
the state, are too important to be lost among the rhetoric. This book
has attempted to provide a clear vantage point from which to view the
subject area without being sucked into the vortex of political argument
or confused by the deliberately contradictory operation of stated law
and legal decision. By providing a basis in political and legal theory, as
well as a sociological understanding of why people protest and what
sorts of people protest in chapter 1 a moral – philosophical foundation
can be found which need not be shaken by practical need or legal nicety.
With an understanding of the history of demonstrations in chapter 2
and the empirical facts of individual demonstration set out there, many
of the real difficulties faced by demonstrators and the competing rights
of other individuals and the state become clearer. From these case
studies, it also becomes clear that the manner and form of policing
demonstrations may be more important than the nature of the
demonstrations or the demonstrators themselves in causing violence or
disorder.

The character of demonstrators and demonstrations must also be
taken into account though, and chapter 7 has given examples of a
particular form of protest and protester which has caused much violence
on demonstrations and has also been the cause of many of the banning
orders which have prevented processions since the passing of the 1936
Public Order Act.

Within the system of all-encompassing discretion, it would be
comforting to find that control of police powers was predictable, strong

and consistent. We have found in chapter 8 that such control is non-existent. This is especially worrying considering the effects of police tactics and behavior in demonstrations.

In the last chapter the question of the simple passing of a Bill of Rights creating a freedom of protest has been considered in detail. That too does not seem to offer easy answers, if the American experience is to be believed.

Legal aspiration and pragmatic reality can be far from each other in dealing with controversy in public order. Freedom of protest is portrayed as a social safety net where other political forms of voicing opinion are insufficient. But if the safety net is not always there (and you cannot see clearly whether it is, or is not) it cannot be relied on and does not, effectively, exist. Our efforts should be concentrated more on controlling police and government than in chasing a failing vision of a non-existent 'freedom'.

Bibliography

Abernathy, G. 1983. 'Should the United Kingdom Adopt a Bill of Rights?' [1983] Am. Jo. Comp. Law, 431.

Acton, H. B. 1982. *J. S. Mill: Utilitarianism, Liberty and Representative Government*, London, Dent.

Agitprop, 1971. *Bust Book. The People* v. *Regina. About Law*, London, Action Books.

Allott, 1979. 'Courts and Parliament' [1979], Camb. LJ, 79–117, April.

Ashworth, A. J. 1976. 'Liability for Carrying Offensive Weapons', [1976] Crim. LR, 725.

Asimow, M. 1983. 'Delegated Legislation: United States and United Kingdom', 3 Ox. Jo. Leg. St., 253.

Baker, J. 1938. *The Law of Political Uniforms, Public Meetings and Private Armies*, London, Gollancz.

Barendt, E. 1985. *Freedom of Speech*, Oxford, Oxford University Press.

Barker, P., Taylor, H., de Kadt, E., Hopper, E. 1968. 'Portrait of a Protest', *New Society*, 31 Oct., 61–4.

Bender, P. A. 1983. 'The Canadian Charter' [1983], 28 McGill LJ, 811.

Benyon, J. 1984 (ed.). *Scarman and After*, Oxford, Pergamon Press.

Benyon, J. and Solomos, J. 1987. *The Roots of Urban Unrest*, Oxford, Pergamon.

Berger, J. 1969. 'The Nature of Mass Demonstrations', *New Society*, 23 May.

Berlin, Sir Isaiah 1969. *Four Essays on Liberty*, London, Oxford University Press.

Bickel, 1975. *The Morality of Consent*, New Haven, Yale University Press.

Birch, R. 1987. 'What Kind of Policeman do you Want?', *The Times*, 12 Oct.

Blackstone, T., Gales, K., Hadley, R. and Lewis, W. 1970. *Students in Conflict*, London, Weiderfeld & Nicolson.

Blundy, D., Gilman, P. Humphry, D. and Knightley, P. 1976. 'The Carnival', *Sunday Times*, 5 Sept.

Boateng, P., Oxford, K. and Simey, M. 1984. In J. Benyon (ed.), *Scarman and After*, Oxford.

Bowes, S. 1966. *The Police and Civil Liberties*, London, Lawrence & Wishart.

Bugler, J. 1968. 'Solidarity with Violence', *New Society*, 21 Mar.

Bust, R. A. 1984. 'Constitutional Law and the Teaching of the Parables', 93 Yale LJ, 455–502, [1984] June.

Cappelletti, M. 1980. 'The "Mighty Problem" of Judicial Review and the Contribution of Comparative Analysis', [1980] 53 So. Cal. LR, 409.

Card, R. 1987. *Public Order: The New Law*, London, Butterworth.

Chafee, Z. 1941. *Free Speech in the United States*, Cambridge, Mass., Harvard University Press.

Clayton, R. and Tomlinson, H. 1987. 'Assessing Damages in Civil Actions Against the Police', LSG, 25 Nov.

Clutterbuck, R. 1973. *Protest and the Urban Guerrilla*, London, Cassell.

Clutterbuck, R. 1975. *Living with Terrorism*, London, Faber.

Clutterbuck, R. 1978. *Britain in Agony*, London, Faber.

Clutterbuck, R. 1981. *The Media and Political Violence*, London, Macmillan.

Clutterbuck, R. 1984. *Industrial Conflict and Democracy*, London, Macmillan.

Clutterbuck, R. (ed.) 1986. *The Future of Political Violence: De-stabilization, Disorder and Terrorism*, RUSI Defence Studies, London, Macmillan.

Cohen, B. 1988. 'Byelaws Under the Military Lands Act 1892', *Legal Action*, April 1988, 14.

Conference on Comparative Constitutional Law, 1986, So. Cal. LR, 53, 401–785, January.

Cover, R. M. 1983. 'The S.C. 1982 Term-Foreword: Nomos & Narrative', [1983] 97 Harvard LR, 68 N.

Cox, B. 1975. *Civil Liberties in Britain*, London, Penguin.

Critchley, T. 1978. *A History of the Police in England and Wales*, London, Constable.

Curtis, M. K. and Berger, R. 1982, 1983. 'Nine Lived Cat – (Incorporation of Bill of Rights', [1982] 43–4 Ohio St. LJ, 89–124, 1–19.

Daintith, T. C. 1966. 'Disobeying a Policeman: a fresh look at Duncan *v.* Jones', [1966] *Public Law*, 248–61.

Dashwood, A. 1977. 'Logic and the Lords in Majewski', [1977] Crim. LR, 532.

Dellows, J. 1977. 'Political Violence and the Response', in R. Clutterbuck, (ed.), *The Future of Political Violence*, 167–76.

Dicey, A. V. 1959. *Introduction to the Study of the Law of the Constitution* (10th edn), London, Macmillan.

Dorsen, N., Bender, P. and Neuborne, B. 1976. *Emerson, Haber and Dorsen's Political and Civil Rights in the United States* (4th edn), Boston, Little, Brown.

Driver, C. 1964. *The Disarmers: A Study in Protest*, London, Hodder & Stoughton.

Dworkin, R. 1977. *Taking Rights Seriously*, London, Duckworth.

East, R. 1987. 'Police Brutality – Lessons of the Holloway Road Assault', NLJ Oct 30.

Ely, J. H. 1983. 'Professor Dworkin's External/Personal Preference Distinction', [1983] Duke LJ, 959–86 N.

Etzioni, A. 1969. *Demonstration Democracy*, New York, Gordon and Breach.

European Convention on Human Rights, Brussels, Council of Europe (annual).

European Parliament, 1985. 'Report into the Rise of Fascism and Racism in Europe', Rapporteur Dimitrios Evrignis, Dec., Doc A 2–160/85.

Farrier, D. 1980. *Drugs and Intoxication*, London, Sweet & Maxwell.

Fitzgerald, P. L. 1982. 'An English Bill of Rights? Some Observations from Her Majesty's Former Colonies in America', [1982] 70 Geo LJ, 1229.

Fortas, Justice A. 1968. *Concerning Dissent and Civil Disobedience*, New York, New American Library.

Fritz, C. G. 1981. 'An Entrenched Bill of Rights for the United Kingdom: The Constitutional Dilemma', [1981] Anglo-Am. LR, .105.

Fulford, R. 1976. *Votes for Women*, London, White Lion Publishers.

Gilbert, T. 1975. *Only One Died – An Account of the Scarman Inquiry into the Events of 15th June 1974, in Red Lion Square*, London, Kay Beauchamp.

Glanville Williams 1961. 'Criminal Law: The General Part' (2nd edn), London, Sweet & Maxwell.

Goldstein, L. 1979. 'Four Alleged Paradoxes of Legal Reasoning', [1979] CLJ, 377.

Goodhart, A. L. 1936. 'Public Meetings and Processions', [1936] 6 Camb. LJ, 22.

Greater London Council, 1985. *The Control of Protest – the New Public Order Bill – The Response of the GLC*, London, Dec.

Griffith, J. 1979. 'The Political Constitution', (1979) 42 MLR, 1.

Grigg, M. 1965. *The Challoner Case*, Harmondsworth, Penguin.

Hall, S. et al. 1978. *Policing the Crisis – Mugging, the State, and Law and Order*, London, Macmillan.

Halloran, J. D., Elliott, P. and Murdock, M. 1970. *Demonstrations and Communications: A Case Study*, London, Penguin.

Hamlin, D. 1978. 'Swastikas and Survivors: Inside the Skokie–Nazi Free Speech Case', Civ. Lib. Rev., Mar./April, p. 8.

Harrison, J. 1985. 'Police Complaints: Pitfalls for the Unwary Litigant', [1985] 135 NLJ 1239, 8/9.

Harrison, 1987. *Police Misconduct: Legal Remedies*, London, Legal Action Group.

Hart, H. L. A. 1963. *Law, Liberty and Morality*, London, Oxford University Press.

Hilliard, B. 1987. 'Holloway Road: Unfinished Business', NLJ, Nov. 6.

Ivamy, E. R. H. 1949. 'The Right of Public Meeting', [1949] *Current Legal Problems*, 183.

Jacobs, F. G. 1975. *The European Convention on Human Rights*, Oxford, Clarendon Press.

Jaconelli, J. 1980. *Enacting a Bill of Rights*, Oxford, Oxford University Press.

Jefferson T. and Grimshaw, R. 1984. *Controlling the Constable*, London, Muller.

Jennings, Sir I. 1956. *Approach to Self Government*, Cambridge, Cambridge University Press.

Jones, S. and Levy, M. 'The Police and the Majority: The Neglect of the Obvious', Police Journal, LV, 1, 4.

Karst, K. 1980. 'Judicial Review and the Channel Tunnel', 53 So. Calif. LR, 401–785.

Kay, R. S. 1984. 'The Creation of Constitutions in Canada and the United States', [1984] 7 Can–US, LJ, 111.

Kenny, J. 1979. 'The Advantages of a Written Constitution Incorporating a Bill of Rights', [1979] 30 NILQ, 189.

Kenny, S. 1966. *Outlines of Criminal Law* (19th edn), Cambridge, Cambridge University Press.

Kettle, M. and Hodges, L. 1982. *Uprising*, London, Pan.

Kidd, R. 1940. *British Liberty in Danger: An Introduction to the Study of Civil Rights*, London, Lawrence & Wishart.

Kidd, H. 1969. *The Trouble at LSE 1966–1967*, London, Oxford University Press.

Kilroy-Silk, R. 1987. 'Riots that Go Unremarked', *The Times*, 22 Aug.

Kretzmer, D. 1984. 'Demonstrations and the Law', 19 Israel LR, 47.

Law Commission Working Paper 103, 1967. 'Criminal Law: Binding Over, The Issues', Sept.

Law Commission Working Paper 82, 1982. 'Offences Against Public Order'.

Law Commission Working Paper 123, 1983. 'Offences Relating to Public Order'.

'Law Relating to Public Order, The', Vol. 1, Home Affairs Committee 5th Report, Session 1979–80, HC 756, 1.

Lester, A. 'Democracy and Individual Rights', Fabian Trust No. 390.

Lester, A. 1984. 'Fundamental Rights: The United Kingdom Isolated?', *Public Law*, 46.

Lustgarten, L. 1980. *Legal Control of Racial Discrimination*, London, Macmillan.

Lustgarten, L. 1986. *The Governance of Police*, London, Sweet & Maxwell.

MacCormick, N. 1978. 'Does the United Kingdom have a Constitution? Reflections on *MacCormick* v. *Lord Advocate*', [1978] 29 NILQ, 1.

MacCormick, N. 1983. 'Jurisprudence and the Constitution' [1983] CLP, 13.

MacGuigan, M. R. 1970. 'Obligation and Obedience', in J. R. Pennock and J. W. Chapman (eds), *Political and Legal Obligation*, New York, New York University Press.

Maddison, *Report on the Virginia Revolution, 1799*.

Marcuse, H. 1969. *An Essay on Liberation*, London, Allen Lane, Penguin Press.

Marshall, G. 'United Kingdom Parliament and British North American Acts', Alberta LR, 19, 352–62.

Marston, J. 1987. *Public Order: A Guide to the 1986 Public Order Act*, London, Fourmat.

Mill, J. S. 1859. 'On Liberty'.

Mitchell, J. D. B. 1986. 'What Happened to the Constitution on 1st January 1973?', [1986] Cambrian LR, 69–86.

Moriarty, C. C. H. 1981. *Police Law* (24th edn), London, Butterworth.

Muggeridge, M. 1972. *Chronicles of Wasted Time*, London, Collins.

Munro, C. 1983. 'What is a Constitution?', [1983] Pub. L., 563.

Pearson, G. 1983. *Hooligan*, London, Macmillan.

Pounder, C. 1985. 'Police Complaints and the Metropolitan Police', *GLC*.

Pritt, D. N. 1966. *The Autobiography of D. N. Pritt: Part II, Brass Hats and Bureaucrats*, London, Lawrence & Wishart.

Reiner, R. 1985. *The Politics of the Police*, Brighton, Wheatsheaf.

Reiss, A. J. 1971. *The Police and the Public*, Newhaven, Yale University Press.
'Report to the Home Secretary from the Commissioner of the Metropolis', 1974, *HMSO*. HC, 357.
'Report of the Inquiry into Events at Red Lion Square on 15th June 1974 before Lord Justice Scarman', 1975, HMSO, Cmnd 5919.
'Report of the Inquiry into Det. Sgt. Challenor', 1965. Cmnd 2735.
'Report of the Tribunal Appointed to Inquire into the Events on Sunday 30th January, 1972, which Led to Loss of Life in Connection with the Procession in Londonderry on that Day', [1972], HL 101, HC 220.
'Report of the Tribunal of Inquiry into Violence and Civil Disturbances in Northern Ireland in 1969', Cmnd 566.
'Review of Public Order Law' – White Paper Cmnd 9510 (1985).
Ross, V. 1977. [1977] Crim. LR, 187.
Rousseau, J.-J. 1974. *Social Contract*, London, Dent.
Russell, W. 1964. *Russell on Crime*, Vol. I. (12th edn), London, Sweet & Maxwell.
Scarman, L. G. 1974. *English Law – the New Dimension*, London, Stevens, 18–21.
Scarman, L. G. 1981. 'Law, Lawyers and Government', [1981] Bracton LJ, 1–6.
Scarman Report, 1981. 'The Brixton Disorders, 10–12 April 1981', Cmnd 8427, London, HMSO.
Schrag, P. G. 1984. 'By the People: The Political Dynamics of a Constitutional Country', 72 Geo LJ, 819–1108 F.
Scraton, P. and Gordon, P. 1984. *Causes for Concern*, Harmondsworth, Pelican.
Sedley, 1970. 'The Garden House Trial', *The Listener*, 6 October.
Sherr, A. H. 1986. 'Client Interviewing for Lawyers: An Analysis and Guide', London, Sweet & Maxwell.
Sherr, A. H. 1985. 'The Scarman Report on "The Brixton Disorders, 10–12 April 1981" – A Retrospective Review' (1985), 7 *Urban Law and Policy*, 227–41.
Smith, A. T. H. 1987. *Offences Against Public Order Including the Public Order Act 1986, Police Review*, London, Sweet & Maxwell.
Smith, De, 1985. *Constitutional and Administrative Law* (5th edn), Harmondsworth, Penguin.
Smith, P. and Gaskill, G. 1981. 'The Crowd in History', *New Society*, 20 Aug.
Smith, J. C. and Hogan, B. 1986. *Criminal Law: Cases and Materials* (6th edn), London, Butterworth.
Stevens, P. and Willis, C. 1981. 'Ethnic Minorities and Complaints against the Police', London, Home Office Research and Planning Unit.
Stephens Digest, (9th edn) art, 114.
Stones' Justices Manual, (annual). London, Shaw Butterworth.
Supperstone, M. 1981. *Brownlie's Law of Public Order and National Security* (2nd edn), London, Butterworth.
Tettenborn, A. M. 1987. 'Universities: A Boost for Free Speech?', [1987] NLJ, 30 Oct., 1021–3.

Thornton, P. 1987. *Public Order Law – Including the Public Order Act 1986*, London, Financial Training.

Thornton, P. 1985. 'We Protest', NCCL.

Tribe, L. W. 1978. *American Constitutional Law*, Mineola, Foundation Press.

Tumber, H. 1982. *Television and the Riots*, London, British Film Institute.

Van Alstyne, W. 1983. 'Interpreting THIS Constitution: The Unhelpful Contribution of Special Theories of Judicial Review', [1983] U. Florida LR, 209.

Wade, H. R. 1938. 'The Law of Public Meetings', (1938) 2 MLR, 177.

Wallington, P. 1976. 'Injunctions and the Right to Demonstrate', (1976) 35 Camb. LR, 82.

Ward, T. 1987. 'Death and Disorder', *Inquest*, London.

Weaver, G. R. and Weaver, J. H. 1969. *The University and Revolution*, New Jersey, Prentice-Hall.

Wedderburn, Lord, 1971. *The Worker and the Law* (2nd edn), Harmondsworth, Penguin.

White, J. 1985. 'The Summer Riots of 1919', *New Society*, 13 Aug.

Wilcox, A. F. 1972. *The Decision to Prosecute*, London, Butterworth.

Williams, D. 1967. *Keeping the Peace: The Police and Public Order*, London, Hutchinson.

Williams, D. G. T. 1970. 'Protest and Public Order', [1970] CLJ, 104–6.

Wolchover, D. 1986. 'Police Perjury in London', NLJ, 28 Feb. 181.

Zander, M. 1979. *A Bill of Rights* (2nd edn), London, Barry Rose.

Zinn, H. 1968. *Disobedience and Democracy: Nine Fallacies on Law and Order*, New York, Vintage Bowes.

Index